The Blue Diamond

Kimberley West Gemstone Mysteries Book 1

By Lynn Franklin

Copyright

The Blue Diamond: Jeweler's Gemstone Mystery #1
by Lynn Franklin
© 2012 by Lynn Franklin

eBook: ISBN 978-0-9855457-0-3
Print: ISBN 978-0-9855457-3-4

This is a work of fiction. Names, characters, businesses,
places, events and incidents are either the products of the
author's imagination or used in a fictitious manner. Any
resemblance to actual persons, living or dead, or actual
events is purely coincidental.
Cover photo: Licensed Material: Comstock/Photos.com

Also by Lynn Franklin

Kimberley West Gemstone Mystery Series

The Blue Diamond
The Pirate's Ruby
The Carolina Emerald
The Turquoise Treasure

Grandpa Max Tall Tales Series

The Poodle Who Picked Pockets
The Poodle Who Ran Away From Home
The Poodle Who Sang Undercover (coming in 2021)

Readers' Specials

The Diamond Digest

Want more fun stories?
Go to LynnFranklin.com

Lynn@LynnFranklin.com.

Dedication

To my Mom, Dolly Scheidhauer
Thank you for teaching me the value of books
and always believing in my ability to write them.
I love you, Mom.

CONTENTS

PROLOGUE

Osprey Beach, Maryland
22 Years ago

"Grandpa, you lied to me!" Kimberley West stomped into the Osprey Beach Jewelry office with all the indignation an eight-year-old could muster.

Max Hershey looked up from the .78 carat diamond he was setting to find his favorite granddaughter glaring up at him. The Chesapeake Bay breezes had pulled strands of brown hair from her ponytail and she'd torn a hole in her new jeans. The flash in her brown eyes prevented him from kissing the dirt smudge on her freckled nose. The little hellion clutched her well-worn stuffed poodle in one arm, a heavy book in the other.

"What do you have there?"

Kim held out The Encyclopedia of Gemstones, the one he'd left sitting on the diamond display case.

"Pretty heavy reading for a little girl," he said, taking the book from her.

Hearing the amusement in his voice, Kim rolled her eyes. Why did adults always assume a kid couldn't use a dictionary? Besides, Grandpa was trying to change the subject.

"You lied," she repeated.

With a sigh, Grandpa removed the specially made glasses with the attached magnifiers and laid them in the center of the workbench. Donning his regular glasses, the ones with the lines across the bottom, he peered down at her.

"What makes you say I lied?"

"You said the colors in opals were made by butterfly wings."

"Uh, huh."

Kim pointed at the book. "It says in there that opal color comes from iron and carbon and mang . . . mang . . ."

"Manganese."

"Yeah."

Kim crossed her arms, Fluffy now forming a barrier between her and the man she'd always trusted.

Grandpa pulled Kim into his lap. It was large, soft and always, always safe. But today, Kim resisted the urge to snuggle against him. She sat rigidly, her sneaker clad feet swinging in the air.

"Didn't you like my stories?" Grandpa said.

Kim reluctantly agreed they were good stories.

"Weren't they more fun than talking about iron and carbon and manganese?"

"Not if they weren't true."

"Nancy Drew isn't true and you like those stories, don't you?"

"Yeah, but no one ever said Nancy Drew was real."

Grandpa sighed, his breath warm on her cheek. "Tell you what, if I promise to tell you when a story is true and when it isn't, will you forgive me?"

Kim's mouth twitched. "Maybe."

"How 'bout if I give you a present and tell you a true story?"

Giggling, Kim threw her arms around his neck. "Definitely."

She heard his chuckle as Grandpa eased her to the floor, then turned to reach into the center drawer of his workbench. Kim set Fluffy down; she needed two hands to accept a fist-sized chunk of golden-brown. The stone was smooth to the touch and emitted a warmth that made it feel alive. She could see through the stone, all the way to the center where a honeybee appeared to be flying in a cloud of gold.

"That's called amber," Grandpa said. "It came from the resin of ancient pine trees, resin that's hardened. The bee was trapped in the resin when it was still sticky. It's been sitting inside the amber for 50 million years waiting for a little girl to appreciate it."

Kim turned the silky stone in her hands. The bee was perfect, its fuzzy shoulders giving way to the gold and black bands just like real bees.

"Oh, Grandpa," she breathed. "It's perfect."

The bell to the store jingled. Grandpa glanced through the window that separated the office from the store front and stood.

"Come say hello to your Aunt Emerald," he said.

Kim grimaced. Aunt Emerald smelled like wet leaves and she treated Kim like a baby.

Grandpa sighed. "I might be able to find a piece of chocolate for a good girl . . ."

"Deal." Setting the amber carefully on Grandpa's desk, Kim lifted her poodle and tagged behind Grandpa into the store. Despite the summer heat, Aunt Emerald was wearing her bossy clothes: high heels, tight skirt and scratchy square-bottomed jacket. Kim wrinkled her nose as her aunt bent to offer a powdered cheek. Feeling Grandpa's fingers tighten on her shoulder, Kim quickly kissed the air near her aunt, then climbed onto a stool.

Aunt Emerald straightened and produced a small jewelry box from the purse Mom said cost as much as a car.

"I found these at an estate sale," Aunt Emerald said. "Are they diamonds?"

As Grandpa opened the box, Kim leaned forward to peer inside. But it contained nothing more than two clear stones set in what Grandpa called studs. Boring.

Grandpa slid the box in front of Kim. "Let's see if you remember your after-school lessons."

"For heaven's sake, Dad, just use that tester thing."

"Gemologists can't depend on gadgets, can they, Kimmy? Besides if the Russians perfect their diamond maker, that tester will be useless." Grandpa smiled down at Kim. "Go ahead, honey, let's see what you remember."

Kim's hand trembled as she removed one of the earrings from the box. The diamond lesson had been last week, but it seemed like long, long ago. He'd begun by telling her what he called "the old wives' tale" about diamond being the only gem that could scratch glass. Anything harder than glass, he'd said, -- even plain old quartz -- will scratch glass. And then he'd told her to . . . to . . .

She closed her eyes, trying to visualize Grandpa's lesson. She could see him standing beside her as he was now, holding a ring. He'd brought the ring towards his mouth and . . .

Opening her eyes, she breathed onto the earring. The gemstone fogged. One-one-thousand, two-one-thousand, three-one-thousand . . . The stone stayed foggy.

Diamonds didn't stay foggy. She smiled up at Grandpa. But before she could say anything, Grandpa placed a finger over her lip. "Remember, don't jump to conclusions. What happens next?"

"I, er, look at it through the . . . the . . ."

"Loupe. Remember?" Grandpa handed her the gadget that would make the gemstone look ten times bigger.

Aunt Emerald snorted. "I did all that. If I can't tell the difference, how do you expect a child to?"

Kim bit her tongue. Grandpa didn't like her sassing her aunts. Which wasn't fair 'cause they sure sassed her.

But Grandpa was doing his own sassing. "If you'd paid attention when you were Kim's age, you wouldn't be asking me to make the identification."

Kim held the . . . the loupe to her eye, just the way Grandpa showed her. She drew the earring towards the loupe until it came into clear view. Look at the edges, Grandpa had taught her. Diamond edges are always sharp. Diamond look-alikes have softer edges.

But without another stone to compare, Kim couldn't tell if these edges were sharp or soft. Looked pretty sharp to her.

She bit her lip and glanced at Grandpa. His smile calmed the butterflies in her stomach.

"Look deeper."

Deeper. Oh, yeah. Diamond look-alikes often had telltale flaws. Like . . . like . . .

"Bubbles!" Kim grinned at Grandpa. "I see bubbles!"

"Nonsense." Aunt Emerald snatched the earring and loupe from Kim's hand and bent to study the stone. With a snort, she looked up. "I see a tiny inclusion. Not a bubble."

Kim wrapped her arms around Fluffy and watched Grandpa bring the loupe and earring to his eye. A slow grin spread across his face.

"Kim's right; it's a bubble." Grandpa set the loupe on the counter and turned to Kim. "And a bubble means?"

"Glass!"

"Excellent." Grandpa turned back to Aunt Emerald. "Better get your contact lenses checked." He tucked the earring back into its case. "Hope you didn't pay diamond prices for these."

Aunt Emerald's nose wrinkled. "I know better than that. Only paid a dollar." She waved her hand over the box. "Maybe you can sell them to someone who doesn't give a sh . . . er, doesn't care."

"These are nice simulants. Sure you don't want them?"

"Absolutely not." Aunt Emerald scooped up her purse. "Tell Mom I couldn't stay; I've got a meeting in Annapolis."

She pecked Grandpa on the cheek, turned and swung the door wide, admitting the fragrance of an Osprey Beach summer: the Bay's brackish water, suntan lotion and sand.

Picking up the earrings, Kim followed Grandpa back into his office and grinned as he pulled a piece of brightly wrapped chocolate from his desk drawer. He handed it to her, touched her cheek, then settled into his chair.

Kim plopped onto the floor and admired the candy's bright blue foil. It was as pretty as anything in Grandpa's store. Grandpa said the candy was made in Switzerland, where he was born. Her mouth watered as she imagined the silky smoothness and deep chocolate flavor.

But . . . she'd peeked into Grandpa's drawer. This was the last piece. Did she really want to eat it now? It came all the way from New York, where Grandpa traveled to buy his gemstones and jewelry. And he wasn't scheduled to go back to New York until next week!

"Don't worry," Grandpa said, "I have more." He peered over his glasses. "Hidden."

Kim giggled. She popped the chocolate into her mouth and carefully refolded the pretty foil. Twirling the satiny dark chocolate around her tongue, she held the open earring box towards the overhead light and rotated it back and forth so the earrings caught the light. She glanced from the earrings to the diamond ring Grandpa held.

"Grandpa?"

"Hmmm?" Grandpa put on his expensive glasses and studied the ring.

"Why didn't Aunt Emerald want the earrings?"

"Because they're not real diamonds."

Kim touched the edge of an earring. "Did someone tell her a story that wasn't true?"

Grandpa chuckled. "No, your aunt makes up her own stories."

Kim looked again from the earrings to the ring. "But they look like diamonds. Aunt Emerald couldn't tell the difference. So why didn't she want them?"

Grandpa peered over his glasses at her. "Wouldn't you rather own something real than something fake?"

Kim shrugged. "Not if they're just as pretty."

"But . . ." Grandpa's eyes darted around the room, finally landing on Fluffy. "Wouldn't you rather have a real dog than a stuffed one?"

Kim giggled. "That's silly. Even a blind person can tell the difference between real and stuffed."

Grandpa stared at her, his expression unreadable. Finally, he reached out and tugged her ponytail.

"Let's be thankful other females aren't as pragmatic."

"What's prag . . pragma . ."

"Pragmatic. It means you have a logical way of looking at the world."

"Is that good?"

Grandpa blinked like something was in his eye. But then he reached out and stroked her cheek.

"Just as long as you can still enjoy my stories."

CHAPTER 1

Crater of Diamonds, Arkansas
Present Day

A loud buzzer shattered the still summer air. All heads turned towards the diamond field.

For a moment, everyone froze, noses lifted, bodies stiff, human setters on point. A second passed, two.

"Mommy, let's go!"

Tension broken, the diamond hunters bundled the remains of their lunch, gathered buckets, pails and screens and hurried towards the Diamond Discovery Center. Within minutes the picnic area was empty except for a pony-tailed woman and a black standard poodle.

Kim West pinched off a piece of hamburger and passed it to Rorschach.

"And that is what they mean by diamond fever."

Rory tilted his head in agreement. Or maybe he just wanted another bite of hamburger.

Kim pushed away her own half-eaten lunch, leaned against the picnic table and turned her face to the sun filtering through the overhead tree branches. After living five years in rainy Oregon, the hot Arkansas air felt glorious.

She wondered briefly if, now that she was moving back to Maryland, she'd tire of summer heat and humidity. Here the air was so heavy it carried the smell of wet dirt from the diamond field across the parking lot and into the picnic area. Kim suppressed a groan of pleasure. She couldn't wait to start digging, looking for amethyst, agate, jasper and quartz.

But not diamonds.

Despite the diamond fever that hung over the park, infiltrating even the youngest child's bloodstream, Kim was immune to diamonds.

Her cell phone announced itself with the theme from Indiana Jones. Kim pawed through her heavy shoulder bag . . . extra glasses, dog treats, wipes for Rory's feet, AAA guide, maps, flashlight, dog-training clicker . . . ah, cell phone. She smiled as she read caller ID and flipped the phone open.

"Hey, Grandpa!"

"Hello there, Monkey. How's your cross-country trip? You didn't try to climb one of those Redwood trees, did you?"

Kim giggled. "Their bottom branches were a little too high to reach. But Rory hiked his leg on one."

"Good for Rory." Only Grandpa, who'd read John Steinbeck's Travels with Charley, would understand the significance of a standard poodle recognizing a giant Redwood as a tree. Unlike Rory, Steinbeck's poodle showed no interest in the trees.

"Where are you now?"

"We just got to Crater of Diamonds . . ."

"Looking for diamonds?"

The excitement in Grandpa's voice made her ache. Poor Grandpa. He'd been so thrilled when she graduated with a degree in geology -- and so disappointed when she went back to school to study psychology. Despite the fact that her dissertation, How the Diamond Industry Brainwashes Women, landed her a coveted professorship, Grandpa still hoped she'd someday return to her roots. He didn't understand her fear that the family's diamond obsession would smother her. Or that she honestly, truly despised diamonds and all they stood for.

As much as she hated diamonds, however, she loved the grandfather who sold them.

Keeping her tone light, she answered "Just looking forward to getting dirty. Wish you were here."

Instead of the expected excuses -- he couldn't trust her aunts to watch the store and couldn't afford to close for a week -- she heard silence. No, not silence. A low hum like . . . traffic? In Osprey Beach?

"Grandpa, where are you?"

"New York."

"But you were in New York last week." Wasn't he? Had she lost track of time in the whirlwind of packing to move back to Maryland?

"Something came up."

Kim straightened and gripped the phone. "What's wrong?"

"Nothing's wrong," Grandpa said. "Just wanted to know how soon you'd be home."

But Kim knew every nuance in her grandfather's voice. The tightness suggested an attempt to suppress anger. Nothing unusual there; Grandpa's four daughters often tested his patience. What worried Kim was the high pitch and quiver.

Almost like he was afraid.

"Something's wrong. I know you too well."

Her own voice must have sounded odd. Whining, Rory shoved something into her free hand -- an acorn he'd retrieved from the ground -- and leaned against her. She stroked his ear reassuringly.

Grandpa sighed. "I never could hide anything from you."

"Yeah, so don't start now. What's going on?"

"Probably nothing. A friend poked at a hornet's nest and I'm supposed to keep him from getting stung."

His voice was still tight with frustration, but the squeakiness was gone. Maybe she just imagined the fear.

Besides, Grandpa's friends were mostly old men whose idea of adventure was wrestling a rockfish into a boat. How much trouble could they get into?

"What can I do to help?" She passed a bite of hamburger to Rory and popped a fry into her own mouth.

"I could sure use another mind to work this through. Maybe put that psychology degree to use."

Kim couldn't help smiling. At long last, Grandpa acknowledged her degree as useful! He'd always dismissed her psychology studies as nothing more than "woo-woo."

"So tell me what's up."

"It's complicated."

"I'm a big girl now. I can handle complicated."

A long sigh. "I don't suppose I could postpone this conversation by enticing you with a new pair of earrings?"

"Nope."

"How 'bout chocolate?"

Kim tried to suppress a giggle. It came out as a snort.

"Seriously, Kim, this really needs to be discussed in person. How soon will you be home?"

There it was again, a tension totally alien to Grandpa's character.

She was, what, eighteen, nineteen hours from Osprey Beach? If she drove. If she flew, however . . . She could probably catch a plane in Little Rock. But that would require crating Rory in cargo. No, better to find a local kennel, fly to Maryland, then fly back to Arkansas to pick up Rory and her van.

"I could catch a plane, be there tonight."

"Thanks, sweetie, but that's not necessary."

Kim breathed out through her mouth. Good. She really didn't want to abandon Rory.

"Well, then, why don't I just drive straight home?"

"Don't cut your trip short. Just get here when you can."

Kim knew better than to argue. Always better to say nothing and do what she wanted.

She changed the subject to her cross-country trip, regaling Grandpa with stories of high desert, towering mountains and plunging canyons. As they chatted, she pictured Grandpa making his way through New York's Diamond District.

She'd been ten years old the first time Grandpa took her on a diamond buying trip, but she could still remember the thrill of stepping out of the taxi onto West 47th Street. The street itself was narrow, making its crowded sidewalks appear wider. Tourists dressed in shorts and t-shirts stood before awning-covered storefronts, gawking at the glittering displays of diamonds. Business-suited men and women clutched jewel-filled briefcases as they wove through the crowd. Hawkers called to passersby while Hasidic diamond buyers in long black coats slipped smoothly through the crowd. Having just read a mystery set in Egypt, Kim likened the scene to a Cairo bazaar.

Only later, as an adult, did she realize the similarities included danger. Pickpockets and would-be thieves haunted the sidewalks, waiting for couriers to exit diamond trading centers, stalking their prey, looking for an opportunity to pounce. In response, merchants hired more security guards. Strategically placed video cameras helped deter impulse snatch-and-runs. But the truly determined simply changed tactics, using disguises and machine guns to rob the stores themselves.

Grandpa, of course, usually dismissed Kim's concerns, saying no one would bother him. After all, who would guess his ratty old briefcase contained a fortune in gems?

Today, however . . . that was tension she heard in his voice.

She opened her mouth to push for an explanation, but Grandpa was already talking.

"Well, I'm here, they're waiting, drive carefully, love you." Click.

Kim frowned at the phone. That stinker! He knew she was going to push for more information. She punched in Grandpa's number on her speed dial. The phone went immediately to voice mail.

Sighing, she closed her phone. At 76, Grandpa could still outsmart her.

Rory stood, his tail wagging furiously. Kim looked across the parking lot, towards the diamond field. Some of the diamond hunters were returning.

Though crowded by Arkansas standards, the Crater of Diamonds park was worlds away from New York. No hawkers, no business suits, no shady looking characters. Just a bunch of sun-burned families covered in the diamond field's odd greenish colored dirt.

Next to her, a mother laid out Kentucky Fried Chicken while her son and daughter -- good heavens, they couldn't be more than five or six years old -- arranged a collection of stones.

Seeing Kim's interest, the mother flashed a weary smile. "Did you see the yellow diamond the little girl found? They said it's 10 points."

Ten points. The size of a match head.

Still the child who found it would long remember today, digging in the dirt, finding the stone, hearing the buzzer announcing a diamond find -- her diamond find -- watching the people crowd around to see what she'd discovered. Maybe she'd grow up to respect geology.

Or maybe she'd just become another diamond-crazed airhead.

Kim sighed and gazed longingly towards the plowed field. From this angle, however, she could see nothing but parking lot, trees and excited families entering the Diamond Discovery Center.

Grandpa should be here, darn it, not traipsing around New York with a battered briefcase full of jewels.

After all, the trip to Crater of Diamonds State Park had been Grandpa's idea. He'd talked about bringing her here ever since she was six years old and he caught her digging up his backyard looking for gemstones.

Instead of chastising her for messing up his rose garden, he'd taken her into the house, cleaned the dirt off her face and began teaching her the natural history of gemstones. He'd placed a piece of black coal in one of her hands and a glittering diamond in the other and explained how -- though they looked totally different -- they were composed of the exact same chemical element: carbon. Calling the diamond a miracle of nature, he'd snagged a jewelry catalog and sketched pictures to show how high pressure and extreme temperatures deep in the earth transformed carbon into the world's most precious gemstone.

Though she understood only half of his words, she'd grasped the idea that there were diamonds in Arkansas and some day she and Grandpa would hunt for them.

But the promised trip never occurred. As sole proprietor of Osprey Beach Jewelry, Grandpa was reluctant to leave his business in someone else's hands. Of his four daughters only one -- Kim's mother -- was dependable.

Mom, however, had her own job teaching high school English and, in any event, she'd never been able to control her three younger sisters. If Aunt Emerald, Sapphire and Ruby decided to use the store as a personal jewelry box, Mom would stand by helplessly. And Dad had more sense than to get involved.

This time Kim suggested Grandpa ask Aunt Ginny to watch the store. What Dad's older sister lacked in height, she more than made up for in attitude. She'd have no problem standing up to the other aunts. And now that Ginny had retired from the Motor Vehicle Administration, she was desperate for distractions.

Grandpa, however, was paranoid. Kim couldn't blame him, really; if she was sitting on all those diamonds, rubies and other gems, she probably would be, too. In the end, he'd refused Aunt Ginny's help and once again the promised trip fizzled. Kim set off across country, alone.

Dreams, however, never die easily. Despite Kim's aversion to all things diamond, she couldn't resist the opportunity to dig in the field that had captured her childhood imagination.

But not today. Today she needed to get on the road, drive as fast as she dared to reach Grandpa. He said he needed her.

And she couldn't shake the sense that when he called, he'd been truly frightened.

CHAPTER 2

Kim pushed the old minivan all day and through the night, thrumming tires keeping time with the chanting in her head: Grandpa needs me, Grandpa needs me, Grandpa . . . Her brain devised and dismissed scenarios that would make Grandpa afraid. Family illness. Lawsuit against the store. Robbery. But Grandpa wouldn't hesitate to reveal those over the phone. What would make him secretive?

Her brain whirred. The miles ticked away, the tedium interrupted only by ammonia-scented rest areas and machines stocked with stale crackers and expensive drinks. Grandpa needs me, Grandpa . . .

At noon on the second day, she pulled into a sun-scorched rest area just north of the

Tennessee/Virginia border. Heat radiated from the asphalt parking lot and the moisture-laden air wrapped her bare shoulders and made it difficult to breathe. For the first time, she longed for Oregon's dry, low-heat summers.

While Rory sniffed a patch of brown grass, she dialed Grandpa's cell phone.

She pictured Grandpa puttering in the light-filled kitchen above the store, pouring iced tea or assembling one of the crazy sandwiches they'd invented together. As the phone rang, her mouth watered with the memory of peanut butter, banana and chocolate syrup sandwiches. She hadn't had one since she last visited Grandpa; it just didn't taste the same without him.

When Grandpa answered, however, the background clank of trucks running over manhole covers revealed a totally different location: Manhattan.

"You spent the night?" Grandpa never stayed in New York. Too expensive, too noisy, too unlike home.

A chuckle filled her ears. "And hello to you, too. Find any diamonds?"

"Actually, I just crossed into Virginia."

"I'm sorry; I didn't mean to cut your trip short."

But she could hear the delight in his voice. "Don't worry; you now owe me a trip to Crater of Diamonds. Together. Like we planned."

Grandpa's musical laugh made her smile. Calling to Rory, she headed back to the van.

"So why are you still in New York?"

"Long story." There it was again; that back-of-the-throat rumble. Grandpa's worry voice.

Before she could quiz him, he added "When I get home I'll need your advice."

"Well, you know I always have opinions." Good, he laughed. "So how soon will you be home?"

"Train gets into Baltimore around seven, so unless traffic is bad, I should be there by eight."

Perfect. Her GPS estimated the final leg of her trip at eight hours.

Anxious now to get on the road, she wished him a safe trip, closed the phone and strapped Rory into his seatbelt.

"Wanna go see Grandpa?"

Rory responded with a lick and a grin.

Seven hours and fifty-four minutes later, the four-lane narrowed to two and the twilight gray water of the Chesapeake Bay came into view. Sensing the nearness of the water -- or maybe Kim's excitement -- Rory stood and snuffled at the back window. Kim cracked the windows and joined the big poodle in inhaling deeply.

Honeysuckle, fresh-mown grass and wet sand. The water itself, however, seemed odorless. So different from the wild, salty odors that emanated from the Pacific Ocean.

But she'd grown up near the Chesapeake Bay, splashed in its brackish water, explored its fossil-rich shores. The Pacific might trigger a deep sense of awe, but she preferred the soothing rhythms of life on the bay.

The speed limit dropped to thirty and the water loomed larger. A freighter chugged across the horizon, but the water just offshore showed nary a ripple. As she neared the intersection with Bayside Road, the street that paralleled the bay, the traffic light turned red.

Kim groaned. Since leaving the Virginia rest stop, she'd encountered an endless succession of red lights, construction gridlocks and kamikaze commuters. Now a steady stream of cars prevented right-turn-on-red. Where had all these people come from? Had the Three Beaches -- Osprey, North and Chesapeake -- changed that much in the two years since she'd last visited?

She squinted at a license plate. Virginia. And the one behind it was Pennsylvania and beyond that was Delaware and . . . Tourists. Why so many tourists . . .

"Yes!" Kim punched a fist in the air as she figured it out. "Do you know what next week is?" In the rear view mirror, Rory's eyes met hers and his head cocked. "Fourth of July!"

Grandpa's favorite holiday.

"There'll be concerts and parades and parties and fireworks . . ." Oops, Rory hated fireworks. "These are good fireworks. They shoot them from barges out in the bay. Ours are the best. The Washington Post says so."

Ours. After all these years, Kim still felt her town's desperate competition with the other two beaches. Tourist dollars were scarce and Osprey Beach lacked North Beach's antique shops and Chesapeake Beach's water park and resort. Without the annual designation of "best place to watch fireworks over the Bay," Grandpa and other Osprey Beach merchants would struggle for survival. Income from Independence Day sales were needed to carry Grandpa's store through the lazy summer into holiday gift-buying season.

So hurray for the fireworks. Rory would just have to adapt.

"Did I ever tell you about the summer Grandpa and I won the sand sculpture contest?" Okay, so she was babbling at a dog. The memories flooding her brain needed an outlet. Freud would love it.

"Several people sculpted adult sea turtles," she told Rory. "But we made baby turtles, fifty-one of them running from their nest into the water. They looked so real we had to keep the sea gulls away until the judges got to us!"

She smiled, remembering that lazy, happy summer. The last summer for childhood fun. The following year she entered Middle School, a hormone-laden nightmare where childhood friends metamorphosed into boy-chasing, blithering idiots.

The light turned green and she eased into traffic. Fifty yards later, brake lights flashed. Kim peered through the windshield and groaned. The Chesapeake Beach geese had waddled into the road, spreading across both lanes and stopping all traffic.

The car ahead of her honked. The geese turned beady eyes towards the offender but didn't move.

Kim sighed. The proper way to deal with the geese was to drift forward, if necessary bumping the ring leader with the car. Tourists, of course, didn't know this.

On the sidewalk beside her, a group of girls, maybe eleven or twelve years old, giggled and whispered as they watched three boys chase one another with snapping beach towels.

Kim winced and looked away, but images of the summer following her sand-sculpture win surfaced. Debbie Abrams and Beth Woods -- her best friends since elementary school -- strutting the boardwalk clad in tiny bikinis, giggling whenever some testosterone-crazed boy did something stupid. No, they didn't want to enter the egg-toss contest. No, they didn't want to go swimming. And, no, they most certainly did not want to sit around listening to some dumb band playing elevator music.

New images: The after-fireworks party complete with live D.J. Michael Todd, quarterback extraordinaire, asking her to dance. Debbie and Beth poking fun of her dancing, then later shunning her. Moping around Grandpa's store. Grandpa's confession of the bullies in his own childhood.

Behind her, someone leaned on a horn. As a group, the geese honked back but didn't yield an inch. Rory woofed and hung over the back seat.

"Yeah, I'm sure you'd do a good job of clearing the road," she told him. "Then we'd have the tourists mad at you for picking on the poor birds."

Poor birds, indeed. She watched a shop owner march into the road, brandishing a broom. The geese lined up facing her. The broom swung. The nearest geese skipped aside while their partners in crime maintained control of the two-lane road. Goose honks joined more car horns.

On the sidewalk, the clowning boys suddenly froze, noses pointed at a smaller boy shuffling from the water park. An official Mickey Mouse backpack hung from the boy's boney shoulders, Hawaiian-style swim trunks fell to knobby knees. He stared at his feet as he walked and didn't see the older boys until they surrounded him. The boy's eyes widened as the leader of the gang shoved him into another boy, who pushed him back toward the center of the circle. The leader's hand raised, fist clenched.

Kim threw the car into park and reached for the door handle. As she stepped out of the car, however, the shop owner descended on the boys. The bullies scattered, leaving the small boy alone and trembling. A slanting ray of light illuminated chubby, tear-streaked cheeks.

Biting her lip, Kim crawled back into the car. The boy wouldn't welcome a stranger's attention. An image surfaced. Another gang, another target. Grandpa, age eleven, newly arrived from Switzerland. Grandpa's confession.

Once upon a time, the confident, successful man she'd known all her life had been targeted by bullies. They ridiculed the way Grandpa dressed, snickered at his French accent, belittled his work ethic. When they discovered he couldn't swim, they tossed him into the bay. Like the boy on the sidewalk, Grandpa's only crime was being different.

Even after all the psychology classes explaining childhood angst, children's cruelty sickened her.

But they could also be useful, as demonstrated by the trio of girls skipping down the sidewalk, waving slices of stale bread and calling "here ducky, ducky, ducky." Two sets of parents, arms laden with beach bags, wet towels and an open bag of bread, followed.

The geese turned towards the girls. Ah yes, tourist training 101.

The geese flocked around the children, clearing the road in seconds. And, mercy of mercies, the traffic light at the other end of Chesapeake Beach stayed green long enough for Kim to zip through.

She eased her grip on the wheel. In just a few minutes she'd get to hug Grandpa . . . and make him reveal whatever worried him.

The road turned inland and the bay briefly disappeared. A left turn onto Osprey Beach's First Avenue carried Kim back towards the water. As she passed Main Street, the boardwalk parking lot came into view. Normally empty at this time of the evening, the lot was dotted with Toyotas, Fords and even what looked like a black Mercedes.

Or was it a BMW? Kim sighed. Didn't matter anymore; she'd dumped the car-crazy boyfriend months ago.

Tapping the brake, she turned right onto the gravel alley that'd been the bane of her growing up years; after the third tumble from her new Schwinn destroyed the front wheel, she'd begun calling the pothole-laden street "bike-eating alley." It ran behind the backs of the houses and shops that lined the boardwalk. Small stones clinked against the van's undercarriage. Kim slowed, her eyes drawn to the tall, narrow homes that blocked her view of the bay.

Gone were the cottage bungalows of her childhood, the ones with the shops in the front, living quarters behind, postage-stamp yards out back. Hurricane Isabel's watery assault forced Grandpa and his neighbors to raise their homes above flood level. The new houses thrust three and four stories high, each floor sporting balconies with wonderful views of the bay, the bottom level reserved for garages or utility rooms that could survive hurricane induced floods.

The old cottages she'd loved were gone, but the bike-eating alley that dented bikes, flattened tires and lodged in knees and elbows remained.

As the car neared Grandpa's driveway, Kim shifted in her seat, conflicting emotions making it difficult to breathe. Excitement, concern, joy, apprehension, anticipation, dread.

The psychologist in her recognized the emotional tug-of-war as a classic response to returning home. But academic understanding didn't stop the turmoil in her gut.

The next few days would be stressful. Her bossy aunts would descend and she needed to prevent them from pushing her around or triggering an angry outburst. She'd help Grandpa in the store, but needed to resist getting caught in the feeding frenzy that always surrounds diamonds. And Grandpa would push to make the current living arrangement permanent and she needed to that resist, too.

She groaned. Oh, to avoid the disappointment she'd see in Grandpa's eyes.

Especially after he'd gone ahead and renovated the top floor, turning three bedrooms and one bath into two luxurious master suites. He'd even fenced the back yard for Rory.

When Grandpa told her what he'd done, she'd pretended to share his enthusiasm. She accepted his offer to stay with him until her Oregon home sold; she couldn't afford to pay the mortgage and the high rents in College Park at the same time. But she'd warned Grandpa that her ultimate goal was to buy a house closer to the University of Maryland, where she'd be teaching in the fall. He'd responded with a "we'll see."

Grandpa didn't understand that after living on her own for ten years, the idea of sharing a place with anyone gave her chills. And she certainly couldn't tell him that his nosiness and matchmaking attempts would drive her crazy.

Whenever she visited him, he arranged for a succession of his buddies' sons to "drop in." Knowing her weakness for "bad boys" -- and her disastrous high school attraction to Jason White -- Grandpa carefully selected for the more wholesome: doctors, lawyers, business executives. Unfortunately, they'd all been too self-absorbed to notice their date's eyes glazing over.

His latest enthusiasm was a Pulitzer Prize winning journalist turned college professor. Grandpa had bombarded her with articles the man had written. Kim filed the stories away, unread. There was plenty of time to make her excuses.

While she could handle Grandpa's matchmaking, however, she was less efficient at quashing his dream that someday she'd join him as co-owner of Osprey Beach Jewelry. He couldn't understand her reluctance, her fear of being smothered by the large, extended family. Three aunts, eight cousins, all named after gemstones, all consumed by diamond fever . . . She shuddered to think she'd almost become one of them. One of the mindless masses dazzled by sparkle, blind to reality.

The job offer in Oregon had delayed that confrontation with Grandpa.

Now she was back in Maryland. Distance was no longer an excuse. The time for the painful confrontation loomed nearer.

Turning into Grandpa's driveway, she was surprised to see the garage door standing open. He must have just arrived.

She started to pull the van beside Grandpa's Camry, then noticed the open garden gate on her left. Now why would he enter through the backyard? From the garage, he could use the interior elevator to reach the living quarters above the shop. So why climb the outside stairs?

From the backseat, Rory whined. Probably needed to relieve himself.

She parked in the driveway, removed Rory's seatbelt and followed him into the backyard, closing the gate behind her. As she neared the outside staircase, she heard voices coming from the downstairs office.

Grandpa! And suddenly she was ten again, bounding up the steps two at a time, swinging open the screen door and . . .

Kim screeched to a halt, her mind trying to process what she saw. A figure dressed in black bent over a pile of clothes in front of Grandpa's workbench. The figure stood, turned towards her . .

. Kim registered the ski mask, the snarled lips, the dilated eyes. Time slowed. He took a step, lifted his right hand. Something caught the office light, flashed . . . knife. He was raising a knife . . .

Rory sped by. Rear legs propelled him into the air. His mouth closed over the arm holding the weapon.

The man stumbled, roared and swung a battered briefcase. It caught Rory in the side. Fabric tore as the black dog dropped to the ground. The man raised the blood-spattered knife.

"No!"

Kim started for Rory, her feet slipping on the tiled floor. Oh god, oh god, she'd never make it in time. Tensing her muscles, she hurled her purse at the knife arm. It thunked against the blade, ripping the weapon from the assailant's fingers. The knife went flying.

The man swore and charged towards her. His free arm hit her shoulders and sent her sprawling. Feet thudded down the outside stairs.

Rory struggled to stand. Kim crawled to him, ran anxious hands down his sides. No blood, no protruding bones. He stood, shook himself and licked the right lens of her glasses.

Police. She needed police.

Pushing herself to her feet, she turned towards the phone on the workbench. Her eyes fell on the clothes. No, not clothes . . .Her heart stopped.

"Grandpa!"

CHAPTER 3

Grandpa lay on his side, his breath ragged, one hand clutched to his chest. Blood oozed between his fingers.

Dropping beside him, Kim stroked his face. Clammy. But he was alive.

"Grandpa?"

His eyes fluttered open, glassy, then focused on her. A small smile formed. He struggled to sit up. His fingers turned red with blood.

"No! Lay still." Whipping off her t-shirt, she pressed it against the wound. Grandpa groaned. But the blood flow slowed.

"Can you hold this in place for a minute?"

When he nodded and moved his hand onto the reddening cloth, Kim scrambled to her feet and snagged the portable phone. Fingers trembling, she reached for the 9, hit the 8 instead, no, no, no, punch the off, now, more slowly 9-1-1.

"My grandfather, he's been stabbed." The words came from her mouth, but she didn't recognize the squeaky voice. Taking a deep breath, she gave the emergency operator Grandpa's address.

"The house sits beside the boardwalk, so they'll need to drive down the alley that connects First and Second. Come in the back."

"I have an ambulance leaving Dunkirk right now."

Dunkirk. Fifteen minutes away if you drove the speed limit. Rory nudged Kim's arm. Kim glanced down, saying "Not now, swee . . ." Something glimmered in his mouth. The knife. Oh, gawd, he was carrying the knife.

Kim dropped the phone and lunged for Rory. Startled, he jumped out of her reach. Feet planted, tail up, he appeared ready to bolt. If he reached the interior stairs, she'd never catch him.

Pitching her voice low, she tried to calm the young dog. "It's okay, sweetie. Bring it here." Cooing softly, she extended her right hand. Rory's tail began to lower. Babbling nonsense, she took a step towards him. His tail raised. Kim froze.

"Bring it, sweetie. You want a cookie?" Rory cocked his head. Slowly, Kim reached her left hand into a jeans pocket, found a dog treat, showed it to him. "Bring it here, sweetie."

Tension drained from the poodle's body. He trotted forward, laid the knife in the extended hand, accepted the cookie. She threw the knife onto the workbench, out of Rory's reach.

Rushing back to Grandpa, she dropped to her knees. His breath was ragged, but his eyes were open and alert. The t-shirt over his wound was solid red. Kim gently lifted his hand, prepared to continue applying pressure. But the blood had stopped flowing.

She stroked Grandpa's hand. "It's going to be okay. Ambulance should be here soon."

His skin was so gray, so cold. Maybe a blanket would help.

Grandpa grabbed her hand.

"Don't leave."

"But you need . . ."

"Need you here . . ."

Before she could protest, he reached into his suit coat pocket and pulled out a package of Swiss chocolates. He muttered something and passed the chocolate to Kim.

Where was that ambulance?

"Grandpa, lay still. You're going to start bleeding again."

But he ignored her, intent on extracting something from the inside pocket of his coat.

"Here. Let me get it."

With a nod, he slumped to the floor. Kim opened his jacket, found the pocket and pulled out a small brown envelope. The kind jewelers used to carry gemstones.

"This it?" She held it up.

Grandpa nodded, pushed at her hand. "Hide."

Huh?

He pushed again. "Hide!"

He watched as she tucked the envelope into her jeans pocket, then grabbed her hand.

"Jim . . ."

"Shhhh. You need to preserve your strength."

Grandpa gripped her hand. Tight. "But . . ."

"Grandpa, please!"

Hearing the panic in her voice, he coughed and closed his eyes, murmuring "bossy . . ."

Were those sirens? Please, let those be sirens.

Grandpa's grip loosened. His hand fell to the ground, limp. Rory licked her tears.

"Grandpa? Grandpa, don't you dare die on me!"

An hour later, Kim peeled the bloody jeans from her body. Beyond the bathroom door, she could hear the policewoman moving around Grandpa's guest room. She gritted her teeth, welcoming the rage that had replaced the terror.

Anger was good. She could function while angry. Fear, however . . . fear turned her brain to mush.

Especially when she feared for Grandpa's life.

No. Don't go there. Focus on the anger.

Anger at the sheriff's deputy who prohibited her from accompanying Grandpa to the hospital. At the older cop who demanded her bloody clothes as evidence. At herself for not thinking when the policewoman ordered her to change clothes.

She'd grabbed the first pair of shorts she'd found in her suitcase, only now realizing they contained no pockets, no place to transfer the stuff from her jeans pockets.

Snatching the discarded jeans, she reached into the pockets for her cell phone, dog treats, clicker, poo bag, clean tissues, brown envelope . . .

She froze, staring down at the jewelers' envelope. Remembering Grandpa's words.

Hide.

Spiders ran up her spine.

"Are you all right in there?" The woman cop sounded annoyed.

"Yes, just a minute."

Hide.

From who? The crook? The emergency workers? Did he want her to hide it from the cops?

"Ma'am?"

Get rid of the cop.

Kim peeled off her bra and panties -- they wanted those, too! -- and bundled them into the jeans. Poking her head around the bathroom door, she shoved the clothes at the cop.

"I need to wash the blood off . . ." Grandpa's blood. Don't go there! "I . . . I'll be a few minutes longer."

The woman nodded. "I'll just wait here. Supposed to escort you back downstairs."

Kim answered with her own nod, resisted the urge to slam the door as she pushed it shut. Anger was good. Unless it made you do something stupid.

Turning on the water in the sink, she snagged a clean washcloth and scrubbed until her skin turned pink. She pulled on underwear, tee and the pocketless shorts. Leaving the water running to give her some time, she scanned the bathroom for a hiding place.

Though the renovation had enabled Grandpa to create two bedroom/bath suites, the bathrooms were small. This one contained just the basics: toilet, walk-in shower, pedestal sink. There wasn't even a linen closet; a single shelf over the toilet held clean towels. The only space to hide anything was the medicine cabinet. And that was too obvious.

Her eyes dropped to Rory. But she'd removed his seatbelt harness when they arrived. He wasn't even wearing a collar.

Which meant she needed hide the envelope in her clothes. Her pocketless clothes. Which left . . . her bra?

She folded the envelope in half, than in half again, creating a one-inch square. Leaning into the mirror, she lifted her shirt to study her low-cut t-shirt bra. There was just enough elastic between the breasts to tuck in the envelope. But when she lowered the shirt, the envelope outline clearly showed.

Elizabeth Taylor never had this problem.

Of course, Elizabeth Taylor had bigger boobs.

Maybe if she shifted the envelope to the bra cup? No, that showed even worse. Plus the envelope scratched.

She removed the envelope, glared at it. Okay, the bra was out. Ditto the bikini underpants; she could just imagine the envelope falling out as she walked. Movie spies hid things in their mouths. But the cops wanted to talk with her and she sure couldn't do that with paper in her cheek.

She shifted her glare from the envelope to the mirror. Thick hunks of brown hair had managed to escape the ponytail elastic. Great. She could just hear Aunt Emerald's voice. Why don't you comb your hair? You could lose a horse in that mess . . .

Huh. She leaned closer. Could she hide the envelope in the long tangle?

Setting the envelope on the back of the sink, she opened the medicine cabinet. Yes! Grandpa had put her bobby pins on the bottom shelf.

She tugged the elastic from her hair. Using her fingers, she smoothed the hair as best she could, wrapped the elastic around it to create a low ponytail. She pushed the envelope into the elastic and pinned it securely. Then she twisted the loose hair and wrapped it around the rubber band, hiding the envelope. She used every bobby pin, but when she was done, the messy bun stayed in place no matter how hard she shook her head. And the envelope was invisible.

Turning off the water, she grabbed her cell phone and checked to make sure she hadn't missed a call from Mom. Nothing yet. What was taking so long for a report on Grandpa's condition?

She pushed that thought aside and reached for the doorknob. Right now, she needed to concentrate on not looking guilty while the cops interviewed her.

CHAPTER 4

Kim and Rory entered Grandpa's living room to find a sheriff's deputy, crime scene tape dangling from one hand, talking to a man dressed all in black. Kim recognized the deputy as the man who'd prevented her from riding to the hospital with Grandpa. He was just a kid, didn't look old enough to shave. Short and skinny with a sparse attempt at a goatee, his cocky stance reminded her of a Banty rooster she'd once seen challenge a Rottweiler. While the rooster had gone to that great henhouse in the sky, she suspected kid cop would be harder to remove.

She couldn't see the new guy's face, but the confident tilt of his head screamed cop.

The policewoman announced their arrival. Both men turned. Kid cop spread his legs and placed a hand on his gun belt. Though the bright yellow tape he held diminished the tough-guy look, Kim avoided his eyes. Best not to challenge a bully with a gun.

Instead she studied the newcomer. New cop stood with his legs together, hands in his pockets, confident in himself. As he should be. With his tousled dark hair, broad shoulders, small waist and lean muscles, he was every woman's bad-boy dream.

Kim had long ago sworn off bad boys.

And then he smiled, revealing Clint Eastwood creases. Kim's breath caught, her heart beat faster. He could be a dark-haired version of Jason White, her high-school flame.

She dug her fingers into Rory's warm wool. She would not, not, not succumb to the wiles of this new guy and confess all. Grandpa said to hide the envelope and she would do just that until he told her otherwise.

"Huh," new cop drawled. "You and your dog have the same accusing expressions."

Before Kim could create an intelligent response, Rory leaped from her side. Snatching the end of the crime scene tape, he raced towards the balcony.

"Rory, come!"

Rory wheeled around and tore back towards her, yellow tape streaming behind. As he passed kid cop, the man lunged at him.

Kim groaned. The deputy clearly knew nothing about young dogs.

Never, ever chase a playful dog. Especially one that's been cooped up in a car for days, called on to defend his people, then subjected to the tense aftermath. Rory needed to release pent-up emotions. And kid cop had just provided the means.

With the game afoot, Rory circled the room. The older cop had the good sense to stand still. Kid cop, however, ran after the poodle. Rory was in his element. He dodged, leaped and twirled. Yellow tape swirled through the air. It never occurred to kid cop to drop his end of the tape. So each poodle circuit of the room wound tape around the cop's legs.

Hmm . . . If the guy tripped, could Rory be arrested for assault?

The older cop turned to Kim. "Can't you stop this?"

She noted the slight grin on his face. "Look at Rory's glazed eyes. His adrenaline is too high; he can't hear me. He might stop if no one was chasing him."

The grin became the full-on smile that should have made her knees weak. Rory's antics, however, had given her time to get her emotions in check. She met the man's eyes, allowed her own humor to show.

"Jacobs!" The older cop raised his voice just enough to be heard about stampeding poodle feet. "Stand still!"

Officer Jacobs stopped, hands on his knees, panting. Rory dropped into a play bow.

Kim waited a few seconds to give Rory's heart a chance to slow, then called his name. He trotted over, yellow tape trailing behind. Battling a smile, she removed the tape from his clenched teeth and tossed it to the ground. Rory licked her hand, leaned against her and cast innocent eyes upward. Oh, yeah, baby, there was more than one bad boy in this room.

The human version introduced himself as Lieutenant Bill Brockley and motioned to the sofa. Kim sat, laid the cell phone beside her and watched Officer Jacobs gather the yellow tape. With a final glare at Rory, he stomped from the room.

She turned her attention to the man sitting across from her in a winged-back chair. Intelligent blue eyes studied her. She stiffened, resisting the urge to touch her hair to make sure the envelope was still hidden. This guy could make you feel guilty even if you had nothing to hide.

Which she didn't. Whatever Grandpa had given her, it had nothing to do with finding his attacker.

"I know you're anxious to get to the hospital," Lieutenant Brockley said, his voice huskier than she expected. Not that she noticed. "But I'm investigating a series of burglaries in the Three Beaches. You're the first to actually see the thief. If we're going to catch him, I need information while it's still fresh in your mind."

Kim frowned. Grandpa hadn't mentioned any nearby robberies. Is that why he'd sounded so anxious on the phone?

"Let's start at the beginning," Brockley continued. "You told Officer Jacobs that you entered through your grandfather's office. Why didn't you go straight to the living quarters?"

"The back gate was open. Sometimes clients come in that way after hours so I decided to go to Grandpa's work area first."

At his urging, she again described climbing the outside stairs to the office on the second floor, opening the door, seeing the man, the knife, the briefcase . . .

The briefcase. Why did the thief take Grandpa's old briefcase?

But Lieutenant Brockley was plowing ahead, asking her to describe the attacker. She pushed aside the image of briefcase and knife, focused on the dark-clad man.

"I'm not sure how much I can tell you," she said. "He was wearing a ski mask, gloves, long pants and long-sleeved shirt. All I saw was black."

Brockley stood, motioning for her to do the same and to come closer. "Taller or shorter than me?" he asked.

But the musky fragrance of Brockley's aftershave played havoc with Kim's neurons. She stepped back, her heels banging the front of the sofa.

Swallowing, Kim lifted her chin to meet Brockley's eyes. Fortunately, they weren't mocking her awkwardness.

"He was about your height, but heavier on top. Like he lifted weights or something."

"Eye color?" When Kim hesitated, he added "Were the eyes darker or lighter than the mask?"

"Lighter. Definitely lighter."

Motioning for her to sit, Brockley returned to his chair. Kim released the breath she'd been holding and ran fingers through her hair. A bobby pin dislodged and dropped onto her shirt collar. She froze.

The envelope. She'd forgotten about the hidden envelope.

Even as the thought formed, a lock of hair pulled loose and flopped onto her shoulder. Kim reached behind her neck, searching for the errant bobby pin. The movement caused another pin to fall.

Brockley scribbled in his notebook, oblivious. As he looked up, Kim's fingers closed over a pin. She snagged it and returned her hands to her lap.

"How 'bout skin color?" Brockley said. "Any skin showing, maybe around the mask's eye holes or where the gloves and sleeves met?"

The pin dug into her palm as she forced herself to think back. She pictured Rory hanging on the assailant, the knife glinting, the hand holding the briefcase swinging . . . a flash of skin as the sleeve pulled back.

"He was white. I saw skin when he attacked Rory."

She shuddered, remembering the thud of the briefcase as it smashed against Rory's side. She hoped the man's arm throbbed, that her soft-mouthed poodle had actually drawn blood when he defended her.

And if he did draw blood?

"Can you get blood DNA from a dog's mouth? I don't know if Rory actually broke the man's skin, but if he did . . ." She shrugged, hoping she hadn't asked a stupid question.

But Brockley was pulling out a cell phone, punching a button. "Has Rodriguez arrived? Send her up with her kit. I need her to swab the dog's mouth. Yeah, the poodle."

Closing the phone, Brockley said, "Might be a long shot, but it's worth a try. Is there anything else you can tell me?"

Kim shook her head, dislodging another lock of hair. She froze. Was the envelope showing?

Rory barked and raced down the hall towards the kitchen. A knock sounded. Brockley motioned her to stay seated, then followed Rory. As soon as he was out of sight, Kim reached back and frantically began stuffing hunks of hair back into the make-shift bun.

She heard the Dutch door open and low voices, but couldn't make out the words. Her fingers fumbled, another pin fell out. She grabbed it and jabbed it back in just as Rory reappeared.

Lieutenant Brockley was close behind, followed by a short, attractive Hispanic woman. He introduced her as Officer Rodriguez.

"Think you can hold the hero dog while I swab his mouth?" The woman's soft smile contrasted with her crisp uniform and no-nonsense voice.

"Before you do that . . ." Brockley pulled out a wallet, extracted a business card and wrote something on the back. "You need to beef up security," he said, He handed her the card. "There's no alarm on the patio or kitchen doors. Do you even lock the interior door to the store?"

She stared at him blankly.

"I didn't think so," he said. "Give these people a call. They'll give you a good price on a decent security system. Be warned; he's my brother-in-law. My cell number's on the front. Call if you think of anything else."

Kim watched him disappear down the hall. When she turned back to Officer Rodriguez, she found the woman smiling.

"Quite a hunk, huh?" Then, before Kim could answer, the woman added, "Could you hold your dog's head like this . . . thanks." She wiped the inside of Rory's mouth, tucked the swab into a small plastic bag, then pulled out another. "Too bad Brockley's shell-shocked. He's had a rough time since moving here. C'mon big boy, open your mouth for me."

Rory allowed the woman to open his mouth. She reached in with the second swab.

"How hard can it be working in Calvert County?" Kim said, turning over the woman's words. "There didn't used to be much crime here."

"Still isn't. And that's part of the problem." Rodriguez slipped the swab into a bag, grabbed another and returned to Rory's mouth. "He was a hotshot homicide detective in Baltimore County. This was a real step down."

"So why's he here?"

"Wife insisted. Wanted a safe place to raise the kids." She released Rory's muzzle and gave him a vigorous ear scratch. "What a good boy. You sure showed that nasty old man, didn't you?"

Kim focused on what the woman had been doing and not on the word "wife." "Did you get anything? I'd have thought he would swallow any blood."

"Blood is surprisingly persistent." Rodriguez tucked the swabs into her bag, closed it and stood. "We won't run DNA tests until we get a solid suspect -- don't have the budget. But this should help nail the guy if we find him."

Kim followed Rodriguez into the kitchen. Hating herself, she asked "So. Brockley's bored in Calvert County. I hope the wife is happy."

Rodriguez grinned. "Wouldn't know. Right after Brock made the transfer, she took the kids and moved home to Maine." The officer reached for the door knob, smiled over her shoulder. "Which makes him the hottest bachelor in the county."

Rodriguez swung the door wide to reveal a scowling Lieutenant Brockley.

CHAPTER 5

Officer Rodriguez gasped, a raw red color spreading up her neck and across her face. Lieutenant Brockley fixed her with cold eyes, then transferred his scowl to Kim. Kim resisted the urge to step back. After all, she wasn't the one gossiping.

"Rodriguez, if you're through, go help the others pack up." Brockley's emphasis on "through" left no doubt that he'd heard the woman's comments.

As Rodriguez scurried outside, Kim assumed an innocent face and forced herself to meet Brockley's eyes.

"Can I go to the hospital now?" she asked.

Brockley's mouth softened. "We're just about finished. We've sealed off the office, so don't go in there. But you can use the rest of the house."

"How long will you have the office roped off? Grandpa will want to open the store as soon as he leaves the hospital."

"I suspect we'll be able to release it tomorrow."

Kim nodded, felt her hair shift. Two more bobby pins fell to the tiled floor with a clink. She reached back, but the remaining pins could no longer support the heavy locks. Hair cascaded against her neck. She felt the edge of the envelope sticking out of the elastic band.

Brockley grinned. "I always wondered how women held their hair up. I guess the answer is they don't."

Kim palmed the envelope with her left hand and forced a smile. "Yeah, well, I'm less competent with these things than most women." She held out her right hand. "But I really need to go to Grandpa. Thank you for coming."

Thank you for coming? Oh, she really needed sleep.

Fortunately, Brockley either didn't notice her nervousness or assumed it stemmed from the need to rush to the hospital. Or that she was just a flake.

"We'll lock up downstairs," Brockley said, shaking her hand, "But make sure you reset the alarm." Turning, he trotted down the outside stairs.

Kim closed the door, leaned against it and let out a long sigh. Great. Just great. The hottest guy in Calvert County thought she was a bimbo like cousin Tiffany.

A car door slammed. Kim turned and peered through the window into the deepening dusk. The sheriff department's black-and-white pulled away, followed by Brockley's unmarked sedan. For a minute she could hear the clack of gravel against the cars' undercarriages. Then silence.

Opening her clenched left fist, she stared at the now crumpled envelope. Time to find out what Grandpa wanted her to hide.

She locked the door and with Rory trotting beside her returned to the living room. Plopping onto the couch, she unfolded the envelope.

Odd. There was writing on the front. Grandpa's writing.

The words blurred. Kim removed her glasses and pinched the bridge of her nose. Grandpa wasn't going to die. There were good reasons Mom hadn't called. Grandpa was probably still in surgery. When Kim got to the hospital, she'd find him sitting up in bed complaining that he was bored.

Slowly, the urge to cry diminished. She replaced her glasses and studied the envelope.

Grandpa had written "Will it pass DiamondView?" Underneath, someone else had scrawled "yes."

Kim frowned. Why in the world would Grandpa send something to New York for a DiamondView test?

When De Beers announced the creation of DiamondView, an instrument that measured a gemstone's fluorescence, Grandpa had scoffed. There were other, less expensive ways to distinguish natural diamonds from man-made, he'd told Kim. Look at the stone's inclusions, study the facets and grain lines. If all else failed, use the darn diamond tester. Nothing conducted heat as well as diamond and the hand-held tester not only measured heat conductivity, it was inexpensive. Grandpa kept one in his office.

No, Grandpa told her, De Beers might claim DiamondView was a jeweler's last line of defense against lab-made diamonds. But that was just another marketing ploy designed to separate a fool from his money.

And yet . . . Grandpa had actually requested a DiamondView test? Why? What made the contents of this envelope so special?

Only one way to find out.

Kim slipped the tissue-wrapped stone from the envelope and teased the paper apart. Her breath caught.

Blue. The diamond that winked in her hand was a lustrous, Caribbean blue.

She'd never seen a blue diamond. Well, okay, she'd seen the Hope and other fancy colored diamonds at the Smithsonian. But she'd never held one in her hand. Grandpa's clients couldn't afford blue diamonds.

This one had been cut in the classic round style. It was larger than a pea, maybe lima bean size. Which made it . . . four carats? Five?

Large for a diamond. Outrageously large for a fancy colored diamond.

As she held the stone to the light, her fingers trembled. The color was more vivid than sapphire, more like her favorite London Blue topaz. Unlike sapphire or topaz, however, this stone appeared alive, flashing rays of light across the room. Nothing sparkled like diamond.

As she studied it, the striking color pulled at her, luring her into a sea where light twinkled. She could imagine diving into those depths, swimming through the glistening color . . .

She dropped the stone onto the tissue as if she'd been burned.

Closing her eyes, she forced her breath to slow. What was she doing? She'd never been tempted by diamonds. Diamonds were for gullible women like her aunts or airheads like cousin Tiffany. Kim took pride in being the pragmatic one in the family.

Yet, for a moment, she'd coveted this diamond as she'd never yearned for anything in her life.

She heard Rory snuffle, felt his cold nose on her hand.

She opened her eyes and smiled down at him. Okay, she'd desired this diamond almost as much as she'd wanted a standard poodle.

She raised the stone to the light again, considering. Blue diamonds were rare, so rare that throughout most of history only kings and queens were allowed to own them. Of every ten thousand diamonds the earth created, only one would be fancy colored -- and that, most likely, would be yellow. Probably because nitrogen, which created the yellow hue, was more common than boron, which made the diamond blue.

The rarity prevented most of Grandpa's gemstone sources from stocking natural colored diamonds. If a billionaire walked into the store tomorrow and wanted to buy a natural blue diamond, Grandpa would refer the love-besotted sucker to someone else.

Unfortunately, customers demanded the rare or unique and Grandpa's clients were no exception. Two years ago, Mrs. Johnstone, Grandpa's wealthiest patron, told him she'd seen blue diamonds on the internet selling for thousands, not millions. But she didn't trust the internet.

Could he find one of those blue diamonds for her?

Grandpa distrusted computers, so he'd called Kim in Oregon. Could she search the internet, figure out what his best customer was talking about?

Kim recognized the request as yet another opportunity to entice her back into the family business. But Grandpa had caught her moping around on a rainy Sunday afternoon, so she'd agreed to investigate.

Internet searches gave Kim a Nancy Drew kind of thrill, and this one was no exception. She easily found listings for blue diamonds like the ones Mrs. Johnstone had mentioned, most often accompanied by complaints: The earring colors didn't match, the color wasn't deep enough, the stones were chipped, flawed, foggy. Even people who'd received exactly what they expected commented on problems with shipping or seller honesty.

A good reason to forego buying diamonds on the internet.

Kim, however, was more interested in where the colored diamonds originated. As she dug deeper into her research, she discovered the blue diamonds sold online weren't naturally blue. The color had been created through irradiation.

Turns out that heating or irradiating off-color, inferior diamonds could turn them into spectacular shades of blue, yellow, pink and brown. Because the color came from human intervention, however, the "enhanced" diamonds were considerably less expensive than naturally colored ones.

The blue diamond she held in her hand had probably been heated or irradiated and, therefore, would sell for tens of thousands instead of millions.

Kim dropped it into the tissue. Still too rich for her blood. But now she understood why Grandpa was willing to pay for DiamondView. If he was going to sell a ten or twenty thousand dollar diamond to Mrs. Johnstone, he'd want to make darn sure the stone was real, that the irradiation was the only treatment used on the diamond.

Thank goodness he'd had the foresight to carry the diamond in his pocket instead of tucking it into the now-stolen briefcase.

Something tugged at the back of Kim's mind, a whispered voice. Grandpa's?

The grandfather clock began chiming. She needed to get to the hospital. But what could she do with the diamond? The police had roped off the office, so she couldn't put it in the safe. And she certainly couldn't carry a precious diamond in her purse and risk losing it to a petty thief.

Besides, as Grandpa liked to tease, she could lose a camel in her purse. No, she needed an interim place to hide the diamond.

Hide.

Hide? Kim stared down at the diamond. Why did Grandpa want her to hide this? And hide it from who?

The Raiders March from Indiana Jones played. Kim snatched her cell phone and glanced at caller I.D. Mom.

"Mom, how's Grandpa?"

Her mother burst into tears.

CHAPTER 6

Kim had never been good at waiting. Sitting in an emergency room with wailing babies, coughing children and glassy-eyed adults would try her patience under the best of circumstances. Add in her own shell-shocked mother, three angry aunts and an assortment of cousins, husbands and boyfriends and Kim had to consciously resist the urge to go screaming into the night.

Falling apart, however, wouldn't help Grandpa. He was fighting for his life. The doctors needed to focus their attention on him, not hysterical family members.

She'd arrived at the hospital in time to hear the young surgeon attempt to explain Grandpa's condition. Upon arrival, they'd whisked Grandpa into surgery. The knife had plunged deep; the damage was severe. The operation was going well when, an hour into the surgery, Grandpa's heart stopped.

They'd resuscitated him, but he was still in danger. The rest of the surgery went as planned. They were now transferring Grandpa to the intensive care unit.

At least, that's what she thought the surgeon said. Her aunts were so busy bombarding the poor man with accusatory questions, it was difficult to hear him. As he stuttered partial answers, her aunts' questions turned into a rant. Kim watched the doctor's eyes widen, his shoulders hunch, his right foot turn towards the exit.

Before he could flee, Kim interrupted the verbal assault with the piercing, two-finger whistle Grandpa taught her when she was eight. Silence descended throughout the room.

"How soon can we see him?" she asked.

The surgeon turned tired brown eyes on her. "Once we get him settled, you can visit one at a time. But please be aware that because of the cardiac arrest, we've put him into a medically induced coma . . ."

"Coma!" Cousin Amber buried her pierced-nosed face into the chest of the latest boyfriend, another of what Kim had dubbed "thug of the month."

The latest outburst proved too much for the doctor. Turning, he fled the room.

"Coma!" Amber repeated, her voice muffled in ... What was his name? Darin, that's right ... in Darin's leather jacket. He awkwardly patted her back.

"Medically induced coma," Kim clarified. "It's to keep his brain from swelling while he heals . . ."

"Nooooooo . . ."

"For heaven's sake, Amber, pull yourself together," Aunt Ruby hissed at her daughter. "You're making a spectacle of yourself."

Kim winced. A would-be actress, Amber's melodramatic tendencies had become a family joke. But Aunt Ruby's obsession with appearances, another family joke, was totally misplaced right now.

"Just think of it as enforced sleeping," she told Amber's back.

Amber sniffed and turned her head. "Sleeping?"

"Yeah, sleep of the dead," Darin said.

Kim glared up at Amber's new flame. Like Amber's previous boyfriends, Darin sported too-tight jeans, too-large muscles, too-little brains and a perpetual sneer.

He glowered back at her, the challenge unmistakable in his eyes. Kim's heart beat faster, but she resisted the urge to step away from this towering hunk of menace. Showing weakness only encouraged bullies.

Instead, she spread her legs, weight on the balls of her feet, and lifted her chin. "Why are you being such an ass?"

"Hey, it was a joke." He gave Kim what he clearly thought was an innocent expression. But his eyes remained icy.

Kim frowned. Darin's deeply tanned skin contrasted so sharply with his pale blue eyes, he could have been wearing a mask . . .

Were the eyes lighter or darker than the mask? Lieutenant Brockley had asked.

Kim's breath caught, her chest muscles constricting. The thought that had started to form while Brockley interviewed her crystallized: No thief would steal an old briefcase -- unless he knew Grandpa transported jewelry in the case.

Misinterpreting her silence as victory, Darin snagged Amber's hand and led her to the other side of the room, where cousins Tiffany and Goldie had saved seats.

Kim watched Darin strut away, her mind racing.

Had Amber told Darin about Grandpa's New York trips? It wouldn't be the smartest thing to say to someone who looked like a wanted poster. But Amber wasn't known for discretion.

Okay, in all fairness, they'd all spilled the beans at some point in their lives. Kim herself had once broadcast Grandpa's trips to a schoolyard of twelve-year-olds.

Her face grew warm as she remembered that first day of Middle School. She'd been desperate to fit in with the coiffed, designer-clad sons and daughters of lawyers, doctors and business hotshots.

Conscious of her Walmart jeans, she'd stared at the ground while her new classmates tried to one-up each other with tales of summer vacations in Paris, Rome and Venice.

Kim scuffed her tennis shoe on the ground, wishing the darn school bell would ring before her turn arrived. How could she confess to her new friends that her school-teacher parents couldn't afford exotic vacations? Heck, she wouldn't have traveled anywhere that summer if Grandpa hadn't bought a train ticket for her to accompany him on one of his New York trips ...

New York, train, jewels ... Kim had read enough mystery novels to recognize a winning combination.

At last, the moment she'd been dreading arrived and the group turned expectant eyes onto Kim. Confident now, she'd launched into an elaborate tale of intrigue, spies and adroit evasion. By the time she finished, the one-day business trip rivaled any James Bond tale. Even Jason White, heir to the White Jewelry dynasty, had been impressed.

At no point in the story had she actually lied. There had, indeed, been a man on the train wearing a trench coat. And he was reading a newspaper and he did keep looking at them. Probably because Kim was giggling too loudly. But Agatha Christie never revealed all, so why should Kim?

For that one glorious day, Kim reigned as sixth-grade queen.

The glory ended that evening, however, when she confessed to Grandpa that she'd revealed his monthly jewelry buying trips to an entire crowd. To this day, she could close her eyes and see the disappointment on his face. He didn't need to vocalize the words that clearly passed through his mind: He could expect such carelessness from Amber, Tiffany or even Opal. But not Kim.

That same night she'd dreamed of the man in the trench coat. This time, however, he followed them from the train station, down Fashion Avenue, into a dark, mist-shrouded alley. Kim grabbed Grandpa's hand, told him to run. But their legs wouldn't move fast enough and she pulled Grandpa along through quicksand and a trench coat clad arm raised and a knife glistened and Kim woke up, screaming.

The morning sun did little to dispel the lingering fear. She was certain her careless brag had endangered Grandpa. She could think of only one way to protect him.

That day at school, she gathered her new friends together and told her first, and last, lie. Not only did she make up the entire story, she said, Grandpa didn't transport jewels from New York. He relied on FedEx just like everyone else.

For the next three years, her former "friends" made Middle School a living nightmare.

But Grandpa was safe and the nightmare never returned.

Until tonight.

Tonight a childhood fear had materialized into reality. Someone who knew Grandpa carried jewels in that briefcase had attacked him with a knife.

So who knew about the briefcase? Grandpa's business associates, of course. Family members. Family members' friends?

Had someone, maybe Amber, trusted the wrong person?

Kim studied Amber's leather-clad boyfriend. Height and weight matched her memory of the man who'd attacked Grandpa. As did those cold eyes.

Darin slouched in his chair, legs stretched into the aisle, ignoring a woman trying to push a walker past him. The woman hesitated, clearly torn between asking him to move his feet and retreating. A second passed, two.

Amber slapped Darin's knee. "Your big feet are in the way."

"Oh?" Darin pulled his legs away and bowed in the woman's direction.

As the poor woman shuffled passed Darin, he draped an arm around Amber, his jacket opening to reveal a black t-shirt imprinted with a skull and cross bones.

Why was he still wearing that heavy jacket? The hospital's air conditioning had long ago succumbed to the hot air generated by the crowd. Kim regretted exchanging those pocketless shorts for jeans. Surely Darin was stifling in all that leather.

Was he sacrificing comfort for looking cool? Or trying to hide dog bite marks?

She frowned, considering. It'd taken, what, twenty minutes for the ambulance and police to arrive? Then another hour and a half of police questioning. Twenty minutes to reach the hospital. Amber and Darin had arrived a few minutes after her.

She computed the times in her head. If Darin was Grandpa's assailant, he'd had a solid two hours to return home, hide the briefcase, change clothes and respond to Amber's distress call.

Should she call Brockley, tell him her suspicions? She shuddered, imagining her family's reaction to police storming the room. Especially if Darin was guilty of nothing more than bad manners.

Best to confirm Darin's involvement before calling Brockley. But how did she convince a thug to remove his jacket?

She glanced back at Mom and her aunts. They'd found seats together in the corner of the room. Mom leaned against Dad's shoulder, eyes closed. Aunt Emerald's ramrod posture and Botox mask belied her white-knuckled hold on Uncle Tom. Aunt Sapphire and Aunt Ruby sat side-by-side, Sapphire's blond head tipped toward her sister's newly red one. Their husbands book-ended them. Uncle Walt absently patted Ruby's knee. Uncle Don stared into the distance, the crystal mobile Aunt

Sapphire planned to hang in Grandpa's room dangling from his hands.

For the moment everyone seemed too exhausted to fight. If she was going to investigate Darin, now was the time.

Donning what she hoped was a neutral expression, she wove her way past a sniffling toddler, a groaning pre-teen and a dozen exhausted mothers. Tiffany spotted her first.

"Oh, Kim, wait till I show you . . ."

But Kim tuned out the rest of Tiffany's words. Tiff's ability to babble nonstop nonsense was legendary. Family members learned long ago to smile, nod and tune her out. Right now, however, Kim didn't have the core space to play along.

Holding up a hand to stop the flow of words, Kim smiled at Tiffany. "Tell me later, okay?"

She knelt in front of Amber and patted her hand. "How you holding up?"

Amber sniffed. "Okay, I guess. It's just such a shock, ya know?"

"It's a good thing you had Darin with you when Aunt Ruby called."

"Oh, Darin wasn't with me, were you honey?" Amber squeezed Darin's knee. "But you came right away when I called."

Darin's eyes narrowed. "You make me sound like a dog."

"Oh, she didn't mean that." If this guy had attacked Grandpa, she sure didn't want him angry with Amber. "She's just grateful to you for, er, coming so quickly to her rescue."

"That's right." Amber giggled. "My knight in black leather."

Darin's shoulders relaxed and Kim hastened to use the opening Amber had unwittingly provided.

"Aren't you hot in that jacket?" Kim fanned her own face. "A/C isn't working real well."

The sneer returned to Darin's face. "I can take it."

As if sitting in a stifling hot jacket was a macho thing to do.

Okay, the direct approach didn't work. Time to use her psychology degree.

Problem was, she didn't know much about Darin. From his behavior tonight, she could assume he was quick to take offense, prone to snide remarks and concerned about his masculinity. He reminded her of a character from the movie Grease. On the plus side, he seemed to enjoy Amber calling him her knight.

So let's try the chivalrous approach.

Kim reached out and touched her cousin's bare arms.

"My goodness, Amber, your skin is so cold."

"Really?" Amber touched her arm. "I guess you're right."

"Did you bring a jacket or anything?" Kim looked from Amber to Darin. Now was his chance.

Instead of removing his jacket, however, Darin pulled Amber onto his lap.

"I can keep you warm, babe."

Amber giggled and snuggled against him. Kim sat back on her heels, trying to keep the frustration from showing in her face. Maybe she should just call the police, let them handle Darin.

No. She could do this. She just needed to . . . to think like a thug. Yeah. Heaven knows she'd observed plenty. For the last five years Amber had paraded a new one at every holiday dinner.

Okay. So what did they have in common aside from the clothes, sneers and tattoos? Tattoos . . . Surely Darin had one somewhere. And he'd have to take off his jacket to show it off.

"So, Darin, tell me about yourself." Better come at this sideways. "Do you work around here?"

"Nah."

Oh, great, a real talker.

Fortunately, Amber wasn't shy about talking. "He works for that Harley store, you know, the one in College Park?"

"Didn't what's his name, your last boyfriend, work there?"

"Yeah." Amber nodded her head. "You're thinking of Tom."

Darin stiffened, then slid Amber off his lap and back onto the empty chair. "Well, he's not there anymore. Got fired."

"Really?" Amber's eyes widened. "I thought he moved to D.C."

The muscles in Darin's neck tightened. "Moved there after he was fired."

Watching the exchange, Kim remembered something else Amber's boyfriends all had in common: They were competitive. Maybe she could use that.

"Tom was always showing off his tattoos," she said. "He had some pretty neat ones."

"Yeah, well, some guys are just insecure," Darin replied.

Huh. Did that mean Darin didn't have tattoos? Or was he afraid to take off his jacket?

Darin's hands clenched and unclenched, clenched and unclenched. Like he was squeezing an exercise ball.

"Exercise."

Had she spoken the word aloud? No, that had been Goldie's voice. Sitting on the other side of Amber, Goldie was describing the Zumba class she and Tiffany were taking.

"I never knew exercising could be such fun," Goldie said. "I've lost five pounds already!"

Kim rolled her eyes and looked away. Like Goldie needed to lose weight. She'd been blessed with the metabolism of Grandma's side of the family.

"So is it, like, a dance class?" Amber said.

"Sort of. I mean, we're learning steps and doing them to music. But the emphasis is on getting a cardio workout."

"I've heard dancers have a hard time keeping weight on," Kim offered.

Goldie turned to her. "That's true. But that's only if you work out four, five hours a day."

"Aren't you worried about getting too muscular?" Amber said.

"Heck, no. A little bit of muscle is good for you." Goldie rolled up her t-shirt, formed a fist and flexed her arm. "See?"

Darin scoffed. "That's not muscle!"

And suddenly Kim knew exactly how to get that jacket off.

"Sure it is," Kim said. She turned to Tiffany. "Let's see your muscle."

Giggling, Tiff flexed her arm.

"Hmm . . . I think Goldie's is bigger," Kim said.

"What about mine?" Amber was now flexing. "I lift a lot of boxes at work."

"Oh, wow, that's a great muscle." Kim flexed her own arm. "Mine's pretty good, too, from wrestling Rory."

Now Tiffany was laughing. "Wrestling poodles! Who'd have thought that'd be good exercise?"

Kim slid her eyes towards Darin. He'd scooted forward on his chair and was watching them intently. This might actually work.

"Let's have a contest, decide what makes the best muscle," she said, "Zumba, lifting boxes or poodle wrestling. Tiff, you be the judge."

Tiffany clapped.

"Okay, ladies, on three we all make a muscle and Tiffany will tell us which is the best. Ready? One, two . . ."

Darin couldn't resist. Before Kim said the final number, he whipped off his jacket and flexed his right arm. His bare, non-bruised right arm.

"There," he said. "This is what a muscle should look at."

As her cousins cooed over Darin's muscled arm, Kim slouched over, suddenly feeling the effects of a long drive, no sleep and constant worry. Rory's teeth hadn't touched this man. At least she hadn't needlessly called the police.

Of course, just because Darin was innocent didn't mean Amber's past boyfriends were. Maybe she should ask Darin why what's-his-name . . . Tom . . . why Tom had been fired. Or maybe she should just tell the police and let them interview Amber's former beaus.

What was keeping the doctor so long? Shouldn't Grandpa be in his room now?

"I insist we move Dad to Anne Arundel." Aunt Emerald's piercing voice cut across the room. Kim looked up in time to see her aunt leap to her feet. "This podunk hospital is going to kill him."

"Keep your voice down," Aunt Ruby said. "You're going to get us thrown out of here."

"Good. And we'll take Dad with us."

Sighing, Kim stood and began making her way back across the room. Under the circumstances, the truce had lasted longer than she had any right to hope. Even so, she struggled to quash her rising annoyance.

She loved her aunts. Really, she did. But all the psychology courses in the world would never enable her to empathize with them.

She now understood intellectually that many of their idiosyncrasies began when Grandma named her four daughters Diamondtina, Emerald, Ruby and Sapphire. When Kim was a child she'd assumed this naming convention came from a craziness peculiar to her family. Later, in college, she was fascinated to learn that it was quite common. She'd met women who'd been named for flowers, days of the week, cities, characters from Greek drama. Parents seemed to think unique names would make their children special. Heck, she'd named Rory for the man who invented the ink blot.

All that was harmless except for one thing: Children, unlike poodles, often fixated on the origins and meaning of their names. So it was no surprise that Mom and her sisters developed an early interest in gemstones.

Grandpa, however, magnified their infatuation by bestowing each of them with real gemstones to match their namesakes. The sisters continued what they considered family tradition by naming their own children in honor of Grandpa's trade. By the time Kim came along, all of her relatives were so obsessed with jewelry they reminded Kim of bunch of black holes, ravenously sucking in every glittering thing within reach.

Despite their common obsession, however, the four sisters were temperamentally quite distinct. No one was surprised when practical Mom, the oldest, not only became a school teacher, but married one. The other three sisters snagged wealthy husbands, which allowed them to indulge their eccentricities. Emerald grew more bossy, Ruby more concerned with what the neighbors were thinking, Sapphire more convinced that gemstones possessed mystical powers that, properly harnessed, would heal the world.

But while temperaments defined the sisters' separate paths, their infatuation with all things jewelry held them in orbit around Grandpa. Given the women's idiosyncrasies, it wasn't surprising for the natural balance to become disrupted by periodic explosions.

"The doctor said Dad was too sick to move." Though Mom's voice was calm, Kim could hear the strain.

"Anne Arundel's a better hospital." Aunt Emerald crossed her arms and raised her chin.

"Don't worry, Emmy, these will protect Dad." Sapphire flicked a finger at the mobile Uncle Don held, creating a soft tinkle as the crystals connected.

"Don't call me Emmy."

Kim opened her mouth, closed it. Though she agreed with Aunt Emerald's comparison of the two hospitals -- how could a hospital in low-populated Calvert County compete with the big guys in Annapolis? -- she suspected Grandpa was too weak to transport elsewhere. If the doctors thought it necessary to induce coma, the trip to Annapolis could kill him.

"Dad isn't the only thing we need to worry about." Ruby stood and faced her sisters. "If we don't get the store open, we'll lose a ton of business."

Oh, no. Grandpa would hate having the aunts dealing with his customers.

But Ruby plowed on. Pulling out a sheet of paper, she announced "We can take turns manning the store. I've made a timetable. Tomorrow I'll take the first shift . . ."

Grandpa's words swam into Kim's mind: I can't join you, honey. Ruby would steal me blind, Emerald's pushiness and Sapphire's flakiness would chase away my regulars, and your mom would be helpless to stop them.

The doctors were doing all they could to save Grandpa's life. She needed to ensure Grandpa had a life to return to. Which meant she had to put a stop to this.

"I'll take care of the store," she heard herself saying. Four pairs of eyes shifted her way. Kim tried a casual shrug. "I'm staying there anyway, so it only makes sense . . ."

"And that's another thing," Aunt Ruby said, "We can't have a dog running through Dad's house. Filthy beast."

Filthy! How many dogs were bathed two or three times a month and brushed almost constantly? And as for presentable ...

"At least Rorschach has good manners," Kim snapped without thinking. She bit her lip, cutting off her next remark, as Grandpa's words swam into her head: Think before you speak.

Her superego, however, had waited too long to assert itself. Kim should have known better than to challenge Aunt Ruby's authority. The others were sure to take offense.

Sure enough, all three aunts were now on their feet, united in their effort to remove Kim not only from the conversation, but from Grandpa's house. The unfairness left Kim momentarily speechless.

"You all know Dad invited Kim to stay with him." Mom's calm voice belied the tightness around her mouth. "You've got no say in this."

"Yeah, well, Dad can't say a whole lot now, can he?" Aunt Emerald's sweeping arm aimed towards the Intensive Care Unit. "We need to prepare in case Dad doesn't make it."

Kim clenched her fists and moved into Aunt Emerald's personal space. Startled, Emerald shifted back.

"Don't even think that!" Hearing the panic in her voice, Kim swallowed and tried to pitch her voice lower. "Grandpa is in a medically induced coma to keep his brain from swelling. Not a real coma. He will survive."

"He's 76 years old." Dad's gentle voice brought tears to Kim's eyes. "He's fighting an uphill battle."

Removing her glasses, she pinched the bridge of her nose.

"Don't forget his heart attack during surgery." Aunt Ruby's voice caught. Clearing her throat, she continued. "We've got to prepare for the worse."

Kim shook her head. No. No way. Grandpa would survive.

He might be 76, but . . . His family practice doc recently declared him healthy. Sure, he was at risk for heart attack. But the blood-pressure and anti-cholesterol medicines should fix that.

Grandpa had grumbled about the new meds, but with pressure from Kim, he'd filled the prescriptions. And whenever she asked about it, he'd assured her he was taking the medicine. Grandpa never lied to her.

No, her aunts were wrong. Aunt Ruby's idea of "prepare for the worse" was nothing more than her typical gloom and doom. The others were going along because . . . because they wanted access to the store and its contents.

Access Grandpa had prevented when he turned down Kim's invitation to join her in Arkansas.

Kim clenched her fists. If Grandpa had come to Crater of Diamonds, he wouldn't have been alone and helpless when the thief arrived. The attack on Grandpa was partly her aunts' fault and there was no way she was going to let them take advantage of Grandpa's incapacity and destroy his business.

Replacing her glasses, she broke into the conversation. "Grandpa doesn't want any of you helping in the store."

Her audacious honesty stopped the argument cold. Everyone stared. Even Mom looked a bit shocked.

Well, in for a penny . . . "He told me to handle things if . . . if he ever caught a cold or something."

Aunt Emerald snorted and wagged her finger. "Just because he favors you, young lady, does not give you the right to sass your elders."

"I didn't mean . . ."

But Aunt Emerald rode right over her. "Dad had no business spoiling you, ignoring his other grandchildren."

"He didn't . . ."

"Emerald's right," Aunt Ruby said. "Just because he let you hang around the store doesn't give you special privileges."

"That's not . . ."

"There's nothing to discuss," Aunt Ruby continued. "Dad's in a coma and can't speak for himself. That means his next of kin make the decisions." Her eyes shot arrows at Kim. "His children. Grandchildren have no say in this." She smiled a phony smile. "Even spoiled brats like you can't change the law."

LYNN FRANKLIN

CHAPTER 7

The next morning, Rory's barking woke her. As Kim struggled from a deep sleep, the big poodle leaped from her side and raced through the bedroom door. Kim groaned. Her back ached, her head throbbed and dried tears had glued her eyes shut. Rubbing her eyes, she reached for her glasses and peered at the bedside clock. Nine a.m. She'd been asleep exactly three hours.

Rory's barking now mingled with pounding on the back door.

She sat up, suddenly alert. Grandpa?

No, anyone with news about Grandpa would have a key. And Rory wouldn't bark at family.

Swinging her bare legs off the bed, she decided whoever was at the door could wait while she used the bathroom.

Minutes later, she opened the kitchen door to reveal Lieutenant Brockley. His rumpled clothes and chin stubble indicated he'd been awake all night. She resisted the urge to straighten his tie.

Instead, she pulled the robe tighter.

"Did you find the thug who attacked Grandpa?"

"The alleged thug." Brockley's tone was flat, cold.

Rory sniffed his pant leg, then trotted down the stairs to do his own morning business.

"What do you mean 'alleged'?"

"The only fingerprints on the weapon were yours."

Kim gritted her teeth. "I told you that! The man wore gloves . . ."

"And your poodle just happened to pick up the knife, and you just happened to remove it from his mouth."

Said poodle trotted back up the stairs, hesitated, then placed himself between Kim and Brockley.

"Did you look for dog saliva on the knife?"

Brockley nodded. "But that could have come from your hand."

"Are you saying I stabbed Grandpa?" She fought the wave of fear, anger and frustration that had been threatening to consume her ever since Grandpa was attacked. He lay in the hospital fighting for his life, her aunts wanted to take over his treasured business and there was nothing she could do about any of it. And now the police suspected her?

"I'm saying it's hard to believe Mr. Curly here picked up the weapon."

"He's a retriever!"

Brockley had the nerve to laugh. "Labs are retrievers, setters are retrievers, but this?" He waved a hand at Rory.

"Take out your wallet."

"What?"

Kim took a deep breath, stepped aside and gestured towards the kitchen. "Drop your wallet on the floor. Anywhere."

Frowning, Brockley crossed to the stove, hesitated, then flipped the wallet onto the floor.

Kim said Rory's name and when she had his attention, pointed to the object on the other side of the room. "Rory, get it."

Without hesitation, Rory ran across the floor, his feet sliding on the tile. He snatched the wallet and trotted back to her. She pulled a dog treat from the robe's pocket and exchanged the treat for wallet.

"Good boy." When she looked up, Brockley was leaning against the sink, arms crossed.

"So you told him to retrieve the knife?" The coldness was gone from Brockley's voice.

Kim ran fingers through her hair. "Of course not. Rory's always bringing me things. That's why my fingerprints are on the knife. I was afraid he'd cut himself." She glared at Brockley. "I'm not dumb enough to handle evidence."

"The dog brings you things?"

Oh, jeez, there was no way she could continue this conversation without caffeine.

Crossing the room, she handed Brockley his wallet, holding it in such a way that their hands wouldn't touch. She filled the tea kettle, pulled tea and coffee fixings from the cupboard.

"Obviously, we need to talk. I don't know how to make coffee, so if you want some here's the stuff." She pointed at the bread and toaster. "Make yourself something to eat while I go put some clothes on. There's butter and jelly in the refrigerator."

Without waiting for his reply, she turned and headed for the bedroom. She'd taken a hot shower last night before flopping into bed, so she simply pulled on clean jeans and a t-shirt, then ran a brush through her hair.

The smell of toast made her mouth water. The tea kettle started to whistle as she entered the kitchen. Brockley was sitting at the table, Rory's chin on his lap. He'd set out two plates and knives, the butter and jelly. A plate of toast sat in the middle of the table. He started to rise, but she waved him to his seat.

The coffee pot finished dripping as she poured her tea, so she filled Brockley's mug as well.

"To answer your question," Kim said as she sat across from Brockley, "I taught Rory to bring me things." She reached for the sugar bowl, which Grandpa had filled with her favorite sweetener. "When he was a puppy, he was always picking things off the floor. I was worried that he'd swallow something, so I taught him to exchange whatever he picked up for a cookie.

"That's why he picked up the knife."

Brockley nodded and reached for the toast. "Thank you for this. Haven't eaten anything since last night."

"Do you really think I stabbed my own grandfather?"

Brockley swallowed a bite of toast. "You've made a decent argument for why your prints are on the knife."

Kim frowned. That wasn't what she'd asked, but she probably shouldn't push it.

"Any sign of the guy who attacked Grandpa?"

"No one showed up at a nearby emergency room to have stitches."

"But Rory must have broken the guy's skin. Officer Rodriguez swabbed blood from his mouth."

"Could have been blood from the knife."

Grandpa's blood. No, don't go there.

"Can't you compare the DNA you found in Rory's mouth with Grandpa's? That would at least confirm Rory broke the guy's skin." And that there was an attacker.

Brockley nodded. "We could. But DNA takes a long time to process and there's no reason to run the test at this time."

"But . . ."

Brockley held up a hand. "The test is expensive and the lab is overworked. We'll wait to talk with your grandfather when he, er, wakes up."

Kim slumped into her seat, her stomach churning from the acid in the tea.

"Don't worry, we'll get this guy. Now that he's progressed from burglary to assault, we can put more guys onto this."

"Uh, I had a thought last night." Before she could lose courage, she explained the significance of Grandpa's briefcase, her theory that he'd been attacked by someone who knew Grandpa carried jewelry in it.

"A thief who followed Mr. Hershey from New York to Maryland before attacking him?" Brockley smiled. "More likely our burglar planned to use the briefcase to carry away the jewelry. And you arrived before he could open the safe."

Kim frowned. That didn't sound right either. Didn't crooks bring their own loot bags? Besides, he'd need to get into the safe . . .

Oh, no, had he opened the safe, stolen everything? She'd been so worried about Grandpa, she hadn't even glanced at the safe.

"So he got the safe open?"

"No. We think you interrupted him."

Kim sighed in relief and reached for her tea. Grandpa purchased good insurance, but even so, the paperwork could occupy her for decades. . .

"Wait a minute." She set her cup down, untasted. "If the thief didn't steal anything, why'd he take the briefcase?"

"What do you mean he didn't steal anything? The showcases were bare."

"Of course they were. Grandpa empties them every night, puts the jewelry back into the safe. He'd never leave stuff in the showcases while he went to New York." She shook her head. "There's just no reason for the thief to take Grandpa's briefcase."

Brockley shrugged. "Thieves don't tend to be the brightest bulbs. And before you ask we did look for the briefcase, but he didn't drop it anywhere nearby."

He reached for another piece of toast. Kim's stomach growled. She needed to convince this guy that no ordinary thief had assaulted Grandpa. But he'd never take her seriously if her gurgling stomach kept interrupting.

Snagging a piece of toast, she smeared it with raspberry jam and bit into it. A few seconds later, her brain registered what she was tasting: Boysenberry. Not raspberry. The jam was sweet, tart, incredibly rich with just a hint of cinnamon -- Grandma's secret ingredient.

The unmarked jar of jam sitting on the table was one of the few remaining jars Grandma had made before she died.

Kim dropped the toast onto her plate. Sliding fingers beneath her glasses, she pinched the bridge of her nose. But the flavor of Grandma's jam remained on her tongue, bringing with it memories of happier days. Picking the boysenberries, one for the basket, one for the mouth. The feel of sunshine on bare shoulders, the smell of ripening fruit, the sound of Grandpa's laughter, the sight of Grandma's gentle face as she accepted the fragrant berries.

Cancer claimed Grandma five years ago. And now Grandpa hovered near death.

Pushing back her chair, Kim stumbled blindly to the kitchen sink. She turned on the water, removed her glasses and wet a paper towel. The cold water removed the tears and soothed her flushed skin. But nothing would remove the vision from last night, Grandpa lying in the hospital bed, his skin thin and white, so fragile, so like Grandma during her last days.

No. Grandpa would not die. And he needed her to stay strong, to fight his battles until he was healthy enough to take over. She could do this. For Grandpa.

She cleaned her glasses, blew her nose and inhaled deeply. Turning to face Brockley, she said

"What would convince you the briefcase is significant?"

Brockley dusted crumbs onto the table. "Were there gemstones in the case? For all we know, it was empty."

Kim returned to the table, sat and reached for her tea. "I can call Grandpa's suppliers, ask them what he picked up. But I'll need to get into his office." She took a sip, savoring the malty flavor.

"We're done with the room, so you can go in now." He leaned back, studied her. "Okay, let's assume for a moment our guy was after the briefcase. Who knew Mr. Hershey carried jewels in it?"

"Grandpa's business associates . . ."

"Any of them here in Calvert?"

Kim sighed and ran fingers through her hair. "Not really, no. I mean, he knows the owners of the local stores, but they really only talk at conferences and things . . ." Kim broke off, remembering a phone conversation. "Last fall, Grandpa sat on a panel discussion at one of the jewelry conferences. I don't remember which one, but it was held in Annapolis. The panel topic was something about competing with the Internet. Grandpa argued you can compete with the internet by personally selecting gemstones for customers. He might have mentioned that he travels to New York . . ."

"To a crowd of hundreds." Shaking his head, Brockley jotted something in his notebook. "I'll talk to the local store owners. I assume your family knows about the briefcase."

"My family had nothing to do with this."

Hearing the anger in her voice, Brockley's eyes widened. But Kim plowed on. "We have our differences like most families. But we all love Grandpa." She leaned forward. "No one would ever harm him.

"Besides, none of the men in the family are tall and muscular like that thug. Well, okay, my cousin Tony is tall, but he's built like a swimmer, not a body builder."

"So maybe whoever set this up had a partner."

Kim stilled, willing her face to go blank. She'd been about to tell Brockley about Amber's slimy boyfriends. It never occurred to her, however, that he'd suspect her cousin of conspiring to steal from Grandpa. Amber might be a drama queen, but she wasn't a thief.

"My family has no motivation to steal from Grandpa." Seeing Brockley's incredulous expression, she added, "When a family member wants something, Grandpa discounts the price so far he actually loses money."

Brockley shrugged, saying he'd learned to never underestimate people's greed.

Kim mentally kicked herself. She'd wanted to point the police in the correct direction so they'd catch the guy who stabbed Grandpa -- not make everyone in her family suspects. Why hadn't she predicted Brockley's response to her theory? Better to have the police looking in the wrong direction than suspecting her own family.

Time to backpedal.

"You know, as we talk, the idea that someone broke in here just to steal Grandpa's briefcase sounds farfetched. Much more likely Grandpa's attacker is the same guy you've been chasing."

To her relief, Brockley nodded.

"I'm sorry for wasting your time," she added.

"Best to look at all options." Brockley stood and headed for the door.

Kim watched him trot down the back stairs and into his car. But even after he disappeared from sight, his earlier words hung in the air: Maybe whoever set this up had a partner.

Her mind flashed to the scene at the hospital, to Amber's tears, her excessive wailing.

True sorrow? Or guilt?

CHAPTER 8

Kim poured a new cup of tea and carried it into the living room. Morning sunlight filtered through the sliding-glass doors and illuminated the dust particles that drifted from the sofa as she sat. The toast she'd eaten lay heavy in her stomach. Cradling the warm mug in her hands, she tucked her legs beneath her and fought a wave of despair.

She'd been back in Maryland less than twenty-four hours and the experience was worse than any of her nightmares. Grandpa lay helpless in the ICU. Her aunts were plotting to take over his store. And she just gave Brockley reason to suspect her family of burglary.

Good going, Kim.

And yet . . . she couldn't shake Brockley's words from her mind. Never underestimate greed.

Kim would never describe a family member as greedy. Avaricious was more appropriate. Or at least that had been her decision when she learned the word for a third-grade spelling contest. She'd loved the way the word filled her mouth and ended with the hissing sound of a snake.

That's what her aunts and cousins reminded her of, greedy snakes who consumed diamonds, emeralds and rubies as fast as Grandpa could stock them. What they couldn't afford they tried to "borrow". Diamonds, of course. Always diamonds. Like her female relatives were movie stars or something.

But the borrowed necklace Meryl Streep wore to the Oscars could later be sold for the same or even higher than the original price. Her aunts' borrowed jewelry had to be cleaned and sold as used. Which meant every time his daughters "borrowed" something, Grandpa lost money.

Her aunts, of course, suggested he sell the jewelry as new. After all, no one would ever know.

Grandpa, however, refused to lie to his customers. Her aunts argued. Finally, Grandpa abandoned reason and simply forbid his daughters from borrowing jewelry. To their outraged "why?" he replied with the stock answer from their childhood: Because I'm the father and I said so.

Good thing her aunts eventually snagged wealthy husbands. While they weren't millionaires, they'd married into Annapolis society and had both the resources and the special occasions to justify buying new jewelry.

Still. Diamonds were as expensive as her aunts were stingy and her aunts never understood why Grandpa wouldn't resell borrowed jewelry as new. Kim had seen Grandpa invoke the I'm-the-father rule many times.

But would they actually try to steal?

As for her cousins . . . She really hadn't spent much time with them. At least as adults. When they'd been children, they'd defined her universe. Weekly family gatherings forced her to "play nice" with a mob of females interested only in clothes, jewelry and boys. Tony, the only boy in the mix, was five years younger than Kim making him too little to do anything interesting like climb trees.

Grandma was an excellent cook, but all the lasagna in the world couldn't compensate for the endless dinner discussions about diamonds, rubies and the latest fashion. Aunt Emerald would inevitably chastise Kim for swinging her legs or putting her elbows on the table or chewing her fingernails. And always, always, someone would suggest an after-dinner trip to the jewelry store so little Tiffany, Goldie or Jade could buy something for an upcoming dance recital.

Amber had been the drama queen. As Aunt Ruby's middle daughter -- neither the big sister nor the coddled baby -- Amber garnered attention by acting out movie scenes. She'd marched around the backyard singing "Heigh Ho," scrunched her face ala Home Alone, mimicked karate moves.

Aunt Ruby, however, remained indifferent to Amber's theatrics, even when Amber landed the female lead in her high school's production of Macbeth. No amount of "out, damn spot" could draw Aunt Ruby's attention from her afternoon teas, tennis matches and benefit balls.

However, the first time Amber arrived home astride the back of a motorcycle, her arms wrapped around a big, burly guy with chains hanging from his shoulders, Aunt Ruby's outrage could be heard in the next county.

Thus began the thug-of-the-month game. Whenever Aunt Ruby began taking her middle daughter for granted, Amber produced a new boyfriend. Kim suspected a lot of these guys were fellow actors, drawn from Amber's drama classes. Especially the one who showed up in guy-liner. That was so over the top Aunt Ruby didn't blink an eye; it was almost as if she didn't see the fellow.

Kim always assumed Amber's boyfriends weren't actual law-breakers. And yet . . . She could remember Amber's reaction to a television re-run of "To Catch a Thief." While Amber's sisters dissected

Grace Kelly's wardrobe, Amber swooned over Cary Grant's suave burglar character.

Had the adult Amber become involved with an actual thief?

She needed to talk to Amber. Preferably today.

She needed to do a lot of things today. Starting with figuring out a way to prevent her aunts from destroying Grandpa's business while he recovered.

Last night she'd postponed her ejection from Grandpa's house by pointing out the dangers of letting it stand empty. But she'd been unable to convince her aunts to stay away from the store. They'd argued that Grandpa needed the July Fourth sales to sustain him until the Christmas holiday rush. And since the doctors planned to keep Grandpa for a week . . .

On the surface, their desire to open the store appeared considerate. But Kim knew her aunts all too well.

They couldn't balance their own checkbooks, let alone a business ledger. And forget about operating the cash register. The one time Aunt Sapphire attempted it, she'd jammed everything so thoroughly Grandpa had to call in a repairman. Then there was her aunts' better-than-thou attitude. Not a good way to sell jewelry.

Add all that to the way they viewed Grandpa's store as a personal jewelry box and the whole thing spelled disaster.

Grandpa had put his heart and soul into Osprey Beach Jewelry, building a solid customer base, creating a reputation for honesty and integrity. He'd nursed the store through stagflation, recession and Hurricane Isabel. But could the store survive his avaricious daughters?

There it was again, that lovely word: avaricious. Sssssss. . .

She could see the reptilian gleam in her aunts' eyes last night when they'd nastily pointed out Kim had no legal say in what happened to Grandpa or his store.

She frowned. Was that really true? Surely Maryland law wouldn't allow someone's children to tear apart their livelihood. Kim might not be next of kin, but there ought to be some other way to stop her aunts.

Tony would know. As the lawyer in the family, her cousin was accustomed to family members calling with "just a quick question." And Kim's question really would be quick. She hoped.

She reached for the phone, hesitated, then instead snatched the notebook and pencil Grandpa kept beside it. Before she did anything she needed to make a list so she wouldn't forget anything important.

Number one was something she'd never forget: Call hospital. Calling Tony and then Amber were two and three. No, with Amber, better make that a face-to-face meeting. Without the presence of Darin/Derwood or whatever his name was.

And she'd probably have to clean the office. She hadn't seen it since the police left, but she'd read enough mysteries to know there'd be fingerprint dust everywhere. Fingerprint dust and blood. Grandpa's blood.

The pencil snapped in half and she was back in the hospital again. Grandpa lay in the bed surrounding by monitors, a breathing tube strapped to his white face. Small, frail, not at all the vibrant man she new. Worse, there'd been no response when she'd touched his hand.

Of course, he was in a coma -- a medically induced coma -- and shouldn't have responded. But this was Grandpa!

Forget the list. She needed to talk to the hospital. Now.

Grandpa's nurse assured her he was "resting comfortably." With some probing, the woman admitted that the fact he'd survived the night was a good sign. The next 48 hours, however, would be critical. But, no, sitting by his side all day wouldn't help. The whole idea of the induced coma was to force Mr. Hershey to rest.

The woman must have heard the panic in Kim's voice, because she added "The most helpful thing you can do right now is plan for Mr. Hershey's return. He'll probably need some assistance for the first couple of weeks . . ." Her voice trailed off, the woman clearly wondering if she'd overstepped.

Kim reassured her that this was exactly the kind of information she needed. She made careful note of the woman's name and, after hanging up the phone, added to her list: Buy gift for Grandpa's nurse.

Across the room, the grandfather clock chimed. Ten thirty. Her sleep deprived brain begged for a few hours' rest. But she knew she wouldn't sleep while Grandpa was in danger. Best to keep busy.

Okay, what else did she need to do today? Probably should check the business phone answering machine, see if there were any important calls. While she was at it, she could contact Grandpa's dealers, track his movements in New York. The insurance company would need to know exactly what had been in the stolen briefcase . . .

And then there was the blue diamond.

Setting the notebook on the coffee table, Kim crossed to the grandfather clock. She reached up and swept her fingers across the clock's bonnet, searching for the envelope she'd hidden behind the swirling finial. A moment of panic, then her fingers closed on the jeweler's envelope.

She stared down at Grandpa's writing: "Will it pass DiamondView?" And the answer: yes.

Grandpa told her to hide the diamond. She'd assumed he didn't want the emergency people to see it. But what if he didn't want anyone to see it? Anyone like her greedy -- avaricious -- family?

She shuddered, remembering her own covetous reaction last night when she looked at the stone. If the blue diamond could have such an effect on her, what would it do to her aunts and cousins, women who valued diamonds above all else?

Or . . . had the diamond already cast its spell on someone? Had someone in her family seen the blue diamond, decided she absolutely had to own it? Even Aunt Emerald, the wealthiest of her aunts, couldn't click her fingers and magically produce ten or twenty thousand dollars for a blue diamond. But she sure had the money to hire someone to steal it for her.

All of her aunts could afford to hire a thief. Some of her cousins had also married into money and those that hadn't . . . Amber could sweetly ask one of her thug boyfriends for a favor.

Until Grandpa awakened, she needed to assume he'd wanted her to hide the diamond from everyone. Including the family.

But where? It'd be safest in Grandpa's safe. She was the only family member who knew the combination.

However, if her aunts made good on their threat to take over Grandpa's business while he was in the hospital, they'd demand the safe combination. She could claim ignorance. But everyone knew her face flushed whenever she lied. No, she couldn't put the diamond in the safe.

Nor could she carry it with her. Purses could be lost, stolen or mislaid. Pants pockets weren't deep enough to ensure the envelope wouldn't fall out. And as she'd found out last night, her bra was of no use.

The clock started chiming, startling her. Ten forty-five. No telling when her aunts might suddenly appear.

Maybe the diamond was safest right where she'd hidden it, on top of the clock.

With a sigh, she returned the envelope to its hiding place.

Returning to the sofa, she picked up her to-do list. She should probably call Tony, find out if there was a way to stop her aunts. . .

A furry paw whapped her knee, almost knocking her over. She braced herself as Rory leaned his full weight against her leg and gazed up at her, his brown eyes filled with longing. His leash dangled from his mouth.

She laughed and tweaked his topknot. "Okay, stinker. Let's talk a walk." She could call Tony from her cell, clean Grandpa's office when they returned.

As she slipped the collar over Rory's head, her cell phone rang.

Aunt Ruby.

Kim flushed the last bucket of dirty water down the toilet. Tucking the bucket, mop and scrub brush into the broom closet, she returned to Grandpa's now-clean office.

She settled into the chair behind Grandpa's workbench and, ignoring the irritating beep of the answering machine, began arranging Grandpa's tools. Everything had its precise place, almost like the instruments on a surgical table. To remove the thick layer of fingerprint powder, however, she'd had to clear the bench, scrub the top, then wipe down every single tool.

Thank goodness Grandpa had covered the microscope before leaving for New York. Kim shuddered to think of the damage fingerprint powder could have done to the intricate workings.

Unfortunately Grandpa's expensive glasses, the ones with the assortment of magnifying lenses clipped to the temple, had been laying smack in the middle of the desk. They took the full brunt of the powdery fingerprint dust. Reaching for the special cleaner, she sprayed the lenses and began meticulously wiping away the black gook.

As she worked, her mind flicked back to the recent conversation with Aunt Ruby.

Aunt Ruby had ordered -- ordered! -- her to fill the display cases. Her three aunts intended to open the store after lunch.

Kim glanced at the wall clock, the only non-ornamental clock in the house. In five minutes, both of its functional black hands would point straight up. Noon. At this moment, her aunts would be sitting down at a fancy Annapolis restaurant. Once finished, it would take them forty minutes to reach Osprey Beach.

Kim had two hours -- two and a half at the most -- to circle the wagons.

Laying the now clean glasses in the exact center of the bench, she reached for Grandpa's collection of pliers.

Would calling Tony again help? He specialized in white collar crime, but if there was a legal way to thwart the weird sisters, Tony would find it. Even if one of the sisters was his own mother.

She'd already left a panicked message on Tony's answering machine. Surely he'd recognizer the concern in her voice and return her call when he picked up his messages.

Kim began arranging the tiny pliers in a fan shape on the right side of the bench. Handles pointed towards the chair so Grandpa could grab them without looking up from whatever delicate piece of jewelry he was repairing.

Of course, Tony might tell her exactly what she feared: That while Grandpa was unconscious, her aunts as next of kin had the legal right to manage his affairs. If that was the case, Kim's options were limited.

Grandpa had given Kim -- and only Kim -- the combination to his safe. No one knew she had the combination, though they probably all suspected. So theoretically, she could tell her aunts she didn't know the combination. No combination, no jewelry, no way to open the store.

Problem was, her aunts would see right through her.

Okay, she couldn't lie. Nor could she recraft Grandpa's ultimate argument: Because I'm the granddaughter and I said so. There was always her preferred method, direct confrontation. But without legal standing, her aunts would charge right over her.

What was left?

Be nice, Grandpa's voice whispered in her head.

Be nice to them?

Sighing, she grabbed the small screwdrivers and positioned them above the pliers.

Thirty-two years old and she couldn't stop the eight-year-old inside of her from responding to Grandpa's admonition. Was she doomed to reverting to childhood now that she'd moved back to Maryland?

Five years ago, she'd fled her smothering family by accepting an assistant professorship at the University of Oregon -- as far away as she could get. There she'd blossomed, spread her wings, all of those stereotypes that were stereotypes because they were so darned real. She'd rewritten her dissertation and sold it to a large New York publisher. She'd published professional papers, chaired department committees, sang (badly) in a community choir. She adopted her first standard poodle, hiked through the rain forest, befriended an ever-growing flock of Rufus hummingbirds.

And she never once had to justify her lack of interest in diamonds, jewelry or the people who coveted them.

But she'd missed Grandpa's chuckle, Aunt Ginny's tomfoolery, Mom's lasagna, Dad's discourses on cell biology. As she tramped in the gray winter rain, she coveted sunshine. Faculty meetings triggered an ache for intellectually stimulating conversation. She'd learned to fix steelhead trout, but longed to sink her teeth into sweet Maryland blue crabs.

Mostly, though, she missed sitting on Grandpa's balcony, watching sailboats cruise the Bay, listening to his stories. Visits with Grandpa always brought back the sweet innocence of childhood.

Which was why, when the University of Maryland actually offered an associate professorship and tenure within a year, she'd jumped at the opportunity.

She knew, however, that returning to Maryland would force her to confront her fear that Mom's extended family would stifle her. Running to Oregon hadn't resolved anything. She needed to find a way to deal with the rest of her family while retaining her independence. She'd counted on

Grandpa's moral support. With him out of commission . . .

Kim gathered Grandpa's assortment of hand-held loupes and laid them beside the microscope. Leaning back, she studied her work. Shifted the microscope more to the left. There, now it looked exactly the way Grandpa liked it.

Her heart ached. She'd missed him so.

No, she'd made the right choice to return to Maryland. To be near Grandpa. She just needed to learn to deal with her crazy family without getting caught up in the madness.

Starting with preventing her aunts from destroying Grandpa's business.

So. Lying about the combination was out. Direct confrontation was out. Being nice . . .

As a child, she'd tried to "be nice" and her aunts had responded by taking advantage of her. She was an adult now. A psychologist no less. Was she so insecure that she assumed being nice would automatically give her aunts power?

Yep.

Kim eyes drifted to the answering machine. The darn beeping was making it difficult to think and the light was mesmerizing.

Hmmm . . . Kim reached out, blocked the light with her hand. Maybe she could hypnotize her aunts, plant some sort of aversion to Grandpa's store. Grandpa probably had a pocket watch laying around somewhere. She'd dangle it in front of her aunts' eyes and intone: Stay away from the store. Stay away . . .

Okay, being silly wasn't helping. But maybe . . . She sat up. Maybe this wasn't so silly. After all, she was trained in psychology. Could she use psychology to trick her aunts into staying away?

It wasn't as if her aunts actually wanted to work. Heaven forbid. They just liked the idea of being in charge. If Kim offered to do the actual work, to deal with customers, arrange for repairs, handle the cash register. . . heck, they'd welcome the chance to boss someone around.

Kim shivered. Just the thought of spending time with her aunts made her claustrophobic. But if that was the only way to protect Grandpa's interests, maybe she could do it. Just this once.

However, she wouldn't tolerate too much bossing.

Knowing it was childish, she decided to deal with the answering machine before following Aunt Ruby's orders to load the jewelry cases.

She reached for a notepad and pen and pressed the play button.

"You have ten new messages," the mechanical voice said. "First message."

A New York dealer said he'd acquired an exceptional lot of Madagascar rubies and would Grandpa like a few on consignment? Kim noted the dealer's name and number.

"Next message."

Mrs. Johnstone, one of Grandpa's long-time customers, inquired about a ring she'd left to be resized. Kim wrote down her phone number. The ring should be in the safe with a tag on it.

"Next message."

Another New York dealer, this one saying he'd received the princess-cut diamonds Grandpa had requested. Kim groaned. Those were probably in the stolen briefcase.

If the local thief had, in fact, been the man who attacked Grandpa, he must have been astonished when he opened that ratty old briefcase.

The next message made her smile. Mrs. Lombardi, Grandpa's next-door neighbor, said she'd be out of town for a few weeks and could Max please keep an eye on her house? The white-haired woman had pursued Grandpa for years and sought any excuse to call him.

Next message. "Max? Maxie are you there? . . . I guess not. Listen, this is important. You need to watch your back. I think I'm being followed." Click.

Huh?

Kim stopped the machine, rewound, hit the play button.

" . . . watch your back. I think I'm being followed." Click.

A man's voice. But fear had tightened his vocal chords, pitching the words into a high, child-like level. And yet, there was something vaguely familiar . . .

She checked the date and time. The message had been left the day Grandpa left for New York.

The tape continued to play, but Kim ignored it.

If the man hadn't specifically said Grandpa's name, she'd have assumed it was a wrong number. Or a prank call.

There was nothing fake, however, about the fear in the voice.

And that voice . . . it was so familiar. Not an old-time friend. Someone Grandpa recently met?

"Arf, arf, arwoo. . ."

Kim jumped and stared at the answering machine. The barking was coming from message number ten.

Rory slinked beneath the workbench. The dog on the machine continued to bark, a high-pitched yip ending in a hound-like howl. Beagle?

"Maxie," a man whispered, "They hired thugs." A cough, then the voice continued. "They're gone now but . . . Listen, you gotta hide . . ."

"Hey! Whatdoya thinks ya're doin'?" The new voice was lower, growling, filled with menace. "Gimme that . . . Shit, that hurt! Get that damn dog, will ya?"

A crash. Silence.

"End of new messages."

Something moved into Kim's peripheral vision. A hand appeared. She screamed.

CHAPTER 9

"You don't have to break my eardrums," a familiar voice whined. "I was only trying to show you something."

Tiffany.

Kim's mind registered the name as her heart continued to beat furiously. Leaning away from the answering machine and its frightening messages, she glared up at her glamorous cousin.

The Bay breeze had whipped Tiffany's blond layers into cover-girl perfection. An intricately pleated skort and matching shrunken top showed off Tiff's hour-glass figure and long legs while screaming designer. Probably Armani. Her makeup -- if she wore any -- was immaculate. Right now her bow-shaped mouth formed a glossy pout.

No way could she deal with Tiffany right now. She needed to identify the voice on those messages, make sure the caller was okay, talk to Tony, get ready for her aunts . . .

Her aunts.

"Are you alone?" Kim's eyes darted to the glass window that separated Grandpa's office from the store front. The room was empty.

Of course, her aunts could be hovering upstairs waiting for an unsuspecting niece to flutter into their web. If only Grandpa hadn't given everyone a house key . . .

Tiffany rolled her eyes, misinterpreting Kim's question. "Of course I'm alone. Dickie works on Wednesdays. I just dropped in to show you my new diamond."

Kim's eyes automatically dropped to the 3-carat, Gabrielle-cut diamond on Tiffany's left hand. Every time Tiff moved, the diamond's 105 facets -- twice as many as the traditional brilliant cut -- sparkled and flashed.

"Not that diamond, silly. This one." Tiffany shoved her right hand at Kim, waggling her fingers to make the yellow stone dance.

Kim felt her jaw drop. The canary-colored diamond caught the light and sent golden flashes across the room. Kim leaned forward, unable to take her eyes from the stone.

She'd never seen a fancy-colored diamond and now, in less than 24 hours, she was confronted with two? That couldn't be a coincidence. Could it?

She grabbed Tiffany's hand, holding it still so she could study the stone. The yellow color was as saturated as Grandpa's blue diamond. Tiffany's diamond, however, lacked the perfection of the blue. Even without a loupe, she could see several dark pinpoints deep in the stone's center. Tiffany snatched her hand away.

"Don't look at it so closely! You'll see the flaws."

"Good heavens, Tiff, I can see the inclusions without magnification. Why in the world did you buy this?" While almost all diamonds had inclusions -- the industry used the benign phrase "clarity characteristics" -- visible flaws in the stone's center greatly reduced a diamond's value. Maybe that was how Tiffany could afford a fancy color?

"I didn't buy it, silly." Tiffany waggled her hand, making the overhead light dance across the diamond. "I had it made. This is Desmond."

Huh?

"You named your diamond after your first husband?" While cousin Amber collected thugs, Tiffany collected wealthy husbands. Desmond, the first, died skiing in the Alps. Husband number two suffered a heart attack while jogging. Richard, the current husband, wisely chose to avoid all physical activity.

"No, silly. This is made from Desmond's ashes."

"Ohmygosh, I've never seen one of these." Kim snatched her cousin's hand and leaned closer to the diamond.

She'd read about the so-called "memorial diamonds" -- diamonds made in a laboratory using cremains. The latest fad used advances in diamond making to turn people's deceased loved ones into diamonds. Real diamonds, made of pure carbon, not zirconium oxide powder like some diamond simulants.

In this case, the carbon was extracted from human ashes. Desmond's ashes.

Tiffany had cremated husband number one and husband number two. Instead of burying the ashes or scattering them, she'd placed the ashes in decorative urns. The gaudy vessels squatted like gargoyles on opposite ends of the mantel over Tiffany's fireplace. Kim had a sudden vision of Tiffany, standing on a step ladder, using a flour scoop to remove ashes from Desmond's urn.

"Desmond was such a cheapskate in life," Tiffany said, "I decided to make him useful now that he's dead."

Removing her hand from Kim's, Tiffany waggled her fingers, making the yellow stone glitter.

As Tiffany admired her ring, Kim fought a flash of jealousy. Tiffany had inherited Grandma's blond tresses while Kim was stuck with Hershey brown curls. Tiffany's blue eyes sparkled with 20/20 vision; Kim's brown eyes required glasses. At family gatherings, Tiffany wolfed down everything in sight, yet remained slender. Kim could live on lettuce and still have to fight off extra pounds.

But while Tiffany had inherited the family's best physical traits, her mind could never keep up with Kim's. Perhaps Tiff's obsession with jewelry had destroyed any neurons she'd been born with.

However . . . memorial diamonds, especially one-carat ones, weren't cheap. This one probably cost twenty thousand or more. Did that mean Tiffany could afford the blue diamond hidden upstairs?

"Tiff, did you ever ask Grandpa to find a blue diamond?"

"Blue?" Tiffany wrinkled her nose. "The salesman said most grave diamonds were blue, so I had Desmond made into a yellow."

It took Kim a moment to figure out the logic. Fancy colored diamonds occurred when minerals other than carbon were present when the diamond formed -- boron made diamonds blue while nitrogen created the canary color of Tiffany's ring. And since boron was rarer than nitrogen, blue diamonds were rarer than yellow.

Of course, that was in nature. Kim knew nothing about colors in synthetic diamonds, so maybe the salesman was correct.

"I had the diamond inscribed," Tiffany said. "Oh, here, you can't see it unless you use your loupey thing." Yanking off the ring, she shoved it at Kim.

Kim accepted the ring and, holding the loupe at her eye, turned it to study the side.

"I don't see . . . is the inscription on the girdle?"

"The what?"

"The narrow rim just below the top . . . I see something . . ." The words, whatever they were, disappeared behind prongs, only to reappear again.

"It says 'Here lies Desmond, useful at last.'"

Kim laughed. Tiffany might be a few points short of a carat, but there was nothing wrong with her sense of humor.

"Opal says I shouldn't have bought this," Tiffany continued. "She says if fake diamonds get popular, the price of real ones would drop and we'd all lose money." She paused to tuck a piece of expertly cut hair behind one ear. "But Mr. White thought it was a good idea, and he ought to know."

Kim gasped. "Mr. White? Bradford White?" Kim's fist clenched over the ring she still held. "Did you buy this from him? How could you!"

"I didn't, I didn't!" Tiffany held up her hands.

"Then why were you talking to him?" Tiffany knew -- heck, everyone in the family knew -- about Grandpa's feud with the patriarch of White Family Jewelry.

For as long as she could remember, Grandpa had grumbled about the way Bradford White's marketing practices "pushed the limit of what's legal." When Kim started helping in the store, Grandpa had emphasized the importance of total honesty with customers. He'd instructed her to reveal all gemstone treatments, even those routinely used. When someone asked the size of a gemstone, she was to say ".45 carats" not "half a carat." And she was to always, always show the customer the gemstone's gemology report and explain what it means.

He didn't need to add "unlike the White family."

Of course, knowing Grandpa's feelings about the Whites hadn't stopped Kim from dating Bradford's grandson in high school. The memory made her shudder.

"All I did was ask him where to send Desmond's ashes," Tiffany said. "Oh, and then he set the ring for me. I'd have brought the diamond to Grandpa, but he lives so far away."

Forty minutes from Annapolis to Osprey Beach didn't seem that "far away" to Kim, but she decided to let it go.

Just as well since Tiff was already onto another topic.

"You didn't forget about Dickie's party tonight, did you?"

"Uh . . ." Party? What party?

Tiffany rolled her eyes. "I told you about it last night. At the hospital? There's this fellow from the lab I want you to meet." Before Kim could protest, Tiffany hurried on. "He's single. Doesn't have much hair, but you two could talk about rocks and minerals and things."

Oh, no, one Tiffany fix-up was one too many.

Last summer, when visiting Grandpa, she'd allowed Tiffany to arrange a dinner date with a lawyer from Dick's firm. Kim had just broken up with an ornithologist whose idea of a date was to sneak through the forest in the middle of the night searching for wild turkeys. The plan, he'd said, was to toss a net over the sleeping birds and relocate them.

But turkeys slept in high trees and when Kim saw the turkey capture contraption -- a net attached to a kid's rocket -- she'd laughed so loudly she woke the birds and scared them away.

In light of that disaster, Tiffany's offer of an evening with a lawyer had sounded civilized. Dinner was excellent and the man even showed interest in her dissertation on the psychology behind the diamond myth. She'd had high expectations when he'd paused to kiss her goodnight. It was like kissing a door knob.

Best to get Tiffany out of matchmaking mode.

"So what brings you to Osprey Beach?"

"Dickie had a client down this way, so I decided to try out that new spa. Oh, look at the time! My appointment's in five." Tiffany headed towards the back office door.

But there was something she should ask Tiff . . . Oh. "Tiff, wait! Tony. Do you know where I can find your brother?"

"I think he's in court all day," Tiffany said.

Kim's shoulders drooped. So she'd have to face her aunts without any ammunition.

"Oh, I forgot," Tiffany continued. "Tony called last night. Said to tell you to look on the top shelf of Grandpa's safe."

"Why?"

Tiffany shrugged, then disappeared outside. Leaving Kim with yet another mystery.

Kim knelt in front of Grandpa's safe, silently cursing the insurance company that required him to buy a high-end model. Unlike more familiar combination locks, where sloppy dialing would still open the lock, this safe required total accuracy. Land a bit too short or too far from a number and the thing wouldn't open. Great for stopping crooks.

Unfortunately, the sensitivity made it difficult for everyone to open. Which was why during store hours Grandpa left the safe in "day lock" -- the safe was locked, but you need dial only one number to open it.

Right now, however, Kim needed to dial all seven numbers accurately. To her disgust, her fingers trembled. Anticipation over what Tony wanted her to find in the safe? Or fear of her aunts' imminent arrival?

Whatever the cause, she missed the third number in the sequence and needed to start over.

Finally, she heard the telltale click. The handle moved. Pulling the door open she stared at the top shelf.

But there was nothing more than the normal jewelry trays, ready to be carried into the storefront for display. Kim reached for the first stack of five trays. On top was a collection of diamond engagement rings. The second tray contained an assortment of rings set with semi-precious stones. Frustrated, Kim flipped through the last three trays. Nothing unexpected.

Setting those aside, she pulled out another stack of jewelry trays . . . revealing a legal-sized manila envelope. With her name on it.

Inside she found a stack of legal looking documents. The first was a Living Will. Kim's breath caught. Oh, please, please, please don't make this document necessary.

She flipped through the pages, noting Tony had been the attorney of record. That explained why her cousin knew about the documents.

But there was nothing unexpected here. Grandpa had checked off all of the boxes that gave permission to remove life support if he was in a permanent vegetative state.

Shuddering, Kim set the document aside, revealing a second document: Durable Power of Attorney.

Kim frowned and tried to translate the legal jargon. If she was reading this correctly, the document only went into effect if Grandpa was incapacitated and couldn't manage his affairs. Like if he was in a medically induced coma.

If something like that happened, the document said, Grandpa designated "my granddaughter Kimberley West" to act as his attorney/agent.

The detailed list that followed gave Kim responsibility for all of Grandpa's personal and business transactions. It also specifically entitled her to live in Grandpa's house for as long as she deemed necessary.

It took a moment for the implication to sink in. Somehow Grandpa, or maybe Tony, had foreseen a time when he might need legal protection from his legal heirs. He'd given Kim exactly what she needed: Legal power to thwart her aunts.

"Why aren't these showcases ready?" Aunt Ruby's voice.

Kim looked up. Her three aunts hovered in the doorway to Grandpa's office, glaring down at her.

CHAPTER 10

Late afternoon sun streamed through the store window as Kim carried the last of the jewelry trays into the showroom. While she'd argued with her aunts, the day had turned blistering hot. Maybe the heat would drive tourists into the air-conditioned shops.

She set the trays on top of a showcase and turned to smile at the room she'd help create. She'd been -- what? twelve? -- when Grandpa complained about the expensive glass and steel display cases the insurance company demanded he install. Not only did the cases make the store look like a dentist office, he said, but they did little to slow shoplifters. Turn your back for one moment and thieves jimmied the top of a case with a metal nail file, grabbed a diamond ring and were out the front door before you could say Jack Robinson.

Kim had suggested arranging the cases in a U and turning them sideways so the opening hugged the right wall. The U allowed Grandpa to stand in the middle and help customers while keeping an eye on what he called "lookee-loos." Placing the cases against a wall freed the rest of the store for the homey touch Grandpa craved.

They'd found three antique china cabinets -- walnut, mahogany and pine -- at a yard sale and spent a joyous week refinishing them before tucking them against the wall opposite the displays. The cabinets emitted a warm wood smell and their glass doors, which rattled when opened, helped protect contents from thieves.

Kim claimed a corner for two overstuffed chairs, their chenille upholstery worn and soft. They finished the room by hanging antique and modern chiming clocks on the wall near the front door. The combination of modern and antique created the friendly yet professional aura Grandpa desired.

Without Grandpa's presence, however . . . She bit her lip. Grandpa would come home, despite her aunts' gloom and doom predictions.

And his durable power of attorney gave her responsibility for keeping the store solvent until he was well enough to take over. Not an easy task for someone who'd never been able to sell Girl Scout cookies.

But Grandpa trusted her, so she needed to fill the display cases, open the store and get busy. She gazed across the trays of glitter to the velvet stands waiting to display them: Necklace busts, risers, bangle pillows, bracelet ramps, earring and ring stands. Decapitated velvet heads, torsos and hands.

She sighed and mentally kicked herself. If she was going to help Grandpa, she needed to shake off the melancholy.

Reaching for a simple velvet board, she tried to remember Grandpa's lessons. She could hear his gentle, patient tenor.

"You want a customer to picture herself wearing this," he'd said, laying a diamond necklace on a board and gently curving the sides so it appeared to adorn a woman's neck. He'd positioned the matching earrings inside the curve, then lifted three diamond bracelets from their trays. "Give her the chance to make the set unique by offering a choice of bracelets." He'd fanned the bracelets out from the necklace in wavy lines. "Now you try it."

Kim stared down at the board, suddenly aware that she'd exactly recreated Grandpa's arrangement.

Shrugging, she slipped the finished board into a case, then reached for a velvet hand.

"Don't put all of the most expensive pieces in one case," Grandpa had cautioned. "That makes it too easy for thieves. Best to scatter the expensive jewelry throughout the store."

Kim selected three bracelets from the semi-precious tray: amethyst, citrine and amber. By placing the purple bracelet between the yellow and orange, she accented all three gemstones. After a moment's hesitation, she slipped an amethyst ring onto a velvet finger. Satisfied, she bent to place the hand beside the diamond necklace display. From the corner of her eye, a black shape with a tail appeared.

"Don't even think it," she told Rory. "This is not a toy."

With a sigh, Rory trotted from the room, returning a few moments later carrying a stuffed hedgehog. Tossing it in the air, he raced across the room to retrieve it. His feet slid on the tiled floor.

"Rory, you need to settle."

He squeaked his toy.

"That's not a settle."

With an enormous sigh, Rory threw himself to the floor and began using his front teeth to groom the hedgehog.

Kim rolled her eyes and returned to the displays. She really should ban her rambunctious buddy from the store, but she hadn't the heart. From puppyhood on, Rory had been her constant companion. She joked that he provided sanity in an insane world, and heaven knew she needed sanity today after the confrontation with her aunts.

They'd been furious when she showed them Grandpa's durable power of attorney. As a group, the anger had been palpable, worse than she'd anticipated. Individually, however, they followed Kim's predictions.

Aunt Emerald's "This is an outrage" was immediately followed by a sniffed "We'll see about this."

Aunt Ruby looked for someone to blame, first accusing Kim of mesmerizing Grandpa, then blaming Aunt Sapphire for "not controlling your son." As if Tony should have denied Grandpa's request to prepare the document.

In the meantime, Aunt Sapphire appeared oblivious to her sisters' rantings. She'd been too intent on arranging a set of clear crystals on Grandpa's desk. The only outward sign of emotion was the thin set of her lips.

Kim had refrained from responding to the verbal assault. Nothing she said would change her aunts and the legal document prevented them from doing more than venting their rage.

Unable to intimidate their niece, the aunts finally swept from the store, leaving behind an anger-charged atmosphere and Aunt Sapphire's crystals.

Kim still didn't know if the crystal arrangement was intended to heal or curse.

But her aunts were gone and she'd completed the first display case. One down, two to go.

First, however, she needed to select the jewelry for the front window.

The window display, Grandpa said, provided the only opportunity to entice passersby into the store. He liked to use the window to reflect the seasons or holiday or mood of customers.

Independence day, Kim thought. Maybe red, white and blue? Rubies, diamonds and sapphires?

She studied the jewelry trays. Her hand hovered over a tray of diamond necklaces. Grandpa liked to put diamonds in the window.

But look at that sapphire bracelet.

The tennis-style design featured small pink, yellow, green and orange sapphires set in 14k gold. Diamond melee separated the stones, enhancing the colors.

While most tennis bracelets were fashioned of uniform-sized gems, this one broke from tradition with a central 2 x 4 mm marquise-cut blue sapphire. Cornflower blue. Montana blue.

Kim's heart quickened as she reached for a loupe and held the bracelet to the light. The blue-purple color saturated the stone and she could see no inclusions or color zoning. There was only one place in the world that produced sapphires like this: the Yogo Gulch in Montana.

When she was little, Grandpa had tweaked her interest in gemstones with tales of jewels discovered in the United States. He described the great diamond hoax in Montana, the discovery of diamonds in Arkansas, emeralds in North Carolina, turquoise in Arizona, California tourmaline, Tennessee freshwater pearls and Montana sapphire.

Over the years, Kim had successfully squelched any desire for diamonds; however, her heartbeat still quickened whenever she encountered gemstones mined in the U.S.

Like the ones in this bracelet.

She draped it over her left wrist. The cheerful multiple colors made the bracelet casual enough to wear with jeans. But the diamond melee elevated it to dressy status. If the central stone came from Montana, most likely the others had been mined there as well.

She reached for the price tag . . .

What was she doing? Even with Grandpa's discount, there was no way she could afford this bracelet. Just as she couldn't afford that other bracelet so long ago.

But this bracelet was even prettier. And she was employed now.

She closed her eyes and gulped in air. Thirty thousand, she reminded herself. She still owed thirty thousand on her college loan. And university professors were not highly paid.

She opened her eyes and, holding the sides of the bracelet, gently returned it to the velvet pad. Her moment of insanity, however, gave her an idea.

What would the window display look like arrayed with multicolored sapphires? Or, maybe, not just sapphires. Maybe she could include London

Blue topaz, mandarin garnet and purple amethyst. A rainbow of colors. Could she use them all without creating a cluttered mess?

Another of Grandpa's lessons: Jewelry arrangements must create a unifying whole without sacrificing the individual beauty of each piece.

Many of Kim's childhood arrangements had come directly from nature. Like the time she combined emeralds and citrine to mimic the green and yellow of daisies.

There was nothing in nature, however, that combined all of the colors in this bracelet.

So. Not nature. Something manmade. Manmade but enticing, something that sparkled, made people ooh and aah . . . Fireworks.

She felt the smile spread across her face, the first real smile since arriving in Maryland.

Fireworks. She could arrange bracelets in the splayed mushroom shape of fireworks.

Moving quickly, she gathered a collection of colored bracelets and began arranging them on a black velvet board. Aquamarine and Swiss Blue topaz became the narrow bottom end of the spray, their pale blue colors suggesting the tail of the bursting rocket. Next came the fiery colors -- ruby, garnet, red spinel. As the fan opened, she mixed in more colors, yellow, purple, orange, green, blue. The multicolored sapphire bracelet became part of the arc, curving upwards, then down as if the burning papers were tearing apart.

Stepping back, she studied the result. The colors harmonized, yet each bracelet glistened with its own unique character.

She frowned. Something was missing. Oh. Fireworks always had white sparks falling from the colors. Snatching several pairs of diamond stud earrings, she removed them from their cases and pressed them into the velvet, using the long fibers to hold the earrings in place. She grinned. Perfect. Grandpa was going to love this.

Now all she had to do was carry the board to the display window without dislodging anything.

Lifting the board, she took shallow breaths as she started towards the window.

A fuzzy stuffed hedgehog smacked her arm. The board wavered. Kim held on and only breathed again when she'd regained her balance.

She scowled down at her playful poodle. "Not now, Rory. I'll throw Tiggy Winkle in a minute."

Unrepentant, Rory squeaked his toy.

Moving more quickly, Kim reached the window and set the display board in the center. She repositioned the bracelets and earrings. She'd need to step outside to see the effect.

First, however . . . She turned back to her oversized puppy. Rory pranced in circles, squeaking the toy.

Sighing, she shook her head and locked the window display. As she began arranging jewelry in the second display case, she considered the rest of the day. She needed to call Grandpa's New York contacts, trace his movements there, make a list of the gems and jewelry that had been in the stolen briefcase.

Surely there'd be time to make those calls. Even at the busiest times of year, jewelry stores were never crowded. And if she kept Rory with her, he'd bark when a customer climbed the front stairs, giving her plenty of time to end the call.

Kim moved to the third case. She should also call Amber, quiz her about her thug boyfriends. And she really needed to identify the frightened voice on the answering machine. The voice had seemed so familiar. Maybe if she played the message several times, a name would come to mind.

She bit her lip and reached for Rory. He leaned against her, allowing her to stroke the silky fur beneath his ear.

Who was she kidding? She wasn't Nancy Drew. She'd made that list of to-do items to distract her from focusing on the horrific possibility that her aunts were right, that Grandpa wouldn't survive.

Removing her glasses, she used two fingers to press the inside corners of her eyes.

Without Grandpa's presence, no amount of wood, velvet or soft lighting would make the store feel warm. She couldn't imagine a world without Grandpa. Yes, it had to happen. Some day. But he was only seventy-six and, until yesterday, had been healthy and active. It wasn't his time to go.

If he didn't make it . . . Kim's left hand clenched into a fist. She'd find that thug. She'd hunt him down and . . .

And what? Beat him over the head with her purse? Sic her poodle on him? Kick him between the legs, turn him into a soprano? Too bad she'd never had time to take those self-defense classes in college.

Replacing her glasses, she realized the anger had removed the urge to cry. And she knew what she had to do: Open the store, sell enough to keep Grandpa's business solvent, use the down-time to make those phone calls. When she learned something, she'd call the police.

Maybe talking to Grandpa's peers would help the police investigation.

An hour later she wanted to scream in frustration. Her jewelry fireworks display drew passersby to the storefront. Then Rory's puffy ears and grinning face enticed them into the showroom.

The combination, however, worked too well. Instead of the slow, steady stream of customers she'd envisioned, the store was overrun with exhausted mothers and their children who wanted to pet the poodle. Kim bustled around the room, answering questions, ensuring nothing was stolen and preventing Rory from accidentally knocking over a child. The chaos made it impossible to sell anything. Plus she had to pee and there'd been no break in traffic to temporarily close the store.

And she hadn't had time to make a single phone call.

How in the world did Grandpa manage on his own?

"Could I please see the purple bracelet that's in the window?" one of the mothers now asked.

Kim pulled the showcase keys from her pocket. "Which one?" She located the key to open the window display.

The woman pointed to a 14k white gold tennis bracelet set in oval amethysts.

Kim inserted the key. As she slid the glass to the side, she glanced at the woman. Unlike Tiffany, this young woman was dressed in cut-offs and a Walmart t-shirt. Her two daughters were similarly attired. No way could this poor woman afford 14k gold. Maybe she should show her the amethysts set in silver.

The bell over the front door jangled. An elegant white-haired woman entered.

Always make eye contact with each customer the Grandpa in her head whispered.

As Kim turned to face the newcomer, Rory streaked to her side and snatched a bracelet from the display window. Kim lunged, but the poodle was too fast; her fingers merely brushed the tips of his puffy tail.

Visions of Rory's keep-away game raced through her mind. Kim charged after him.

Instead of taunting her, however, Rory trotted over and sat in front of the new woman. When Kim saw the bracelet dangling from his mouth, she groaned. He was holding the sapphire bracelet she'd so admired. Six thousand dollars worth of sapphire bracelet.

She started calculating a payment plan to reimburse Grandpa for a chewed bracelet.

"Oh, you think this would look good on me, do you?" The woman lifted the end of the bracelet. To Kim's relief, Rory released his end.

"Actually, this is lovely." She draped the bracelet over her wrist. "The sapphires are small, but that center stone is an unusual color."

"Yogo sapphire. Only found in Montana. Here, let me help you with that."

Kim looked back at the first woman -- "I'm sorry, could you excuse me for a minute?" -- then stepped towards the white-haired lady and secured the bracelet clasp. "Grandpa puts safety chains on all of his bracelets. And this clasp is one of the easiest to use." She demonstrated. "This is my favorite bracelet in the store. The multiple colors make it casual enough to wear with . . . er, to wear every day. But the diamonds dress it up for more formal occasions."

"Very pretty." The woman held her wrist up to the light. The colors glowed. "Will it go on sale?"

Kim kept the smile on her face. How she hated that question. So many "sales" were nothing more than retailers lowering their over-priced stock to normal.

"Grandpa doesn't believe in sales. He'd rather keep his every-day prices low than play games with mark ups." Kim pointed to the bracelet. "That's why the bracelet is only six thousand."

Only. And yet . . . "The sapphires are all vividly colored, their cut is excellent and clarity characteristics range from slightly included to slightly included two. That makes them very rare."

The woman simply frowned. A second passed, two. The woman reached for the bracelet clasp. Kim's shoulders fell. She fought the "no one will buy these stupid cookies" despair.

Stop it. When she was ten, she'd been unable to sell the Girl Scout cookies, but she'd sold jewelry for Grandpa. She'd done that by . . . by displaying her knowledge of geology.

"To me, what makes this special is that all of the sapphires were mined in Montana."

The woman hesitated. "All of these came from Montana?" she said, laying the loose bracelet back across her wrist. "I didn't know there were gem mines in the U.S. Other than the turquoise in Arizona."

Thank goodness. Here was something she could discuss. She turned her body slightly so she could include the young mother in the conversation.

"Compared to some other countries, our mining operations are pretty small. But what we produce is gorgeous. Montana sapphires. . ." She nodded at the bracelet, "often have saturated colors and high clarity. Oregon produces some of the prettiest feldspar in the world; their sunstone really glistens. There are a few small mines in Nevada that produce large, intensely colored opals. There was even a diamond mine in Colorado, but that's been closed."

"Diamonds?"

Ah, jeez, just the mention of those darn stones made the woman's eyes glisten.

"What happened to it?" she said.

Kim sighed. "They had trouble making a profit. Mining is expensive."

"I'd have bought American diamonds."

"Yeah, I think that's what they were counting on. But you get less than half a carat of diamonds for every ton of rock you move." Kim nodded towards the bracelet. "American diamonds aren't available, but you can buy Montana sapphires."

Five minutes later, Kim handed Mrs. Edwin Smythe her receipt and watched the bracelet she coveted leave the store. Well, at least the temptation was now beyond her.

"Excuse me."

Kim turned back to face the woman who'd inquired about the amethyst bracelet. Smiling shyly, the woman held out. She was holding the bracelet.

"You dropped this when your poodle started playing salesman."

For a moment, Kim couldn't breathe. How could she be so stupid? Thank goodness this woman was honest.

"I couldn't afford it anyway," the woman was now saying. "Amethyst is my birthstone, but when I saw the price tag . . ."

Kim accepted the bracelet and checked the price. Four hundred dollars. Squinting, she read the tag's small series of numbers, which indicated what Grandpa had actually paid for the bracelet. Somehow, she needed to reward this young woman for her honesty.

"Could you afford it at three hundred?" At that price, Grandpa would only clear fifty bucks but considering this woman could have walked out of the store with no one noticing, it was a bargain.

The woman's eyes widened. "I thought . . . You told that woman that you never have sales."

Kim smiled. "We don't. I'm offering it to you at just over wholesale to thank you for your honesty." She nodded to the two little girls giggling and petting Rory. "And for your daughters' entertaining Rory."

The woman's face lit up. "Oh, you're so nice! I've always wanted an amethyst bracelet -- I've got earrings to match -- but the bracelets in my price range have pale purple stones and my earrings -- an anniversary gift from my husband -- are dark purple like these and . . ." She continued to babble as she handed Kim her credit card.

A few minutes later Kim watched the woman and her daughters descend to the boardwalk. The young mother was practically skipping.

Smiling, Kim locked the front door. So that's what Grandpa meant when he said the purpose of jewelry was to make people feel good. He'd spent his life doing just that. She just wished she could make Grandpa acknowledge that her work as a psychology professor served the same purpose. To understand the mind was the first step toward understanding oneself. And self understanding enabled people to cope with daily frustrations and challenges, which should ultimately lead to some sort of happiness.

She had to admit, however, that making that young mother's eyes light up felt pretty darn good.

Turning the "open" sign around to read "back in a minute," she raced to the bathroom.

As she washed her hands, she marveled at Grandpa's ability to run the store by himself. Rory's "help" certainly made things more stressful. But even if Rory hadn't been there, she'd have been torn between answering questions and keeping an eye on browsers who might possibly be shoplifters. She'd read somewhere that jewelry thieves often worked in pairs, one to distract the salesperson while the other jiggled open a display case. Today her sleep-deprived brain made it impossible to fully focus. Add to that concern for Grandpa, ignorance of the stock and impatience to play Nancy Drew and she'd have been an easy mark. A pair of thieves could have walked away with thousands of dollars in merchandise and she'd never known.

The grandfather clock chimed four, five, six times. Too late to make those New York calls.

Kim rolled her neck, trying to work out some of the stiffness. The tension -- after only half a day! -- was worse than facing an auditorium of first-day freshmen.

She scanned the bathroom shelves, but couldn't find the bottle of hand lotion she'd left there last summer. Crossing to the bed, she opened her purse and rummaged inside for the hand cream she kept there.

She needed to keep the store open for another hour or so. Then if she grabbed something to eat on the way, she should reach the hospital before visiting hours ended. Though the doctors said Grandpa wouldn't be aware of her presence, she wanted to see him, touch him, reassure herself he was still in this world.

Her hand finally closed over the cold plastic tube. As she pulled the cream from her purse, a postcard fell out. Kim picked it up and smiled. Aunt Ginny had mailed the card from New York, probably purchasing it at the Metropolitan Museum. "Next time you need to come with me," she'd written. The card originally pictured Rembrandt's Mona Lisa.

Over the painting's famous eyes, Aunt Ginny had affixed a plastic googly eye. Kim tilted the card, making the black eyeball roll around.

Grinning, she returned the card to her purse, wondering how many more of the plastic eyes remained. She'd been -- what, ten, eleven? -- when they'd found the package of eyeballs in a dollar store. Somewhere in her moving boxes she had a collection of token gifts from Aunt Ginny -- birthday cards, paper dolls and illustrated bookmarks -- all sporting googly eyes.

The Mona Lisa postcard, however, had to be the best. She needed to call to thank her . . .

Wait a minute. Why wait? Why not call right now, admit defeat with the store and ask for help? Aunt Ginny's cheerful demeanor and gentle nosiness made her a natural for sales. She'd purchased enough jewelry from Grandpa to be able to talk intelligently about the stuff. Plus she wouldn't tolerate any nonsense from Mom's sisters.

But Ginny wasn't home. As Kim left a message, she wondered if her globe-trotting aunt was even in town.

Frustrated, she trudged down the inside stairs. As she turned towards the store, Rory raced passed her, barking.

Kim froze and stared at the man-sized silhouette lurking at the front door.

CHAPTER 11

Kim's breath caught as she tried to discern the features of the man looming outside. But the early evening sun reflected off the door's glass, effectively obscured his face. The man's height and shape, however, matched Grandpa's attacker.

Call the police.

Even as the thought formed, Rory's bark changed to happy yipping. She studied his wagging tail. Normally Rory reflected her own emotions, displaying them for all the world to see. But he didn't share her qualms about this visitor.

Taking a deep breath, Kim pulled her keys from her pocket and crossed to the door.

"I hope you haven't been waiting long . . ."

Something flew from the man's arms and ran into the store. Rory took off in pursuit.

"Al!" The man charged after Rory.

Remembering her mistake with the amethyst bracelet, Kim closed and locked the door before following everyone into Grandpa's office.

From the back, the man didn't look nearly as scary as he did silhouetted against the front door. Though his shoulders were broad, his limbs were more lanky than Grandpa's attacker. His turquoise knit shirt hung loosely around his waist, indicating a recent loss of weight.

Sensing her presence, he leaned aside to allow her into the room.

"I'm afraid to move," he said. "Will he hurt Al?"

Rory had trapped the animal at the back door. Kim smiled as she identified it as a longhaired miniature dachshund. It lay on its back staring up at Rory. Its black face sported red-brown markings much like a Doberman, giving it a droll appearance. It wore a doggy grin as it batted Rory's face with its big feet.

Rory dropped into a play bow and took a fuzzy leg into his mouth.

"Rory, leave it."

Rory looked at Kim then back down at the dog. The dachshund waggled its feet. Rory grabbed the dog's ear.

"Rory, that's enough!"

Sighing, Rory sat down. The dachshund flipped onto its feet and bunched its leg muscles.

"Oh, no you don't." Before the dog could race off, Kim scooped it into her arms. He immediately rolled onto his back and gazed up at her with liquid brown eyes.

"Is he okay?" the stranger asked.

Scratching the dog's belly, Kim turned towards the dachshund's owner. Tall, middle-aged, dressed in khaki pants and knit polo. Gold wire-rimmed glasses, much like her own, framed green, no brown, no hazel eyes. Whatever color, his eyes lacked the menace of Grandpa's attacker. Nothing to fear.

"They were just playing." Shifting Al into her left arm, she held out her right. "Kimberley West. How can I help you?"

As their hands met, the man flashed a crooked smile. The resemblance to Indiana Jones sent a jolt of electricity up her arm. All he needed was a hat to hide his receding hairline, a leather jacket and chin stubble and he could pass for Harrison Ford.

"Max is right; you have lovely eyes." His voice was a deep baritone.

"You know Grandpa?"

"I'm afraid Max and Uncle Jim have been attempting some matchmaking. I hope you won't hold that against me."

Uncle Jim, Uncle Jim . . . "Oh! You're Jim Hampton's nephew!"

The very man Grandpa had been touting for the last six months.

"Guilty. I'm Scott Wilson by the way."

His smile deepened. Kim suddenly realized she still held his hand. Slipping her own away, she plunged it into a jeans pocket.

Mercifully, he ignored her discomfort. "And you must be Rorschach," he said to the poodle now leaning against him. Rory sighed as Scott scratched his ear. Scott turned back to Kim, his smile fading. "Is Max around? I've been leaving messages, but . . ."

"Grandpa's in the hospital."

"Hospital? Why?"

Kim studied Scott's face as she answered. "Someone attacked him. Stabbed him with a knife."

Scott visibly paled. Taking a deep breath, he said "Is he okay?"

"He will be." No matter what her aunts said, Grandpa would get well and come home. "They've got him in a medically induced coma. Because of blood loss."

"We need to talk."

"About what?"

"Uncle Jim and your grandfather."

The grim look on Scott's face announced she wasn't going to like whatever he had to say. "Let me close the shop." She needed to hear this without interruption.

Setting Al onto the floor, she trudged into the store, her thoughts drifting back to last summer when Grandpa first introduced her to Jim Hampton, his new fishing buddy.

A retired thin-film physicist, Jim had spent his professional career researching ways to extend the longevity of artificial knee and hip joints. Most artificial joints lasted only ten to fifteen years, forcing patients to undergo painful repeat surgeries. Jim hoped to create indestructible joints by coating the moving surfaces with a film of diamonds. A heart attack, however, forced Jim into early retirement.

While Jim's research sounded interesting, she feared Grandpa would turn the evening into a pep rally for diamonds. Besides, scientists in general weren't great conversationalists and physicists in particular were notorious for being out of touch with reality.

She needn't have worried. Jim had just returned from a trip to Colorado and they'd spent a delightful evening sharing tales of the American Southwest. Jim described panning for gold in one of the Rocky Mountain's clear rivers. Grandpa recounted his Great Diamond Hoax story, the one where he changed his voice to mimic the devious prospectors and the duped banker. Kim talked about digging for dinosaurs in Colorado.

It was at the end of that delightful evening that Jim first mentioned his nephew. Something about a

Pulitzer prize, a domineering ex-girlfriend and a new job at the University of Maryland. Kim was so used to Grandpa trying to introduce her to men that she hadn't paid much attention.

Too bad no one told her he looked like Indiana Jones.

With a sigh, she flipped the door sign to "closed," turned off the lights and headed back towards the office. She'd empty the display cases later.

As she neared the office, Al ran between her legs, barking. Kim froze, her heart pounding. Al's high-pitched yip turned into a howl.

The hairs on Kim's arms stood at attention. She recognized that bark.

And now she knew why the voice on the answering machine sounded familiar. It belonged to Jim Hampton.

"It's just tourists," Scott said as he peered out the front window. Scooping the little dog into his arms, he turned and frowned. "What's wrong?"

"Your uncle . . ." Her throat muscles were so tight, her voice was high-pitched. She swallowed, tried again. "How is Jim?"

Scott hesitated. "Maybe we should talk about this somewhere else."

"Please. Just answer the question."

He stared at the floor, closed his eyes, opened them, lifted his chin and, finally, met her eyes.

"He died."

Kim gasped. No. No, no, no.

Scott inhaled deeply and looked away. "He tangled with a couple of burglars. I got there too late."

Kim laid a hand on his arm. "There was nothing you could do against hired thugs."

Scott shrugged off her hand, his eyes narrowing. "Hired thugs? What makes you think he was killed by hired thugs?"

"He . . . he left a message. . . ."

The color drained from Scott's face. "The last call Uncle Jim made was to Max?"

"I think you'd better hear this."

Without waiting for an answer she turned, led the way back into Grandpa's office and pointed Scott to a guest chair. He sank into it.

"I removed the tape so it wouldn't record over," she said, replacing the new tape with the old. "There are two messages. I think it's Jim's voice."

She hit the play button.

. . . watch your back. I think I'm being followed.

"My God." Scott brushed a trembling hand across his face. "Uncle Jim sounds terrified."

"I'm afraid it gets worse." She fast-forwarded the tape to Jim's final message.

Maxie, Jim whispered, they hired thugs. They're gone now but they might be back. You gotta . . ."

Hey!

Scott groaned. She reached for the pause button, but Scott waved her off.

Whatdoya thinks ya're doin'? Gimme that . . .

Sounds of struggle.

Shit, that hurt! Get that damn dog, will ya?

Crash.

Silence. Then the line went dead.

Giving Scott time to collect himself, Kim removed the tape and replaced it with a new one. She slipped the used tape into a jewelry envelope, labeled it and tucked it into a drawer.

"I was there." Scott's voice was little more than a croak. "But I was too late."

Kim shuddered, remembering her own inability to protect Grandpa. Fifteen minutes. If she'd have arrived fifteen minutes earlier, she'd have been with Grandpa when the thief arrived. And maybe, just maybe, he wouldn't have attacked. After all, two people were harder to control than one. Plus Rory would have alerted them to the intruder.

She opened her mouth to share her own guilt, but Scott began describing the night Jim died. Reasoning the poor man needed to talk, she remained silent.

"He never said anything about being followed." Scott scraped one hand through his hair, leaving the ends sticking out in all directions. "Seemed kinda odd, though, that he was so anxious for us to go fishing when he just returned from a fishing trip out west."

Scott arrived at the pre-arranged time -- 4 a.m. -- to find the house dark. Normally his uncle turned the front lights on. Figuring Jim had slept in, Scott used his key to open the front door.

That's when he heard the crashing, yelling and barking coming from the basement.

Stumbling through the living room, he swung open the basement door and charged down the gloomy stairs. The light at the bottom temporarily blinded him, which is probably why he crashed right into a large, muscular man. Next thing Scott knew, he was sitting on the ground, gasping for breath and staring up at a bald man with no neck.

The man clutched Jim's laptop. Beyond him, a weasel-like man kicked at Al, cursing when he missed. Al ran in, nipped the man's ankles and zipped away before the thug could land a blow.

"Damn dog," Weasel growled.

"I got the computer," Scott's attacker said.

Weasel looked up and spotted Scott. "What are you standing there for?" With a final kick at Al, again missing, he turned towards the outside basement door.

Scott reached for No-Neck's leg, leaving himself wide open for the kick to his gut. Groaning, he pulled into fetal position, rolled onto his side and spotted his uncle laying behind the work bench. Blood oozed from a head wound.

Scott crawled to Jim, pulled off his shirt and attempted to stop the bleeding while dialing 9-1-1 on his cell.

"And the whole time we waited for the ambulance, Uncle Jim kept muttering Al's name," Scott said. "So I promised to take care of the little beast; had to catch him, put him in a closet so the medics could get in. But they . . . they couldn't save Jim."

Scott took a deep breath and finally looked Kim in the eyes. "The last thing he said was 'tell Max.'"

"Tell Max what?"

"I was hoping Max would know." Scott nodded at the answering machine. "I called, but didn't want to say Jim died on a message."

Kim nodded. A number of messages for Grandpa included no message other than "call me." She'd made notes of those messages, but had put them at the bottom of the call-back list.

But what was so important that Jim's dying words were to tell Grandpa something?

"I think I know," Scott said.

Reaching into his shirt pocket, he pulled out a jewelers' envelope and handed it to her. "Uncle Jim had two safes. The thieves stole the one in Jim's home laboratory. But I found this in his bedroom safe."

There was no writing on this envelope. Kim removed its contents. Her breath caught as she stared down at a small blue diamond.

CHAPTER 12

The diamond Kim now held was miniscule in comparison to the blue diamond Grandpa gave her -- a sesame seed compared to a pea. But the color was the same tropical blue.

"It is a diamond, right?" Scott said.

"I'll have to test it, but I think so." The resemblance to Grandpa's blue diamond was too strong to be a coincidence. Even so, she reached for Grandpa's diamond tester, the one that measured a stone's ability to conduct heat. No natural gemstone conducted heat as well as diamond. And the tester took a lot less time than performing the manual tests Grandpa had taught her -- fogging the stone, weighing it, viewing it under 20x magnification.

"If it's a diamond," Scott said, "then it belongs to Max. No way could Jim afford a blue diamond."

She lifted the diamond with a pair of tweezers, touched the tester's wand to a facet and read the meter. Definitely diamond.

Reaching for a loupe, she held the stone to a light and searched for inclusions. None. Of course, the stone was so tiny, it was hard to see anything. Plus she was way out of practice. She'd need to view it in the microscope under several lighting settings to be certain.

She tilted the tweezers so she could see the side. But the girdle hadn't been laser inscribed with a gemological report number. Disappointing, but no surprise. Normally people didn't demand gemological reports for diamonds under half a carat, so jewelers wouldn't bother with the expense.

Still. The tiny diamond looked pretty darn perfect under a loupe. And with the color, it could almost be from the same rough as Grandpa's diamond . . .

She frowned, trying to remember what Grandpa had said about diamond cutting. To bring out the most sparkle, most rough was fashioned into one large and one small diamond.

Like Grandpa's stone and one she now held?

On the other hand, just because the color of the two stones was so similar didn't mean they came from the same rough. For decades, gemologists theorized that the 45-carat Hope Diamond and the similarly colored 31-carat Wittelsbach-Graff diamond had been cut from the same rough. In 2009 scientists finally had the opportunity to study the two stones side by side. To their disappointment, computer modeling proved the two diamonds could not have been cut from the same rough. Given the resemblance, however, they concluded the Hope and Wittelsbach-Graff had come from the same diamond mine . . .

Could Grandpa's diamond and the one in her hand have come from the same mine? If so, which mine? And why hadn't she heard about a mine producing such high quality blue diamonds? Unless . . . a thrill coursed up her spine. Unless there was a new mine?

No. Ridiculous. She didn't even know if the two diamonds were natural blues. Mostly likely the color had been produced through irradiation and heat and the fact they looked similar was nothing but coincidence . . .

"You know, if Max hadn't told me you hate diamonds, I could swear this one has you mesmerized."

Kim jerked, almost dropping the diamond.

"I am mesmerized. It's not that I don't like beautiful stones. What I hate is the craziness that diamonds always seem to generate." She folded the diamond's paper wrapper around it and tucked it back into the envelope. "I confess that I always get a little carried away when thinking about geology and crystallography."

She held the envelope out, but Scott refused to accept it, saying his uncle couldn't afford a blue diamond; therefore, it must belong to Max.

"Don't be surprised if this is Jim's," Kim assured him. "The color probably isn't natural and irradiated diamonds cost much less than naturally colored ones. You can even find them on the internet. It's still a lovely stone, though. The color, clarity and cut are awfully good . . ."

"Which probably still puts it out of Uncle Jim's budget." Scott nodded at the envelope. "Why don't you keep it here? After those thugs broke into Uncle Jim's house, I'd feel better keeping the stone in Max's safe. We can ask him about it when he gets out of the hospital."

"Speaking of hospital, I'd better secure the store so I can go see Grandpa."

Still holding Al, Scott stood and handed her a business card. "I'm no longer at the Post, but my cell phone still works. Please let me know when Max comes home."

She glanced at the Washington Post business card. That's right, Grandpa had said Scott won a Pulitzer for an investigative story and was now teaching somewhere. Hopkins? Maryland? Why hadn't she paid more attention?

She set the card on Grandpa's desk and led the way back through the store.

"I'm really sorry to hear about Jim." She stepped outside with him. "He was a good man. I know Grandpa will want to attend the funeral, but . . ."

Scott shook his head. "Uncle Jim's will specifically says no funeral. He willed his body to science. Mom and Aunt Cary want to have a memorial service. I'll suggest they wait until Max is out of the hospital."

He extended a hand. This time Kim made a point of shaking it and withdrawing. That produced another crooked smile. Scott turned and trotted down the front steps, Al tucked under his arm.

Kim stepped back inside, closed the door and sighed. Grandpa finally recommends a man that she found interesting and he didn't even ask her out. Of course, she had his phone number. And he did ask her to call when Grandpa came home. So maybe next time . . .

She crossed back into Grandpa's office to find paper and pencil. Before unloading the cases for the night, she intended to make diagrams of where she'd put everything. That way tomorrow morning she wouldn't have to design new displays.

She started with the window display, replacing the bracelets she'd sold with similar colors. As she sketched the case nearest to the front door, her cell phone rang. Aunt Ginny.

"What's this I hear about Max?"

Kim rolled her eyes. Aunt Ginny didn't believe in hello's or goodbye's, saying life was too short for trivia. At less than five feet tall and comfortably overweight, Ginny reminded Kim of a bumblebee, darting from flower to flower in a frenzied attempt to savor every experience before her time on earth ended. When her genius mathematician husband was still alive, this involved traveling to Russia, China and the Galapagos. After Uncle Bruce's death, Aunt Ginny continued traveling, her latest being a cruise down the Nile.

When Grandpa turned down the trip to Crater of Diamonds, Kim considered inviting Aunt Ginny. Somehow, however, that seemed like a betrayal of Grandpa, so she hadn't mentioned it.

Right now, though, she welcomed her aunt's support. Quickly she described the attack on Grandpa and his daughters' plan to take over his business. Before she'd even formed the request, Aunt Ginny announced she'd arrive first thing in the morning. "Unless you need me tonight?"

Relief swept over Kim and for the first time in hours, she actually smiled. "Tomorrow will be perfect."

Hanging up, she hurried through her chores. By the time she'd made her display-case diagram, secured the jewelry in the safe, fed Rory, set the alarm and snagged a drive-through fish sandwich at a nearby fast-food restaurant, however, she didn't reach the hospital until long after visiting hours ended.

Didn't matter. She was determined to see Grandpa. Maybe if she acted as if she belonged, no one would challenge her.

She punched the button to open the ICU doors. As the doors whooshed open, she straightened her shoulders and marched in. The smell of disinfectants assailed her. From somewhere nearby a machine made whooshing sounds, reminding her she was in alien territory. The central nurse's station was empty. So were most of the cubicles arranged around the station. She let out the breath she'd been holding.

Grandpa's bed was located midway around the room. Her sneakers squeaked as she approached. The blue curtain around Grandpa's bed was closed. Now that was odd. Was a nurse with him? Or had something happened to him?

Either way she was here to see Grandpa and, by golly, she would see him.

Inching the curtain open, she peaked inside. A tall, muscular man dressed in scrubs was standing by the bed. He must have just come from surgery because he was still wearing his hair cover and mask.

Was Grandpa okay?

"Doctor, how's he doing?" she said, stepping into the room.

The man beside the bed whipped around. That's when she saw the knife in his hand.

CHAPTER 13

For a heartbeat, Kim stared at the knife. Was she hallucinating, mentally reliving the horrors of last night? But even as the impossibility raced through her mind, the fake doctor raised the knife.

"No!"

Kim swung her heavy purse, heard it connect with a satisfying thunk, watched the knife fly through the air, smack the floor, skitter across the slick tile. As she reared back for another swing, the man lunged for the knife. Her purse bashed the side of his head. He staggered, his right foot bumping the knife and sending it sliding under the bed.

Blue eyes turned toward her. The same savage eyes that had glared from a black ski mask. Only this time a surgical mask hid the bottom of his face.

How? How had he found them?

And why?

Before she could move, the assailant lowered his head and charged. His left shoulder slammed her stomach, knocking the wind from her lungs and flipping her up and over his shoulder. She crashed against the metal side of Grandpa's bed. Alarm bells trilled.

She couldn't breathe. Oh, gawd, she couldn't breathe and Grandpa was helpless and . . .

A nurse pulled back the curtain. "What's going on . . ." The woman's eyes widened as the man lunged at her.

Gasping for air that wouldn't come, Kim watched helplessly as the man raised an arm to shove the woman aside. The motion bared a forearm dotted with dog teeth shaped bruises. The nurse slammed into the wall. The attacker charged out the door. No one tried to stop him.

The nurse pushed away from wall, swept an assessing eye over Kim, then Grandpa. Correctly identifying Grandpa as the patient most in need, she hurried to the bed. A second, younger nurse appeared, gasped, then rushed to Kim's side.

"Lay still," she commanded.

Lay still? Kim couldn't take her hands from her stomach, let alone get up and dance. The nurse's nametag, Clarice, faded in and out of focus until finally -- finally! -- her lungs began to fill. She inhaled the bitter odor of disinfectant, tasted something metallic. The alarms mercifully stopped.

"Can you breathe now?" Kim nodded and allowed the nurse to help her to her feet. She resisted, however, the young woman's attempt to pull her into a chair. Away from Grandpa.

"Grandpa?" The word came out as a whisper.

"He's okay," the first nurse said.

"How . . . how did he find . . ."

"Don't talk right now," Clarice said. "Catch your breath. The police are on the way."

Kim perched by Grandpa's bed, gripping his hand and watching the reassuring rise and fall of his chest. Her confrontation with the fake doctor had dislodged the lead to Grandpa's breathing tube, causing the alarm to sound. Though it seemed like the battle had raged for hours, it'd been less than a minute before the older nurse restored the breathing tube -- which meant there'd be no brain damage.

Still . . . Releasing Grandpa's hand, she removed her glasses and rubbed her eyes.

"Why don't you step out here so we can clean you up?" Clarice, the younger nurse, stood in the doorway clutching a wet cloth and what looked like an assortment of stinging antiseptics.

Kim glanced down at the warm blood oozing from her knees and wrinkled her nose.

"I'd like to spend a few more minutes with my Grandpa." Besides, what was one more scar?

Clarice frowned, shrugged and turned away. Kim reached for Grandpa's hand. But even his warmth couldn't stop the questions churning in her brain.

How?

How had Grandpa's assailant tracked him to this hospital? How had the fake doctor found Grandpa's bed without anyone noticing? And how was she going to keep Grandpa safe from another attack?

And there would be another attack. The man who stole Grandpa's briefcase acted desperate. Did he think Grandpa recognized him? If not, why risk attacking him in the hospital? If the intensive care unit had been crowded, with its full complement of nurses, someone would have spotted the assailant before he reached Grandpa. Yet the man believed it was safer to risk discovery than to allow Grandpa to come out of the medically induced coma.

But desperate or not, the guy was smart. She remembered the long knife. He obviously knew that unhooking Grandpa's breathing tube would set off alarms. Slit someone's throat or wrist, however, and the patient would lose a lot of blood before the heart monitor registered something wrong. In Grandpa's weakened condition, that might have been enough to kill him.

Did that knowledge mean Grandpa's attacker was a doctor? A medic? Someone familiar with hospitals? Or simply someone who watched television?

Then there was the question of how he'd found Grandpa. True, there was only one hospital in Calvert County. The assailant, however, managed to slip past the front desk, into the intensive care unit and all the way to the opposite end to Grandpa's bed without a single person seeing him.

No one saw her, either. But she'd known where to find Grandpa; it'd taken her . . . what? A minute? Less? Say a minute to walk from the ICU door to Grandpa's cubicle. Easy to slip by while the two nurses were with other patients.

The assailant, however, didn't know which bed Grandpa occupied. He'd needed to look in each cubicle to find Grandpa. And not just look in; he'd need to study the patient's faces. In addition to Grandpa, there were three other male patients on the floor. All elderly, all with faces obscured by tubes, wires and gadgets. Given that Grandpa's bed was the farthest from the door, the fake doctor couldn't have found him in less than four or five minutes.

Sheila, the first nurse to arrive on the scene, claimed the central station hadn't been empty for longer than two or three minutes.

Either one of the nurses was lying. Or the assailant knew just where to find Grandpa.

She shivered. Grandpa squeezed her hand. "Grandpa?"

"He can't hear you, honey." Sheila held out a can of orange juice. "Drink this. You need the sugar."

Obediently, Kim took a sip of the juice. "But he just squeezed my hand."

"You've had quite a shock. I'm sure you imagined . . ."

Kim set the can down with a thunk. "I did not imagine it."

The older woman just shook her head. "He's in a coma . . ."

"Medically induced coma. That means you can bring him out of it, right? And . . . and maybe he's not as deep as you think and . . ." Tears burned her eyes. She gulped air, willing herself to not cry. Grandpa squeezed her hand again.

"There! He just did it again."

"Let's go into the other room. We need to let him rest."

Kim choked back angry words. Don't anger Grandpa's nurses. He needed them.

Instead, she forced what she hoped was a timid smile. "Could I please stay with him just a few minutes longer?"

Sheila frowned. Hmm. . . Grandpa always said Kim's attempts at timid mouse looked more like feral cat.

"Well, just one minute longer," the nurse finally said before turning on her heel.

As soon as she was out of earshot, Kim leaned over and whispered in Grandpa's ear.

"Grandpa? Grandpa, I need your help. Squeeze my hand if you recognized the man who attacked you."

She waited one second, two seconds, three . . . Nothing. Did that mean Grandpa didn't recognize the man? Or that the earlier hand squeezes had exhausted Grandpa and he was too weak to respond now?

"So you didn't recognize him, right?" No response. "You did recognize him?" Still no response.

"It's time." The nurse stood in the doorway, arms folded across her chest, chin high.

Kim's shoulders drooped. She kissed Grandpa's cheek. "Don't worry, Grandpa. I won't let anyone hurt you." Even if it meant finding his assailant herself.

Tucking the hand she held beneath the sheet, she followed the nurse into the brightly lit central area. Clarice, the younger nurse, was already sitting in front of a computer screen. As they entered the station, Clarice handed Kim the now cold wet cloth.

Kim swiped at her knees, wincing as the damp touched the scrapes.

"Here, let me do that." Nurse Sheila knelt in front of her.

"So. Any ideas how the fake doctor reached Grandpa without anyone seeing him?" Kim hissed as the nurse scrubbed a particularly sensitive place.

Sheila shrugged. "Probably the same way you did. By sneaking in."

If the nurse thought she'd make Kim feel guilty, she was wrong. Thank goodness Kim arrived when she did! If she hadn't sneaked in . . .

"I knew where Grandpa is. Someone else would have to look in each cubicle to find him. That would take time. So why didn't anyone see him?"

Sheila's jaw muscles tightened. "Are you suggesting one of us helped this monster?"

"Of course not!" Kim consciously turned her palms towards the angry nurse, a conciliatory gesture she'd learned in college. "You didn't do anything wrong. But Grandpa's attacker would only have a minute or two to find Grandpa. Otherwise, one of you would have seen him, right? Which means either the guy was very lucky, or he knew where he was going before he sneaked into the ICU."

"Well, if he knew where your grandfather was, he certainly didn't learn it from us." Sheila ripped open a packet, pulled out gauze soaked in something and applied it to the now clean knee.

Kim bit her lip as a sharp pain pierced her knee.

"We don't give out information," Sheila continued, "unless your name is on an approved list and you know the password."

As the older nurse talked, the younger one's eyes shifted. Feeling Kim's eyes on her, Clarice turned away and began shuffling paper. The back of her ears were bright red.

A beeper sounded from somewhere. A light flashed above the doorway of the cubicle near the exit. Clarice pushed her chair back.

Sheila sighed. "No, no, stay put, Clarice. I'll deal with it."

The older nurse moved soundlessly across the floor, leaving Kim alone with the obviously uncomfortable Clarice.

"You know," Kim said gently, "if someone accidentally provided information to that guy, well, everything turned out okay and no one will get into trouble."

Clarice bit her lip. "Don't know what you're talking about."

"He called didn't he?" Clarice's intake of breath was answer enough. Kim plowed ahead. "And he asked which bed was Grandpa's? Maybe because he was sending flowers or something?" No answer. "Did he have the password?"

Clarice's shoulders slumped, her head drooped. "No," she muttered. She lifted her head and glared defiantly at Kim. "But he was on the approved list!"

Approved list? But she'd seen the list last night. Aunt Emerald had insisted only blood relatives be listed. And the only male linked to Grandpa by blood was . . .

"Tony? He said his name was Tony?"

No. No way. Cousin Tony would never harm Grandpa. Besides, the fake doctor had blue eyes. Tony's were brown like hers.

Unless Tony made the call and an accomplice attacked Grandpa?

"When . . . when did Tony call?"

"I'd just come on duty, so maybe 3, 4 o'clock."

Kim let out the breath she'd been holding. Tiffany said her brother had been in court this afternoon. No way could he have called the hospital.

But relief was soon replaced with a new worry: Someone called the hospital masquerading as Tony. Which meant the attacker knew the names of Grandpa's grandchildren.

The man with the knife was not a local thug or a casual acquaintance. He was closer, much closer. Maybe even someone Grandpa trusted.

CHAPTER 14

Forty minutes later, Kim followed Lieutenant Brockley into the hospital vending area and waited while he fed quarters into the coffee machine. The machine gurgled and belched and finally deposited an empty paper cup onto the platform. More burping before a thin stream of black liquid trickled down. Brockley slouched beside her, his eyes focused on the slowly filling cup.

She studied the detective's unshaved, sleep-creased face and fought a rush of guilt. Maybe she shouldn't have called him.

But, darn it, the state troopers who'd responded to the hospital's 9-1-1 call refused to post a guard. How could she leave Grandpa alone knowing his attacker might return?

So she'd called Lieutenant Brockley. He'd sent a patrol officer to sit outside Grandpa's room and told her to stay at the hospital until he, himself, arrived.

His entrance had produced a new flourish of activity. Kim perched on a straight-backed chair and watched Brockley consult the state troopers, interview the nurses and give instructions to Grandpa's guard. As the adrenalin subsided, her shoulders and right arm began to throb and she fought to keep her eyes open.

Now that Grandpa was safe, she just wanted to go home, pull the sheet over her head and sleep. First, however, Lieutenant Brockley wanted to talk.

"Let's find an empty room," he said, lifting the steaming cup.

Once settled in a Naugahyde chair, the detective asked Kim to describe the fake doctor. But there was little she could add to her earlier account. The cap on the assailant's head hid his hair color and the mask effectively disguised his facial features. The only new information she could provide was the size of the man's arm muscles.

"His arms were solid looking, like people who lift weights," she said. "But it's definitely the same guy. He's got bruises on his forearm where Rory grabbed him."

The detective took a sip of coffee, winced and set it on the coffee table. "The burglars are getting violent. This afternoon, a schoolteacher returned home early and found two men wearing black ski masks, both carrying knifes. They roughed her up, duct taped her to a chair and proceeded to make off with her computer, television and jewelry. The teacher's description of one of these men matches yours."

"So this guy robbed someone this afternoon and then came here to kill Grandpa? Why?"

"My guess is your grandfather recognized him and the man wanted to make sure Mr. Hershey could never identify him."

"But ... " Kim shook her head. "That doesn't make psychological sense. I mean, yeah, if Grandpa identifies him and his DNA matches the swabs from Rory's mouth, you could convict. But convicted burglars are released from jail all the time, right? Why would a thief commit murder in a capital punishment state?"

The detective shrugged. "The contents of your grandfather's stolen briefcase was worth, what? Thousands of dollars? Tens of thousands?"

Kim grimaced. "I haven't had a chance to call Grandpa's suppliers, but, yeah, thousands."

"People have killed for less than that."

"But ... In cold blood?"

"I've seen it all."

Kim was too tired to argue. Stalking Grandpa in the hospital seemed extreme for an ordinary thief, but what did she know? She'd studied abnormal psychology in college, but had zero practical experience. Besides, right now she was so exhausted her brain wasn't functioning.

As if sensing her fatigue, Lieutenant Brockley stood. "I think that's all for right now. And don't worry about your grandfather; he'll be safe tonight."

"Tonight?" Kim leaped to her feet. "But what about tomorrow night?"

Brockley sighed. "I can guard him for twenty-four hours. I don't have the manpower for more than that."

"Twenty-four hours! You've been searching for these crooks for, what? Days? Weeks? How can you be sure you'll catch them in twenty-four hours?"

"I can't spare someone for longer than that."

"So you're going to just let the killer waltz in here and murder Grandpa?" Outrage turned to fury and Kim's body began to tremble.

"Take it easy." Brockley reached out a hand. Kim slapped it away.

"Take it easy? How can I keep Grandpa safe if the police won't help?" Suddenly conscious that she'd pushed a cop, Kim folded her arms across her chest.

But, judging by his soft eyes, the detective seemed to understand.

"I'm sorry," he said, "twenty-four hours is the best I can do."

The next morning a sense of urgency drove Kim into Grandpa's office early. Last night, Lieutenant Brockley had compared her description of Grandpa's attacker to one of the burglars who attacked the school teacher and concluded they were one and the same man. There'd been something wrong with the detective's reasoning, but Kim had been too tired to work it through.

Now, however, she identified her concern: How did a local burglar know about Grandpa's unscheduled buying trip?

From what she'd read in the newspaper, the local burglars targeted people on vacation and folks with regular schedules like the school teacher. Grandpa tried to vary the timing of his New York trips for just this reason. But a few days of spying would have alerted the burglars to the routine trip he took last week.

So why wait until this week to rob Grandpa?

Setting her morning tea on Grandpa's desk, Kim flipped open Grandpa's address book, then reached for the phone. As she punched in a number, the store clocks began to chime, cuckoo and bong. Eight o'clock.

Only one thing made the recent trip different from all the others: the blue diamond. And there was no way a local burglar could know about that.

Somewhere in New York City's Diamond District, a phone began to ring.

"C'mon, c'mon," Kim muttered.

The shops in the Diamond District wouldn't open to the public until nine. Grandpa's suppliers, however, started working before eight. She pictured them there, behind their steel doors, shatter-proof glass and security cameras, helping people like Grandpa find the perfect diamonds for their customers.

But would they answer their phones before nine?

The phone rang nine, ten, eleven times.

Kim's free hand clenched into a fist. She was convinced the answer to who was trying to kill Grandpa lay in New York.

"Levy and Sons," a woman said.

Kim closed her eyes, said a silent thank you, then asked for Mr. Levy senior. A few minutes later, a voice boomed "Little Kimmy! I haven't seen you in years!"

She smiled, remembering the first time she'd met the roly-poly man on the other end of the phone. With his curly black hair and beard and jolly nature, he'd reminded her of a young Santa Claus. Of course, at age ten, she was above such childish beliefs.

"Max said you were moving home," Mr. Levy continued. "Gonna take over the business for him?"

Kim grimaced but kept her reply neutral. After enduring several minutes of the hearty man's questions, she explained that Grandpa had been robbed.

"He's in the hospital, but he's going to be okay." She refused to believe otherwise. "Anyway, the insurance company needs to know what was in his stolen briefcase."

"I'll fax you a list of what I gave him."

Kim took a deep breath. Now came the part that required acting.

Keeping her voice light, she said "Was Grandpa alone when you saw him?"

"Of course. You're the only one he's ever allowed to accompany him. Matter of fact, when he invited me to dinner and said he was spending the night in town, I thought for sure you'd be with him."

"Why?"

"He was just here last week."

So she wasn't wrong; Grandpa had made his regular New York rounds last week.

"Uh, did Grandpa say why he was returning so soon?"

A pause as Mr. Levy thought. "Not really. Said something about dropping a diamond off for testing and wanting to wait for the results. I don't know why he didn't just use Fed Ex like everyone else. But it worked out for the best because I just got in some gorgeous Canadian diamonds and Max said he had a client wanting new earrings . . ."

"Uh, Mr. Levy? Did Grandpa tell you anything about the diamond he was having tested?"

"No, and you can be sure I quizzed him about it. All he'd say is that he was having it tested for a friend."

A friend. Not a customer.

A friend just poked at a hornet's nest, Grandpa had said.

Same friend?

For a few minutes, Kim gently quizzed Mr. Levy. But the jeweler knew nothing more about Grandpa's New York trip. After promising to accompany Grandpa on his next trip to New York, Kim hung up the phone and turned to Rory.

"The reason Grandpa spent the night in New York was to wait for testing results." Rory cocked his head. "Dumb reason, huh? When we saw Phantom of the Opera, I wanted to spend the night in the big city. But, nooooooo, we had to go up on the train, see a matinee and come right home because Grandpa didn't like New York hotels."

Of course, that'd been nineteen, twenty years ago. Still, it rankled that Grandpa wouldn't make an exception for his granddaughter but would babysit a stupid diamond that was being tested. . . Unless . .
.

Unless he thought the diamond might be a natural blue.

For a minute, Kim couldn't breathe. A four or five carat natural blue diamond like the one Grandpa had given her would be worth millions.

Millions of reasons for a thief to kill.

As if sensing her tension, Rory leaped to his feet and raced to the back door, barking.

"It's okay, Rory, I'm just worried . . ." A car door slammed. Rory's bark turned to happy yips.

Kim peered through the rear window in time to see Aunt Ginny swing a rolling suitcase from the backseat of her cherry red Mustang convertible.

Swinging the door open, Kim rushed outside and into Aunt Ginny's waiting arms. As the sun beat on her back, her aunt's familiar fragrance of vanilla, jasmine and green apple allowed her to pretend she was five again and Aunt Ginny had arrived to save her from the monotony of a family reunion.

Except when she was five, she hadn't needed to bend over for a hug.

She kissed her aunt's cheek. "You've gotten shorter!"

"Watch that! You may be taller than me, but I can still paddle your bottom . . . Yes, you're a wondrous dog, but I don't want your ball."

Undaunted, Rory again shoved his saliva covered tennis ball at Ginny.

"I don't want, no, I don't . . . well, alright." Ginny tossed the ball and grinned as Rory bounded across the yard. Rory pranced back to them and offered the now sand-covered ball to Ginny. This time she extended her hand without hesitation and threw the ball in a soft, underhanded arch. Rory leaped into the air and snagged the ball before it touched ground.

As Kim watched, tension drained from her shoulders. If she could package and sell Aunt Ginny's upbeat demeanor, she could pay off her college loans and retire. Just being near Aunt Ginny made her smile.

Which is one reason why, when Grandma died, she'd urged him to invite Dad's older sister to dinner. Though Aunt Ginny was fifteen years younger than Grandpa, she shared his love of Doris Day movies, puppies and chocolate. Surely they could find more common ground if given the opportunity.

And even if they couldn't, Grandpa needed Ginny. All widowed men needed a Ginny. Kim's freshman psychology courses had revealed the grim statistics: After the death of their wives, elderly men often died within the following year.

Well, that wasn't going to happen to her grandfather.

Grandpa resisted the romantic dinner idea, but finally agreed to invite Aunt Ginny to accompany them on a fishing trip. Which is how Kim discovered her favorite aunt lacked the patience to sit still. When Ginny wasn't pacing the river bank, she talked incessantly. That the fish didn't even nibble only exacerbated her aunt's boredom and increased her patter.

Problem was, even a babbling Ginny was interesting. She'd cruised the Nile, climbed Mexican pyramids, tramped through Brazilian rain forests, ridden camels through the desert. Ginny's lively anecdotes made it impossible to simply tune out her monologue.

Grandpa later claimed that Ginny's restless behavior chased all the fish away.

For Kim's sake, the two remained friends. And as the years passed and Grandpa remained upbeat and healthy, Kim quit worrying about marrying him off.

Now, however, she studied her aunt's shrinking frame, rounded shoulders and deepening smile lines and wondered if she should have attempted some matchmaking for Ginny. True, it would have been hard while living in Oregon. But she could have at least encouraged Ginny to date. When had her aunt's mop of curls become more salt than pepper?

Ginny swiveled and sunlight glinted off her earrings -- dangling, upside down fish. Was that . . . Kim leaned closer. Yep. Aunt Ginny had glued googly eyes to the fish's heads.

Giving the ball one final toss, Aunt Ginny turned and wiped her hand on Kim's shorts. Her hand froze and her eyes widened.

"What happened to your knees?" Aunt Ginny said. "Did you fall out of the apple tree again?"

Kim glanced at the gnarled Gravenstein apple tree, rising in the center of Grandpa's yard, its branches laden with small fruit. The tree provided welcome summer shade, luscious autumn apples and year-round, wide-spreading branches just begging to be climbed. As a child, she'd spent hours in the tree, reading Hardy Boys mysteries and avoiding her pesky cousins. That tree had been the center of some of Kim's happiest childhood moments.

Which is probably why, two summers ago, she'd succumbed to the lure of the tree's upper branches. She'd failed to consider the limits of her thirty-year-old body.

When she shuffled into Grandpa's office, blood oozing from elbows and knees, Grandpa had set aside the sapphire ring he was setting and pointed towards the tall stool sitting beside his desk. It was the same stool she'd sat in as a child whenever Grandpa tended the wounds from one mishap or another. As always, he'd cleaned her wounds without hurting.

And unlike some people, he hadn't mentioned her fall again.

Aunt Ginny threw back her head and cackled, the motion setting the earring's googly eyes rolling.

Grinning, Kim reached for the suitcase. "I've got a lot to tell you, but let's get you settled first."

But once she'd carried mugs of tea into the living room and started talking, Kim couldn't seem to stop. Starting with Grandpa's phone call that interrupted her cross-country trip, the frustrations of the past few days poured out. By the time she described the attack in the hospital, Kim itched to do something, anything, to bring life back to normal.

"I'm trying to trace Grandpa's movements in New York," she concluded. "I keep thinking the blue diamond is the key."

"So let's see it."

Kim rose and crossed to the grandfather clock. As she ran her hand across the top, Ginny gasped.

"You're not keeping it there, are you? That's the first place a thief would look."

Kim froze. "Really?"

Ginny nodded. "People hide things on flat surfaces above eye level."

Kim bit her lip and swept her hand over the clock's top. The envelope was exactly where she'd left it. "I'll put it in the safe when we go downstairs."

Returning to the couch, she withdrew the gem and gently unfolded its paper wrapping. Beside her, Ginny gasped. Kim realized with shame that the glistening blue stone made her own heartbeat quicken.

"Betty Grable wore a blue diamond ring." Aunt Ginny held the gem to the light. "My, that is pretty. You think it's a natural blue?"

"I can't think of any other reason for trying to murder Grandpa." Kim shuddered. She reached for a pad and pencil and handed them to her aunt. "I won't know for sure it's natural until I see the lab report. It was probably in the stolen briefcase, but there should be a number on the girdle that will enable me to get a copy. Could you please write down the numbers while I read them?"

A spare set of jeweler's tweezers and a loupe sat on the end table. Using the tweezers, Kim grasped the top and bottom of the diamond, then raised the magnifier to her eye and brought the stone's girdle into focus. A set of numbers swam into view.

"Ready? Nine, six, zero, four, three, eight, two, five, one." Kim set the stone and loupe onto her lap and rubbed her eyes. Darn, she was out of practice.

"How 'bout I read these back to you?"

Kim nodded and repositioned the diamond and tweezers. When she brought the diamond into focus, however, she found herself staring at a symbol instead of numbers. No, not a symbol. A drawing of . . . was that a dinosaur?

"Ginny? Would you look at this please?"

She passed the loupe, tweezers and diamond to her aunt.

"Looks like a T-Rex." Ginny held the diamond to the light, tilting it so it flashed. "What's T-Rex doing on a diamond?"

"Some people like to laser inscribe personal messages on their diamonds. Usually, though, it's something like 'I heart you.'" She grinned, suddenly remembering the inscription on Tiffany's new diamond. "Unless you're Tiffany."

"Oh, goody, a new fluff-for-brains story. Let's hear it."

As Kim described Tiffany's new use for her husbands' ashes, Ginny's uninhibited laugh filled the room. Oh, she'd missed that laugh. Now if only Grandpa were here, life would be perfect.

"So Max bought this diamond for a dinosaur nut?"

"When you put it like that, doesn't sound likely, does it?" Kim retrieved the diamond and again peered at the side. Whoever had operated the laser wasn't much of an artist. The dinosaur's body was too stocky, its arms too long . . . Kim's breath caught. Her mind whirled, pieces of the puzzle suddenly fitting together.

"That's not T-Rex. That's Torvosaurus! Why are you rolling your eyes?"

"You and your dinosaurs." Ginny snatched back the diamond back. "And that still looks like a T-Rex."

Kim shook her head. "Torvosaurus had longer arms and a thicker body. AND it was first discovered in Colorado." She leaned forward and laid a hand over Ginny's. "Some diamond manufacturers laser inscribe symbols to indicate where a diamond was mined. The Canadians, for example, use a maple leaf or polar bear. If I'm right, this diamond came from Colorado!"

"I didn't know there was a diamond mine in Colorado."

"There was one. I don't know if it's still open; it kept closing and re-opening . . . Let me get my computer."

A few minutes later, Kim set her laptop on the coffee table. She couldn't resist typing in "Torvosaurus picture." The web illustrations matched the laser drawing on the blue diamond.

Kim found a drawing of T-Rex and positioned it next to Torvosaurus. "See the differences? . . . Now that's interesting." She pointed at the article on Torvosaurus. "The first jawbone was found in Colorado, but they've since found bones in Wyoming and Utah. Perfect."

"Why perfect?"

Changing the search to "Colorado diamond geology," Kim pulled up a geological map of the state. "You know that diamonds are created by intense heat and pressure of the sort found only deep in the earth, right? That's also where you find kimberlite and lamprolite -- types of igneous rocks. Volcanoes bring diamonds to the surface, as well as kimberlite and lamprolite. Look for kimberlite or lamprolite and you might well find diamonds"

She pointed at the geological map. "The mountains that stretch from Colorado through Wyoming, Montana and into Canada contained kimberlite. I'm not sure why, but kimberlite is more likely to have diamonds than lamprolite."

She changed the search to "Colorado diamonds" and clicked on the first entry.

The Kelsey Lake mine, she read, had been located on the Colorado/Wyoming border. During the five years it was open, the mine produced 17 million tons of diamonds.

"Wow," Ginny said. "That's a lot of diamonds."

"Not really. The Argyle in Australia -- that's the world's largest mine -- produces double that every year. But look at this." Kim pointed at the screen. "Half of the diamonds found at Kelsey Lake were gem quality. Only five percent of Argyle's diamonds are gem quality; the rest are used in industry."

Ginny whistled. "Look at that. They found a 28 carat diamond in Colorado."

"And cut it into a 17-carat light yellow diamond," Kim read. "I'd like to see that . . . darn, they closed the mine in 2002."

"But that makes no sense! Why import diamonds if we have them right here?"

"Diamond mining is expensive." Kim clicked back to the search engine and typed in "Kelsey Mine re-open." "That's one of the reasons the owners of the Arkansas deposit turned it over to the state. Not enough diamonds to make mining there cost-effective. Of course, the vandalism didn't help."

"Vandalism? Who'd want to vandalize a diamond mine?"

"De Beers got blamed . . ." She blew out her breath and leaned back. Google found no mention of the Kelsey mine reopening.

"De Beers." Ginny snorted at the name of the one-time diamond monopoly. "Afraid of the competition I suppose. Is that why Max hates them so much?"

"Grandpa doesn't like cartels, but the Arkansas thing was long ago. Nineteen twenties, maybe . . . You'd think that if the Kelsey mine reopened, the new owners would advertise."

"You're getting off track. Why does Max's face get red whenever someone mentions De Beers?"

"Long story. Grandpa thought they forced one of his suppliers out business . . ." So if the Kelsey mine hadn't reopened, then why was there a Torvosaurus on the blue diamond? Unless . . .

Unless the blue diamond came from somewhere else in Colorado.

"Are you listening to me?" Aunt Ginny's voice was so close to Kim's ear that she jumped.

Kim turned to Ginny and gripped her hand. "The Kesley Lake mine hasn't reopened. But what if the blue diamond came from somewhere else in Colorado? What if there's a deposit of blue diamonds in Colorado?"

"Lovely idea but even I know that a single blue diamond does not a deposit make."

"Two blue diamonds. Jim Hampton's nephew found a small one in his uncle's safe, remember? And when I met Jim, he said he'd just returned from a trip to Colorado." She paused, trying to put the pieces together. "Okay, try this: What if Jim met someone who'd discovered a diamond deposit in Colorado?"

"Why not Jim discovering the deposit?"

"Not likely. I don't know how long Jim stayed on his visit, but I can't imagine him stumbling on a diamond deposit let alone recognizing what it was. Heck, at Crater of Diamonds where everyone's hunting in an actual deposit, prospectors can search for weeks before finding something. It's not impossible that Jim found the stones, but more likely he's got a friend who lives in Colorado or something."

Ginny nodded. "And Jim involved Max to, what, make sure the diamonds are real?"

"Or to get certification so they could attract investors. Remember diamond mines are expensive."

A slow grin spread across Ginny's face and her eyes twinkled. "Guess this means you need to call Jim's nephew so you can compare notes."

Kim turned away so Ginny couldn't see her own smile.

LYNN FRANKLIN

CHAPTER 15

The voice that answered the phone was so low and sexy that for a moment Kim couldn't speak.

"Hello? Is someone there?"

"Scott, it's Kimberley West." Her own voice squeaked. Beside her, Aunt Ginny giggled. Taking a deep breath, Kim pitched her voice lower. "Max Hershey's granddaughter."

"I know which Kimberley." The humor in his voice made her hands clench at the same time that her toes curled. "Good to hear your voice."

"Er, yeah, well, the reason I called . . ." Briefly, Kim told him about Grandpa giving her the blue diamond, finding the Torvosaurus inscribed on it and her theory that Jim had a friend in Colorado who'd discovered a new diamond field.

"Anyway, Jim said he'd been to Colorado and I wondered if he told you anything about the trip," she concluded.

The silence was so long that for a moment she wondered if they'd been cut off. "You know," he finally said, "Uncle Jim was awfully vague about it. He was supposed to be fishing with a friend. But usually after a trip he returns with a bunch of fish stories. This time he didn't want to talk about it. I assumed he didn't catch anything, but . . ."

"Would his friend in Colorado talk to us?"

"Maybe," Scott said. "But I don't remember his name."

"Would you recognize the friend's name if you looked in Jim's address book?"

"Good idea . . . Look, I've got an appointment I need to keep. Why don't you meet me at Uncle Jim's house in, say, two hours? Two of us can go through his paperwork faster than one."

She opened her mouth to accept, then realized she'd be leaving Aunt Ginny alone in the store. With a killer running loose.

"Gee, I'd love that, but I don't want to leave my aunt . . . ow" Kim glared at the woman who'd just smacked her knee and was now gesturing to be allowed to speak. "Hang on."

"Whatever he wants you to do," Ginny said as soon as Kim covered the mouth piece, "do it. I'll call some friends to come help so I won't be alone."

Uh, oh. Aunt Ginny had that matchmaking look in her eyes. Kim made a mental note to keep Scott away from the store while Ginny visited.

She agreed to Scott's suggestion, jotted down Jim's address and gave Scott her cell phone number. It would take forty minutes to reach Jim's house, they were meeting in two hours . . . She did some quick calculations. She had about seventy minutes to do some investigating on her own.

She handed the phone to her aunt. "I need to open the store. Call your friends. If they're still not here when I have to leave, we'll close the store and you can reopen when someone arrives. Agreed? Rory, stay with Aunt Ginny."

Rory sighed and threw himself to the ground with a thump.

As Kim trotted down the stairs, she made a mental list of what she could accomplish before leaving. With Grandpa's police protection limited to one more night, she couldn't waste time.

She flicked on the store lights and smiled in satisfaction as the already-filled showcases glittered. Grandpa would be proud of her creative blending of color. She crossed to the front door, making a mental list of what she could do in seventy minutes.

Highest priority: Obtain a copy of the lab report on the blue diamond. She unlocked the door and hung the Open sign. If the diamond was a natural blue, maybe she could convince Detective Brockley to expand his investigation to include Grandpa's jewelry associates.

In the meantime, she'd quiz cousin Amber about boyfriends, past and present. She could easily imagine one of those thugs figuring out Grandpa carried diamonds in his briefcase and trying to rob him.

Her cousin's boyfriends had never demonstrate excessive neurons; if one of them had robbed Grandpa, there should be a trail to follow. Besides, blaming the attacks on one of Amber's thugs was less frightening than the idea that Grandpa's attacker was specifically after the blue diamond.

If, however, Grandpa's attacker had specifically targeted the blue diamond -- knew it was a natural color worth millions -- she'd be dealing with a more sophisticated and dangerous category of thief.

Taking her place behind the showcases, she reached for the phone. With any luck, the tourists wouldn't arrive until after Aunt Ginny joined her.

A few minutes later a watered-down Beatles song -- this one Yellow Submarine -- filled her ear as she waited for someone at the gemology lab to help her.

The woman who finally answered the phone recorded the inscription number Kim read off then promised to fax the report by the end of the day.

"Uh, I really need it sooner than that. The report may help with a robbery investigation." That sounded professional, right?

But the woman wouldn't commit to anything earlier than five o'clock. Kim's demand for a supervisor proved ineffectual.

Only the jangling of the bell over the front door prevented her from slamming the phone in frustration into its cradle. Forcing a smile on her face, she turned to the customer . . . and froze.

Jason White sauntered toward her, his tall, muscular frame casually elegant in a fitted, long-sleeved shirt and pressed khaki pants. The Bay breeze had tousled his blond hair across his forehead, drawing attention to his cool blue eyes. As he neared, she caught a whiff of his trade-mark cologne, ginger, myrrh and sandalwood.

Kim's hands fisted, her nails digging into her palms. No. No, no, no. After fifteen years, this was not how she'd imagined encountering her old high-school flame. He'd broken her heart and she'd hoped she'd never see him again. But if she did run into him, it had to be perfect. She'd imagined a party scene, a floaty red dress brushing her knees, a glass of white wine in her hand, a crowd of admiring men surrounding her.

Never mind that she didn't drink wine, own a dress or know enough men to make a crowd. It was her fantasy and it had sustained her through a month of sleepless nights after Jason White stood her up for the prom.

Now, instead of that lovely scenario, here she stood, clad in black jeans, turquoise tee and

Sketchers sandals. She'd planned to brush her hair and add some mascara and lipstick before heading off to see Scott. At the moment, however, she wore no makeup and had pulled her hair into a ponytail. Probably looked like she'd just stepped off the boat.

She studied Jason, searching for some sign that he'd aged, that the years had knocked away some of the cockiness or at least created some physical flaw to counteract his inherent sexiness. Was that a couple of lines near his eyes and mouth? If so, they certainly weren't as deep as her own smile lines. Her eyes trailed from his face. Still muscular. Not even the start of a beer belly.

The man could still model for GQ. Except for the beat-up briefcase he set on the showcase . . .

She felt her mouth drop open. "Is that Grandpa's briefcase?"

"You tell me." Jason set the case on the counter. "I found it beside the North Beach boardwalk. Looked like someone tossed it over the rail."

The case sported several more dings, patches of sand and some wet spots, probably from the waves. Kim eagerly reached for it, her hands brushing Jason's. Ignoring the sparks that shot up her arms, she snapped open the case. Empty.

"Whoever stole it took everything, of course." Jason's eyes narrowed. "You look disappointed."

Kim shrugged. "I thought they might have left the paperwork."

Something flashed through Jason's eyes, but it was gone so quickly she might have imagined it.

"How did you know this was Grandpa's?"

"Everyone in the business recognizes the ratty old thing he carries."

Kim sighed. "Well, thanks for returning it. Er, what were you doing on the boardwalk?" Jason lived in Annapolis, a perfect place for rich boys and their toys. It was also forty minutes away from the three beaches.

"Jogging. I get bored if I keep going to the same places."

Kim folded her arms. "Long way to drive just for a run."

He grinned and her knees went weak. "Well, I also heard you were back in town."

"How in the world . . ."

"That's all Max has been able to talk about," Jason said laughing. "And you know how fast gossip spreads in this business."

No, she didn't know. It'd been years since she traveled around with Grandpa and she'd been too young and innocent to notice people gossiping. Kim made a note to caution Grandpa about discussing her affairs.

"Where is Max, by the way? He already rope you into taking over the store?"

"Grandpa's in the hospital." Kim took a deep breath, gripped the handle of Grandpa's briefcase. "The thief stabbed him."

"Oh, Kim." Jason laid a hand over hers. This time she felt nothing.

She pulled her hand away. "He'll be fine. I know he will."

"Of course he will." Jason's smile didn't meet his eyes. Kim looked away. "Hey, why don't you let me take you to lunch? Don't worry, I've showered and changed."

"Can't. I have an appointment."

"Dinner then. There's supposed to be a new five-star seafood place right here in Osprey Beach that's getting great reviews. Have you heard?"

Kim closed her eyes and breathed deeply. Yeah, she'd heard. Grandpa planned to take her there to celebrate her homecoming. He'd been so excited that a fancy restaurant opened so close, as if that proved the town was now cosmopolitan enough for his globe-trotting granddaughter. She hadn't had the heart to tell him she'd prefer to sit on his living room balcony, watching the waves and being near the grandfather who'd lifted her fallen bicycle, wiped her tears and picked gravel from her scabby knees.

There was no way she'd dine at that new restaurant without Grandpa. Especially not with the man who'd stood her up for the prom right in front of Grandpa, her parents, God and everyone.

It should have been her shining moment. After what seemed like centuries of playing wallflower, Jason White -- football star, heartthrob and heir to

White Family Jewelers -- had invited Kimberley West to be his date to the senior prom.

A single trip to the mall confirmed Kim's suspicion that no amount of babysitting money would pay for the gown of her dreams. Instead, she and Grandma spent weeks sewing a long dress that vaguely resembled one in Vogue magazine. At the last minute, Mom surprised her with a trip to the Chesapeake Beach Spa to have her hair styled and makeup applied.

Grandpa used a whole roll of film photographing Kim in all her finery. And then they all sat down to wait for Jason.

They waited. And waited. And waited.

If cell phones had been available then, Kim might have acquiesced to Mom's pressure to call Jason. Instead, Kim would have to call Jason's home and the thought of his distinguished father answering stilled her hand.

In the end, it was Grandpa who called the White household and discovered Jason had left hours ago -- to pick up Cindy McMann, the prom queen.

Dad manfully offered to step in. Before Kim could voice her horror, Grandpa dismissed the idea of the prom as "kids' stuff." But, he added, Kim looked too pretty in her "custom gown" to stay home.

While she washed the mascara from her tear-streaked face, Grandpa wrangled last-minute reservations at the famous Willard Room in downtown D.C. And what started as a nightmare turned into an eye-popping evening of costumed doormen, towering marble columns, massive chandeliers, red carpets and course after course of exotic French food. She got her first taste of white wine (yuk), sea bass (okay) and crepes Suzette (yum). Grandpa regaled her with stories of famous people who'd stayed at the Willard: Martin Luther King, Charles Dickens, Buffalo Bill, P.T. Barnum and Kim's own literary hero, Mark Twain. After dinner, they'd explored the hotel. By the time the parking attendant delivered their car and the doorman handed her into the passenger seat, she'd no longer had to pretend she was having a good time.

It was only later, as an adult, that she recognized Grandpa's genius. He'd provided a face-saving alternative to going to the prom with Dad or to dinner with the entire family. He'd selected a restaurant far from the ones her schoolmates would choose, a place that was elegant without being overly romantic. And he'd spent a small fortune -- money he didn't have -- to protect his granddaughter's fragile ego.

Now Jason White wanted to buy her dinner at the restaurant Grandpa had selected for a special occasion? No, no way.

She opened her mouth to turn down the invitation when everything seemed to happen at once. The front door bell jangled as a white-haired woman stepped inside. On the other side of the room, Rory and Aunt Ginny crossed through the interior door. Jason's eyes widened and he jumped back; his elbow bumped Grandpa's briefcase and sent it to the floor with a loud crash.

Everyone froze. Everyone except the big poodle.

Rory barked and charged into the room. Kim caught him as he started to round the display case.

"It's okay, sweetie, it was just Grandpa's briefcase." Kim pitched her voice low, trying to calm the startled poodle.

But Rory continued to growl, eyes focused on Jason. Every hair on his back stood up.

"Keep him away from me."

Kim glanced at Jason. He stood on the balls of his feet, legs spread, fists clenched, eyes wide enough to see the whites.

Darn, she'd forgotten. Jason was deathly afraid of dogs. As a child, he'd seen a close friend attacked by a pit bull.

Turning back to Rory, she spoke in a soothing voice. Rory barked.

"Jesus, Kim . . ."

Kim ignored Jason. She stroked Rory's chest. Poor dog was trembling. Had it been the loud sound? Or had Rory picked up on the animosity she'd been feeling as she relived prom night?

"It's okay, sweetie." Gently, she led him behind the counter.

Straightening, she turned back to Jason and the new customer . . . oh, no. Mrs. Johnstone. Grandpa's best customer. Mrs. Johnstone hadn't moved. Her wide eyes darted from Rory to Jason.

Great. Rory had frightened Grandpa's best customer.

"I'm sorry, Mrs. Johnstone. Rory's really very friendly. The sound just startled him."

"That's okay." Mrs. Johnstone forced a smile. "I like dogs. If you're busy, I can come back . . ."

"No, I'm just leaving." Jason turned his megawatt smile on the elderly woman. "Or I will be as soon as Kim accepts my dinner invitation."

Oh, smooth, Jason. Now she'd look like a jerk if she didn't accept.

"I'm really not in the mood for some place fancy," she said. "If you'd like to just grab a bite at Doni's . . . " They could walk to the barbecue restaurant. And along the way, maybe she could encourage Jason to reveal some of that jewelry gossip.

Jason nodded. "Meet you here at seven?" He pointed his chin towards the fallen briefcase. Though it lay on the other side of the display case, it was only a few feet from where Rory stood. "I hope you'll excuse me if I don't . . ."

"I'll get it."

The tension in the air dissipated as the door closed behind Jason. The hair on Rory's back slowly returned to normal. He wagged his tail at Mrs. Johnstone.

"I'm really sorry Rory scared you," Kim said. "Honestly, he's very gentle."

Mrs. Johnstone, however, didn't seem to hear. She stared out the window, frowning. "Odd to see a White here . . ." she muttered.

Shaking her head, she turned from the window and smiled. "And how are you, my dear. Max has been so looking forward to your arrival."

Kim reached for the extended hand, trying not to stare at the blinding array of white and black diamonds that circled her wrist. The small, brilliant cut stones had been set in a twisted rope pattern that set off the contrast in the two colors. Stylish, but a bit harsh looking on fair skin. Kim would have replaced the black diamonds with a softer brown -- no, the industry called the most common diamond color "cognac." Yeah, right.

She introduced her aunt, then, trying to forestall the inevitable question and lengthy answer, said "Grandpa's not here right now. Can I help you with something?" With any luck, Mrs. Johnstone's request would be simple and Kim would have time to call Amber before heading off to meet Scott.

"Well, I wanted Max to look at a ring, but I bet you could do it just as well." She reached into her expensive purse -- even Kim recognized the Chanel logo -- and pulled out a robin's egg blue ring box . . . a box adorned with the crest Jason's grandfather designed years ago.

Why had Mrs. Johnstone bought a ring from Grandpa's biggest competitor?

Accepting the box, she flipped open the top to reveal an oval-cut diamond solitaire. The stone couldn't be much more than half a carat. Kim's eyes slid to Mrs. Johnstone's wedding set, which featured a four-carat emerald cut diamond surrounded by diamond melee.

"I just need an estimate on how much this thing is worth," Mrs. Johnstone said.

"I'm sorry, you'll have to wait for Grandpa." Kim held out the box. "I'm not certified in appraising."

Mrs. Johnstone ignored the proffered ring. "Just give me a rough figure. Or better yet, just look at the thing and tell me what you see."

Kim glanced at the wall clock. She still had twenty-five minutes before she had to leave.

After asking Aunt Ginny to watch the store, she called Rory and led the way into Grandpa's office. Affixing the ring to the microscope's stone holder, Kim set the magnification to 10x, illumination to overhead daylight and peered in.

Looked like a nice little diamond with only a few pinpoints, a small feather and . . . She squinted. That was odd.

Removing the ring from the stand, she slowly rotated it side to side. Was that a blue flash?

She replaced the ring in the holder and increased magnification. Yes, there it was. In the center of the table, a hairline crack extended from the surface through the pavilion. The crack had been filled with a clear liquid, making the inclusion invisible to the naked eye.

Kim returned the ring to its box and began describing what she'd seen.

"Wait a minute." Mrs. Johnstone held up a hand, traffic cop style. "Go back to the fracture filling. What's that?"

"Uh, it's when a manufacturer injects glass or clear plastic into an inclusion to mask it. The filling reflects the light better than the air it replaces."

"So fracture filling improves a diamond's clarity?"

"Apparent clarity. That's different from the clarity grade you got on the gem report. Fracture filling isn't necessarily permanent -- it can change color if exposed to intensive heat -- so gemologists grade diamonds as if the fracture is still visible . . . Didn't anyone tell you about the fracture filling?"

"No. Should he have?"

"The FTC requires jewelers to reveal any treatments that affect the value of the stone. Fracture filling improves the look of the stone, but not the value." This time Mrs. Johnstone accepted the ring Kim held out.

"So he finally did something illegal," Mrs. Johnstone said.

Huh? Who was she talking about?

"Uh, filling inclusions to improve a diamond's appearance isn't illegal," she began. "In fact, it's a good way to bring low-cost diamonds into the market . . ." Kim trailed off.

Not only was Mrs. Johnstone not listening, but her eyes had narrowed into a feral slit. She stared over Kim's right shoulder, lips pressed together, one side of her mouth tilted upward. And then her eyes cleared, the tension in her face and shoulders relaxed.

"Thank you, my dear." Kim flinched as the older woman patted her hand. "You've been a great help."

"But . . ."

Mrs. Johnstone scurried away. Kim stood in time to see the front door close behind her.

"Well, that was weird." She hoped she hadn't just cost Grandpa his best customer.

CHAPTER 16

An hour later, Kim slammed on the brakes and cursed the oblivious driver who'd cut her off. She glanced in the van's rear-view mirror and winced as the tailgating car behind her loomed close enough to read the driver's lips as she talked on her phone.

Amazing how much Crofton, a commuter community midway between Baltimore and Washington, had changed in the years Kim lived in Oregon. The four-lane highway that cut through Crofton was now six lanes in places and the sides of the road were lined with outdoor shopping malls. Thank goodness she'd programmed Jim Hampton's address into her GPS.

In point five miles, the GPS said, turn right on Clubhouse Gate Road.

Good. In half a mile she'd be rid of the tailgating idiot. She forced her clenched teeth apart.

Now if she could only figure out a way to reconnect with Amber.

Before leaving Osprey Beach, she'd called her cousin to ask about boyfriends, past and present. In hindsight, Kim should have scheduled a face-to-face meeting instead of trying to quiz Amber on the phone.

But, darn it, she was running out of time. Lieutenant Brockley planned to remove Grandpa's police protection tomorrow morning. There was no way he would arrest Grandpa's stalker by then; the police were looking in the wrong direction.

Kim needed evidence to convince Brockley that the attack on Grandpa was separate from the series of Calvert County burglaries. If that required ratting on one of Amber's thug friends, so be it.

Amber, of course, didn't see it that way. She'd ranted and railed and accused Kim of prejudice against bikers. She denied telling anyone about Grandpa carrying jewels in his battered old briefcase. And she refused to create a list of old boyfriends.

Turn right on Clubhouse Gate Road.

Well, at least one thing was going right today -- the tailgating woman didn't follow the van into the tree-lined neighborhood. Kim breathed deeply and consciously loosened her fingers on the steering wheel. Easing off the accelerator, she prepared for the upcoming series of turns that would lead to Jim Hampton's house.

Given the messages Jim left on the answering machine, she suspected he'd been the friend who needed Grandpa to make a special trip to New York. The friend Grandpa said was in trouble. Somewhere in Jim's house there must be notes, files or other paperwork that would explain why two old men had suddenly attracted the attention of killers.

Arriving at address on right.

Kim pulled into a driveway lined with crape myrtles and stopped in front of what a realtor friend called a "five, four and a door": Five windows upstairs, four windows down with a door in the middle. Stepping into the humid air, she breathed in the fragrance of honeysuckle and tea rose. Off to her left a lawnmower roared to life. A flash of red in a maple tree drew her eye; she smiled as the cardinal called a happy cheer-cheer.

Turning, she studied the row of McMansions, manicured lawns and neat sidewalks, searching for a neighbor with a clear view of Jim's house, someone who might have seen the men who attacked him.

Directly across the street, a lace curtain twitched. Kim could barely make out a figure sitting behind the picture window. The neighborhood busybody?

Her cell phone launched into the Indiana Jones "Raiders March." Flipping it open, she read the caller I.D. Scott Wilson.

"I'm sorry," he said. "My interview ran long. I should be there in thirty minutes."

After assuring him she'd wait, she snapped the phone shut and headed for the house with the lace curtains.

The elderly woman who opened the door was so tiny Kim was tempted to kneel down to talk. She reminded Kim of the apple dolls Aunt Ginny had taught her to make when she was a child. However, when Kim explained she was a friend of Jim's looking into his death, the wrinkled face beamed.

"Oh, good, maybe you can find out who was driving that BMW that followed Mr. Hampton. I'm Mildred Mahoney."

Kim followed Mrs. Mahoney into a sunny living room filled with doily-draped chairs, family photos and -- yes, yes, yes -- a cafe style table positioned right in front of the picture window. The homey atmosphere was enhanced by the fragrance of warm chocolate.

"I was about to make a pot of tea to go with the cookies. Would you join me? . . . No, no I can manage. You sit right here." She gestured to the cafe chairs and disappeared through an arched doorway.

Kim hurried to the front window. To her disappointment, the view of Jim's driveway was partially blocked by the crape myrtles' leaves. In the winter, when the trees lost their leaves, Mrs. Mahoney would have an unobstructed view of not only Jim's driveway, but also his side yard. Right now, however . . .

Kim turned to see Mrs. Mahoney struggling with an overloaded tray of china tea pot, cups, sugar, milk, lemon and ohmygosh, chocolate chip cookies.

"Here, let me help." She crossed the room to collect the tray, then held it while Mrs. Mahoney transferred everything to the cafe table.

"There." Mrs. Mahoney inspected the table. "It needs a bud vase, doesn't it?"

Kim grinned. "All it really needs are those wonderful smelling cookies."

"Then eat, eat." Mrs. Mahoney settled into a chair. "I love afternoon tea but hate eating it alone. Your timing was so perfect."

Setting the tray aside, Kim sat and reached for a cookie. "These are homemade!" Her mouth filled with dark chocolate, butter and real vanilla -- and no stale aftertaste like with the pre-made refrigerator cookies.

Mrs. Mahoney beamed and poured the tea. "I've always wanted to ask 'one lump or two', but I'm afraid my doctor insisted I switch from real sugar to artificial."

Kim frowned at her cookie. "These were made with sweetener?"

Mrs. Mahoney laughed. "Of course not. I figure if I use the fake stuff in my coffee and tea, I can afford to bake with real sugar. Just as long as I limit how much I eat each day."

"I need to introduce you to my Aunt Ginny. She shares your philosophy." Kim reached for a second cookie. "You were saying something about a BMW?"

Mrs. Mahoney nodded and gestured out the window. "As you can see, ours is a quiet street. We all have driveways and garages, so you seldom see people parked on the street. Unless there's a party, of course.

"Anyway, starting about, oh, a week or so ago, I noticed this black BMW parked down by that Bradford pear tree." She pointed towards a location two doors down, on the opposite side of Jim's house. A perfect spot to observe Jim's driveway.

"I thought at first the Maxwells -- they own the house with the tree -- had friends visiting. But they didn't recognize the car, either. We called the police but, of course, the car was gone when they arrived." Mrs. Mahoney leaned forward, her faded blue eyes suddenly glittering. "Then two days later, the BMW followed Jim home."

Kim shivered, remembering Jim's voice on the answering machine: I think I'm being followed.

"I told Mr. Hampton, of course, but he didn't want to call the police." She bit into a cookie and shrugged. "Said he could handle it."

"Did he act like he knew who was following him?"

"No. But his face drained of color. If he'd known the person, he wouldn't have been frightened now would he? So I was surprised when he wouldn't let me call the police."

Maybe Jim didn't know exactly who was following him, but the message he'd left Grandpa indicated he suspected someone. But who?

"I don't suppose you got the license number . . ." Kim felt her mouth falling open as Mrs. Mahoney set a slip of paper in front of her.

"My eyesight isn't what it used to be," she said, "but I had several opportunities to get it right."

"This is wonderful!" Kim picked up the paper and studied the numbers written on it in a cramped hand. "What did the police say?"

"That's the problem. The police weren't interested. They wrote down the number, but I don't think they did anything with it."

Kim gasped. "But . . . but Jim was attacked, robbed . . ."

"And the BMW was nowhere around. The car I saw racing from the driveway that night was more like an SUV."

"I don't suppose you got that number . . ."

Mrs. Mahoney snorted. "I wish. No, I was lucky I even saw the car. I have to take thyroid medicine on an empty stomach. I figure since I never sleep through the night -- bladder always was a bit temperamental -- I'd just take my pills when I did my nightly bathroom run. Normally that would be 1, maybe 2 a.m. But I had trouble falling asleep that night, so it was closer to 4. Saw this dark, truck like thing screech down Mr. Hampton's driveway. No lights on, so I couldn't get a good look at it. Maybe if I had . . ."

Kim reached across the table and squeezed the old woman's vein-covered hand. "You've done beautifully. The police know they're looking for an SUV and maybe they can connect that BMW with it." She reached for her purse and began rummaging inside for a pen and paper. "I'd like to write this number down . . ."

"You can have the paper if you promise to follow through."

"Don't worry, I will." She'd give the number to Scott; if he couldn't convince the police to trace the license plate, she'd ask Aunt Ginny to help. Having worked at the DMV for all those years, surely Ginny could call in some favors. Kim slipped the number into her wallet.

"Oh, look, there's Mr. Hampton's nice young nephew! Is that who you're meeting? You must bring him some cookies."

As Mrs. Mahoney shuffled into the kitchen to prepare a goody bag, Kim watched Scott climb from a blue Subaru Forester. He crossed to her van and peered inside. Turning, he scanned the side yard, presenting an excellent view of a shapely backside encased in tight jeans.

"Nice butt, huh?"

Kim jumped, then looked down at the grinning Mrs. Mahoney. The old woman giggled.

"Don't look so surprised; I may be wrinkled on the outside but I can still appreciate a handsome man."

Kim grinned. "I definitely need to introduce you to Aunt Ginny."

Accepting the plastic bag of cookies, she thanked Mrs. Mahoney and headed across the street.

CHAPTER 17

At the sound of her shoes, Scott turned and his mouth quirked into an Indiana Jones half smile. Kim froze mid step. Shivers chased Scott's gaze as it traveled from her face to her toes and back up again. She opened her mouth in greeting but her tongue had glued itself to the roof of her mouth. Her face grew so warm she feared her lipstick would melt and ooze down her chin.

"I see you've met Mrs. Mahoney," he said.

Grateful for a distraction, she held the bag aloft. "I'm supposed to share these with you, but you'll have to move fast if you want one."

"Ah, that's right. Max said chocolate turns you on."

Scott's warm baritone gave the words added significance and Kim resisted the urge to lean towards him.

Change the subject!

"Jim's neighbor got the license plate of someone she said was following him." Kim held out the slip of paper. "She gave it to the police but got the impression they wouldn't follow through. Maybe they'll listen to you."

Scott reached for the paper. Her hand tingled as his fingers brushed hers.

"Let me call this in while I get Jim's mail." Pulling a cell phone from his pocket, Scott trudged down the driveway towards the mailbox.

Kim watched, frowning. Why in the world did she find this man attractive? He was so not her type.

He wasn't particularly tall -- just shy of six feet. Though he moved with a certain grace, he wasn't muscular or athletic. All in all Scott Wilson was physically just sort of average. Yet he oozed a sensuality she was finding difficult to resist.

Scott paused in front of the mailbox. The tapered fingers holding the phone clenched and his mouth flattened into a thin line. Removing the phone from his ear, he punched the disconnect button and stood silently.

"Everything okay?" Kim called.

Scott tossed her a rueful smile, pulled mail from the box and trudged towards her.

"Police gave me the same run around they gave Mrs. Mahoney," he said.

Kim slipped the paper with the license number from the stack of mail. "I know someone who used to work for the DMV. Let's see if she can do something." She'd give the number to Aunt Ginny. Putting a name to the person following Jim might prove enlightening.

"Could we start our search in Jim's workshop? Maybe the crooks missed something and . . ." She bit off the next word as the teasing glint in Scott's eyes turned sober. How could she be so insensitive? Grandpa was in danger, but at least he was still alive. Unlike Scott's uncle.

"Scott, I'm sorry. Maybe you'd rather . . ."

He held up a hand. "'s okay. I've been avoiding the workshop ever since . . . ever since that night. Might be easier to have someone with me." His eyes dropped to the mail in his hand. A grin formed. "Well I'll be doggone . . ."

Ripping open a letter, he scanned it. When he looked up, the humor had returned to his eyes. "Look at this. Uncle Jim joined a health club! I thought he'd lost some weight, but he denied it."

Kim accepted the proffered envelope. It contained a monthly bill from the new 24-hour gym that just opened in Osprey Beach.

"He sure didn't plan on visiting very often," she said, returning the letter. "It's, what, forty-five minutes to the gym from here?"

Scott shrugged. "Probably intended to bring Max with him."

Grandpa? At an exercise club? That image would take some getting used to.

She followed Scott into the house and paused in the foyer. The layout appeared to be classic colonial: Formal dining room on the right, living room on the left, hallway leading deeper into the home, probably to a kitchen and powder room. Straight ahead, glistening oak stairs led up. With the addition over the garage, the house was the perfect size for a small family.

But Jim had been a bachelor.

"How long did Jim live here?"

Scott adjusted the thermostat. An overhead vent emitted a blast of cold air. "I guess I was ten when he bought the place. Figured Mom could have the bonus room -- it's big enough for a sitting room along with the bedroom and bath. He let me choose one of the other bedrooms.."

"This is where you grew up?"

"Well, from the time my parents split. Before that we followed Dad all over the back country of North Carolina and West Virginia."

"What did your dad do?"

"Doctor. He was too busy saving the world to think about his family."

Kim shot him a look, but his expression remained neutral. Apparently, he held no bitterness.

He turned and opened a hallway door she hadn't noticed. "The lab is down here." He flicked on the light.

As she hesitated, suddenly picturing television crime scenes, he added "Don't worry; I hired forensic cleaners." He started down the stairs, muttering "Never thought I'd ever need them."

The stench of ammonia burned her nose as she followed Scott down the creaky, dimly lit stairs.

Someone had nailed a two-by-four across an exterior door, the ends extending beyond both sides of the door like the crossbars on a crucifix. Naked wires protruded from an empty computer stand. Kim couldn't help scanning the floor in front of the work counters, searching for telltale blood.

Dragging her eyes from the floor, she focused on the only bright spot in the room, a central island supporting a shiny silver contraption. She started to smile; the thing looked like a cross between R2D2 and an upside down fire hydrant.

Following her gaze, Scott smiled. "That's Hank."

"Hank?"

"Jim's CVD machine."

"I'll be darned . . ." Kim strode to Hank and ran a hand over the cold, slick surface. Her breath caught as she stared down at the machine that could turn carbon gas into diamonds.

"Grandpa used to tell bedtime stories about these things. Well, actually about the quest to make diamonds."

"Odd choice for a child."

Kim laughed. "I don't think he knew any kid's stories. So he turned real stories about diamond smuggling, scams and heists into adventures." She patted what passed for Hank's head. "You should get Grandpa to tell you about the diamond makers. He's the only man I know who can make attempts to turn carbon to diamond sound like a mystery novel."

Sometimes, reading in bed with Rory, her mind conjured Grandpa's story-telling voice, the one where he changed pitches to mimic different characters, whispered to build suspense and broke into convincing evil cackles.

She could hear his breathless whisper now as he described the bubbling caldron of minerals deep within the earth. It was here, he'd intone, that heat and pressure transforms carbon into the world's most precious gemstone.

Diamond! she always interjected.

That's right, Grandpa would say, and the diamonds would stay there forever except . . . now the whisper grew menacing . . . sometimes the earth would shake and gasses would push and push and push and . . . Grandpa's hands flew into the air . . . BOOM!

A volcano! she'd squeal.

And Grandpa would mimic a volcano flinging diamonds into the air.

Naturally, Grandpa said, when people figured out diamonds came from volcanoes, they tried to build their own.

Their own volcanoes? she'd giggled. That's silly.

Grandpa nodded, but said greed often overrode common sense. Once people learned heat and pressure could change cheap carbon into priceless diamond, they figured they could become rich by building a miniature volcano and . . .

She grinned as she pictured Grandpa's elaborate knees-high, arm-pumping gait as he impersonated a Victorian gentleman running from his homemade, unexpectedly exploding volcano.

"It was the bedtime stories that triggered my interest in diamond history and lore," she told Scott. "I was so surprised when I went to the library and found out he hadn't exaggerated those explosions."

"Really?" Scott leaned against the counter. Close enough she could feel the heat from his body. "The volcanoes we built in school never exploded."

He smelled like Irish Spring soap. "You weren't trying to turn carbon into diamond with those paper mache things. We're talking extreme heat and pressure here."

Scientists learned the hard way that iron couldn't contain the forces. Neither could steel. A few researchers tried to dodge the problem by manipulating carbon gasses with low pressure. Nothing worked. Over time diamond-making contraptions ranged in size from a test tube to a two-story monster.

As years turned into decades, a new question arose: What would happen if they ever succeeded?

Executives at General Electric envisioned an endless supply of industrial diamonds to coat their cutting and grinding tools. Jewelers fretted about unscrupulous dealers flooding the market with lab-made stones and destroying people's confidence in the industry.

Novelist H. G. Wells predicted that even if someone, somewhere created diamonds, no one would believe him. In his short story, "The Diamond Maker", Wells' fictional diamond creator grew slowly insane as he tried to convince the world he'd succeeded where others failed.

In many ways, Wells' 1911 story proved prophetic.

In 1956, when GE executives called a press conference to unveil the world's first man-made diamonds, they were greeted with scorn.

Kim smiled, remembering Grandpa crossing his arm and lifting his chin to impersonate a reporter.

That's just black sand, Grandpa the reporter scoffed.

Now he widened his eyes, let his cheeks sag to mimic a geeky researcher.

No, not sand. Look through this microscope. See those sharp angles, that eight-sided shape? Diamond. Real diamond. Isn't it wonderful?

H. G. Wells, Grandpa said, must have been chuckling in his grave.

The tiny diamonds did indeed prove useful for coating grinders and other tools; eventually, man-made diamonds captured 20 percent of the industrial diamond market.

But the glorious single crystal, the sparkling stone women coveted, remained out of reach for another 40 years.

Kim was still in elementary school when the Russians announced they'd created gem quality diamonds from carbon gas. The process, called chemical vapor deposition or CVD, used a diamond chip as a "seed" on which to build a larger diamond. Hydrogen and methane gas were heated until they released carbon. The carbon settled onto the diamond chip and built a diamond crystal layer by layer.

To create diamond, the Russians had used a machine very much like Hank.

"Grandpa was so excited about CVD diamonds," she said, walking around the table -- and away from Scott. "Boy, was he pissed when De Beers created the DiamondSure and DiamondView gadgets." Seeing Scott's blank expression, she explained, "Those things can distinguish real diamonds from man-made."

"But why would Max support fake diamonds? Wouldn't that destroy his business?"

She smiled and stroked Hank. "Grandpa cares more about his customers than making money. I mean, yeah, engagement rings bring in most of the store's income. But you wouldn't believe how many people go into debt to buy the darn things."

"Tell me about it."

Hearing the disgust in Scott's voice, she stopped and cocked her head.

"Uncle Jim claimed his mother's diamond ring killed his father."

"Ah, I'm not a fan of diamonds . . ." except that blue one ". . .but I don't think they kill people."

"They do if you can't afford the damn things and start moonlighting to pay for them." Scott ran fingers through his hair and stared at the far wall. "I never met my paternal grandparents. My grandfather was crushed by a large crane when moonlighting at the Baltimore shipyards. Uncle Jim thought he was exhausted from working two jobs and got careless. Blamed the incident on the diamond ring my grandmother craved. And then . . ." He took a deep breath. "Well, it's past history."

Wondering what he'd left out of the story, Kim made a mental note to lead Scott back to the topic later. In the meantime . . . "So what's with Hank?"

Scott sighed. "You know Uncle Jim worked on a team trying to coat artificial hips with diamonds? They had problems keeping the diamond coating thin and smooth; too much build-up and the surface turned into sandpaper.

"Anyway, Jim's funky heart forced him to retire before his team succeeded. He puttered around for a bit, did some traveling, went fishing with Max. But he couldn't settle down. Then one day I found him down here with Hank."

"These things must be expensive. Where'd he get it?"

"No idea. I've always assumed he borrowed it from the company he worked for."

She peered through the microscope-like window into the chamber. There seemed to be a small platform in the center and some metal tubes laying about.

"'Ever watch Hank in action?"

Scott chuckled. "Once. It was boring. You can't see the carbon molecules forming on the diamond. Couldn't see anything, actually. If you're that interested, I'll let you browse through Jim's lab book. Should be somewhere in this mess."

Kim wasn't sure she'd understand what Jim had written, but it'd be fun studying his notes.

"So what are we looking for?" Scott said.

She looked around the lab. Not much paperwork here.

"Anything that can help us trace Jim's movements in the weeks before he died," Kim said. "Doesn't look like there's much here. Does he keep an office somewhere?"

"Upstairs." He pushed off of the counter. "Let's see what's here, find Uncle Jim's notebook. By that time the A/C should have cooled the office."

But the paperwork consisted of nothing but receipts for lab equipment. There was no sign of Jim's lab book.

"Maybe he took the notebook to his office?"

Scott shrugged. "Only one way to find out."

She followed him up the stairs.

The office was little more than a metal desk parked in front of a window, two bookshelves and a single file cabinet. Along the top shelf to her right, a row of composition notebooks held center court between thick, scientific journals. Behind the desk, bright afternoon sun streamed through a double-paned window.

Scott crossed to the bookcase on the right and ran his finger along the composition notebooks.

"He stored the lab books here, oldest on the left, newest on the right." His finger paused to the right of the last notebook. An empty space, about the size of a composition notebook, separated the notebooks from the first of the scientific journals.

Scott frowned at the space, then removed the notebook beside it. "This one ends last December." He slammed the book shut. "Seven months of work missing."

"Don't panic yet," Kim said. "Jim probably took down the current notebook to work on." She nodded at the desk. "Might even be in a drawer."

Sighing, Scott replaced the notebook. "Hope you're right." He swept a hand around the room. "Desk or file cabinet?"

"File cabinet." Searching someone's desk seemed too personal to Kim. Opening the top cabinet drawer, she stared at the neatly labeled files and breathed a sigh of relief. Looked like Jim the scientist's need for order extended to his file system. She reached for the first file.

"Doesn't it seem odd that the crooks broke in while Jim was here?"

Scott pulled open the center desk drawer. "Jim's car was in the shop, so the place probably looked deserted."

"But surely they'd have called first to make sure the house was empty?" At least, that's what they did in the mysteries she read.

"Wouldn't have made any difference. Uncle Jim had just started taking prescription allergy medicine. Said it knocked him out. I don't think he'd have heard the phone." Closing the drawer, he turned to the top right one.

"Did Jim have an answering machine?" When Scott nodded, she smiled. "Well, if they did call, they'd let it ring until the machine picked up, right? They wouldn't leave a message, but there must be a record of the call somewhere. Couldn't the police . . ."

"Of course they could." Scott reached into his pocket and pulled out a cell phone. "Why didn't I think of that?"

"You had other things on your mind."

Scott pulled a business card from his wallet and began dialing. Kim turned back to the files, but allowed part of her mind to eavesdrop. Though it took several minutes to reach the officer in charge of the investigation, the thumbs up Scott shot her indicated success.

"He's going to subpoena Uncle Jim's phone records," he said as he hung up. "With any luck, that'll lead them to the killers."

Kim suppressed a shudder. They continued their search in silence.

In the end, however, Jim's files contained little more than scientific papers: articles about coating artificial joints with crushed diamonds, making tiny diamond wafers to store computer data, using diamonds in semiconductors, abrasives, and lasers. Interesting stuff, but not revealing.

The desk yielded a date book, address book, parking ticket and a plane ticket stub.

Kim reached for the plane ticket and felt her heart quicken. Two weeks ago -- just about the time Mrs. Mahoney spotted the car following Jim -- the scientist returned from a trip to Colorado.

"I didn't realize Jim went back to Colorado." She handed the ticket to Scott.

He glanced at it and shrugged. "Yeah, I told you, remember? He was supposed to be fishing, but wouldn't talk about it afterwards."

"I thought we were talking about the trip he took last summer." She pointed at the ticket stub. "This trip occurred just before someone started following Jim."

Scott sagged against the desk corner. "You think he brought those diamonds back from that trip? And didn't tell me?"

Kim laid a hand on Scott's arm. "If I'm correct and Jim's friend discovered a new diamond field, the friend would have sworn Jim to secrecy."

"'cause of de Beers?"

"De Beers and other prospectors. Jim's friend would need to find the pipe and purchase the land it's on before going public."

"But if you're right, they've already found two diamonds. The one Max gave you and the one I found. Doesn't that mean they've already found the pipe?"

Kim shook her head. "When a volcano erupts, it spews diamonds everywhere. Then you've got erosion and streams carrying the diamonds farther from the source.

"So even when you find diamonds, the pipe could be miles away. Took ten years to find the pipe for the Argyle Mine in Australia. It's amazing they were able to keep the field a secret. The Canadian prospectors weren't so lucky. When they discovered a diamond field, news leaked quickly and the place was flooded with prospectors. Including De Beers, of course. Do you know who Jim was visiting in Colorado?"

Scott shrugged. "Some old college buddy. I'm afraid I wasn't paying attention to names." He tapped a finger on Jim's address book. "The guy's probably in here. But let's search the bookcases before we do anything else."

They each took a bookcase. Kim's contained novels by Elmore Leonard, Ross Thomas, Donald E. Westlake and Lawrence Block as well as a number of nonfiction books.

Normally, she loved nothing better than perusing someone's bookshelves. Today, however . . .

She stole a glance across the room. Scott was reaching for a book on the top shelf, providing a perfect view of his broad shoulders, narrow waist and tight butt. Turning away, she could feel her face flush. Damn. She never understood her friends who flew into ecstasy over a man's butt. Until today.

Best to think of something else.

"So, is your mom older or younger than Jim?" Oh, great, now she was chattering, her fall-back position when nervous.

Fortunately, Scott didn't seem to notice.

"Younger than Uncle Jim, older than Aunt Cary."

"Aunt Cary?" She pulled de Tocqueville's Democracy in America from the shelf and flipped through the pages. Maybe Jim hid papers in his books.

"My grandmother was a Hollywood fanatic."

Ah. Cary Grant. "So Jim was named after James Stewart?" She replaced the de Tocqueville and pulled out Ian Fleming's The Diamond Smugglers.

Scott nodded. "Yep. His full name was James Stewart Hampton. Mom's was Lauren Bacall Hampton and Aunt Cary... well, you get the idea. I always thought it was weird that my grandmother used the stars' last names as middle names."

Kim snorted. "I'm no longer surprised by the names parents burden their children with. Because Grandpa is a jeweler, Grandma named her daughters Emerald, Sapphire, Ruby and Diamondtina. The names must have gone to the girls' heads because my cousins have names like Tiffany, Jade and Goldie. Aunt Sapphire even wanted to name her only son after the world's largest diamond."

"Hope?"

"Nope. The world's largest diamond at the time was the Cullinan."

Scott looked up from the book he was searching. "No way. Some poor kid had to go through life named that?"

"Uncle Don stopped it. Said they should name the only boy in the family after Grandpa. So they christened him Anthony Maxwell Cullinan Anderson."

Scott's eyebrows shot up. "Where'd the Anthony come from?"

"Grandpa's first name. He goes by the middle." She closed the Fleming and reached for Darwin's Origin of Species.

"You must feel lucky to have such a normal name."

Kim slammed the book shut. "Normal? I was name after a big hole in the ground."

"Kimberly?"

"My name is spelled K-i-m-b-e-r-l-E-y. Like the diamond mine."

Scott's face remained blank. A second passed. Two. As understanding dawned, he threw his head back and laughed, a deep, belly laugh almost as infectious as Grandpa's.

"Go ahead and laugh. Have you seen photos of that ugly mine? Try to live with that when you're an overweight twelve years old with zits on your nose."

Scott's smile remained, but the glitter in his eyes burned with more than amusement.

"Well, Kimberley with an E, you sure turned out just fine."

Kim's breath caught and she was suddenly acutely aware of the empty house. How long had it been since she'd kissed a man? After the disastrous date with Tiffany's lawyer friend -- he of the door-knob kiss -- she'd been shy about accepting other dates. Most of the men she'd met in Oregon had been Birkenstock wearing, conspiracy spewing environmentalists or no-necked, proselytizing right-wingers. Something about the Oregon rain seemed to drive people to one political extreme or the other. Since Kim wasn't political at all, she'd tended to keep to herself, to focus on teaching and writing professional articles and completing her PhD. She was successful with the PhD, but not with the men she dated.

But here she was, back in Maryland for only two days, and her hormones had danced the jitterbug for a bad-boy cop, an old flame and, now, a reporter turned professor with a tight butt, lazy smile and smoldering eyes. She needed to get a grip.

"So, how 'bout them Redskins?"

The half grin appeared. "It's baseball season." His eyes held hers. Kim's breath caught and her toes curled. "When we're done here," he purred, "how 'bout I take you to dinner?"

It's time to fish or cut bait, Grandpa's voice whispered in her head. Okay, Grandpa, this one's for you. She opened her mouth to accept, then froze, suddenly remembering her dinner with Jason.

The groan she stifled had nothing to do with the heat coursing through her. The thought of turning down a date with someone she was honestly interested in to go out with the jerk who'd dumped her when the prom queen needed a list-minute escort made her teeth grind.

Maybe she should return the favor, call Jason and say I'm sorry but I got a better offer.

She sighed. No, she'd never be so cruel. The prom was a long time ago and, in any event, she needed to quiz Jason about jewelry world gossip. Maybe she could invite Scott along ... She entertained a vision of Jason's face if she arrived with another man in tow. But she dismissed the idea as counterproductive. She needed to pick Jason's brain, not watch him try to one-up another man.

"I'm sorry. I already have plans for this evening. Business plans."

"Some other time, then." His voice contained disappointment coupled with ... disbelief? Disbelief that she had a date? Or that it was a business meeting?

"Honestly, Jason White is just a, er ..." A friend? Hardly. "Just someone I went to school with. His family owns a jewelry store chain and I figured if anyone has heard scuttlebutt about a new diamond field, the Whites would..."

She broke off and stared at Scott.

The easy-going expression he'd worn all day had disappeared, replaced with a clench-jawed, narrow-eyed, red-faced mask.

CHAPTER 18

"Scott? Are you okay?"

Anger had transformed his face into a stranger's. Why hadn't she realized Scott was the same height as the man who attacked Grandpa?

She only had Scott's word that his uncle was killed by burglars. What if he'd killed Jim for the blue diamond? And when he didn't find the large diamond in Jim's things, stalked Jim's best friend? Grandpa would certainly have recognized his pal's nephew under that ski mask.

Shifting her weight to the balls of her feet, she slid her eyes sideways. The office door was six feet away. Could she reach it before Scott grabbed her?

"Uncle Jim said your family avoided the Whites." His voice was cold, but not threatening.

Keep him talking! "We do avoid them." She suddenly realized she was still holding Darwin's book. Maybe if she threw the heavy tome before running... "Grandpa disagrees with the White's business practices." Clenching the book, she took a baby step to her left. "It's mostly devious stuff like using fractions instead of decimal points to indicate diamond size... That allows them to round up so customers think their diamonds are larger than they really are." Another step towards the door. "The Whites have never actually done anything illegal, but Grandpa says..."

"You don't call exchanging a diamond for a cubic zirconia illegal?"

She halted midstep. "I've never heard anything about that." If someone had accused the Whites of substituting stones when selling, repairing or cleaning a diamond ring, everyone in the business would know. The accusation -- even if later proven invalid -- could destroy a jeweler's reputation.

Scott sighed and crossed his arms. His bare arms, unmarked by dog teeth.

She released the breath she'd been holding.

"I'm sorry," the man who didn't attack Grandpa said. "I know Jim told Max the whole story. I thought you knew."

"Knew what?"

Dropping his arms to his side, he straightened. "Too long of a story to go into now. Let's finish up here so you won't be late for your business meeting."

"Honestly, Scott, I have no interest in Jason White. And even if I did, he made it abundantly clear in high school that I was beneath him."

Scott crossed the room in two strides, trapping her against the bookcase. A shelf edge dug into her spine as he bent over her. "Then he's even a bigger idiot than I thought," he whispered before dropping his mouth onto hers.

For a moment, she froze, her mind a tangle of spaghetti. Her body, however... Her knees weakened, her breath caught, her body pressed against his. Just as she relaxed into the kiss, Scott released her.

"Just be careful tonight, okay?" he said, stroking a finger down her cheek. "I don't trust anyone in the White family."

"Why not?"

"Like I said, it's a long story." He kissed her forehead, turned and crossed to the other bookcase. "Let's finish up here, okay?"

No, it wasn't okay. Kim had no patience for unanswered questions; she wanted closure right now. But Scott was already pulling books from the shelf and flipping through the pages.

Gritting her teeth, she replaced the Darwin and reached for a book at random. Nothing in those pages, either. As she returned it to the shelf, her mind registered the book titles. What an odd collection. Stephen Ambrose's *Undaunted Courage* stood next to Mark Twain's *Roughing It*. *The Path Between The Seas, 1776, Diamonds In the Salt, Blood and Thunder, Sleuthing the Alamo, California Gold Rush* and the *Coming of the Civil War, Buffalo Bill's America, Acres of Diamonds, The Age of Gold* . . . the only common theme seemed to be they were all history books.

"Yeah, Jim really enjoyed history," Scott replied to her question. "He'd have loved the wild west, searching for gold and gemstones, maybe having a few shoot-outs. It's kind of amazing, really. He was only eight when his father died and he became the 'man of the house.' Took his responsibility seriously. Mom's almost sixty and she still complains about Uncle Jim's bossing.

"And yet a part of him never grew up. He still wanted to play cowboys and Indians."

Interesting. She could imagine Grandpa reading some of these books, especially the one on the Alamo and Buffalo Bill and . . . Why did *Diamonds In the Salt* sound familiar?

Pulling the book from the shelf, she gazed down at the blue and white cover. Her mouth fell open as she read the subtitle: The first authentic account of the sensational diamond hoax chicanery.

"Oh, wow, this is the story about that famous diamond scam. Grandpa used to tell it all the time. I loved this story."

Scott looked up from the book he was examining. "Then please take it. I don't have any use for it."

"Are you sure?" When Scott smiled and nodded, Kim cheered and opened the front cover. Grandpa had assured her the story was true, but she never knew the tale came from an actual book... She frowned. On the title page, someone had written a series of numbers and letters: R26L00R7.

She felt her heartbeat quicken. A clue?

"Scott?" When he looked up, she held out the book and pointed at the writing. "Someone wrote numbers in here. Do you think...?"

"Combination to the office safe," Scott said. "Uncle Jim said he had so many numbers in his head, he needed to write down the important ones."

"Oh." Her shoulders slumped. So much for her Nancy Drew moment. "We should probably copy these numbers where you can find them."

"Already put them in my date book."

Kim swallowed the disappointment and set the book beside her purse. At least she'd have something fun to read tonight.

Pulling another book from the shelf, she held it by the spine and shook. A pink envelope fell out.

"Hey, I found something." The stationery smelled like lavender. A single word -- Jim -- had been written on the envelope in a feminine, flowing hand.

Feeling like a Peeping Pauline, she handed it to Scott.

He had no qualms about opening the letter. He studied the note inside, frowned, then passed it to Kim.

I'll do anything you ask of me except one thing. I won't watch you die. -- Etta Place

The letter was unsigned.

"Who's Etta Place?" She turned the letter over, but found nothing written on the back.

"Etta Place? She was the Sundance Kid's girlfriend." Scott crossed to the bookcase behind Kim, removed a DVD and handed it to her.

As soon as she saw the movie's cover -- a mustached Robert Redford and scruffy Paul Newman -- the penny dropped. The two heartthrobs had turned Butch Cassidy and the Sundance Kid into one of the all-time great westerns. Katharine Ross played school teacher Etta Place whose speech about not watching Sundance die had provided pubescent girls everywhere dramatic words to swoon by.

But why was someone sending the famous quote to Jim?

"Almost looks like notes for a television quiz show." She handed the letter back to Scott.

Scott's mouth thinned. "Or a warning."

Kim drove back to Grandpa's on autopilot, her mind a whirlwind of questions. Did the note hidden

in Jim's book relate to the attacks? If so, who sent it? And why would a girlfriend fear for the life of a mild-mannered physicist?

Scott had insisted there was no girlfriend, that his uncle wasn't dating anyone. Kim found that hard to believe. Jim had been an outrageous flirt. With the shortage of eligible bachelors in the sixty and up age range, Jim had his choice of lady friends all old enough to remember Katharine Ross's dramatic movie speech to Robert Redford.

Besides, Scott said the handwriting seemed familiar. Even though he couldn't remember where he'd seen it, Kim suspected the writer knew Jim well. The movie quote was too intimate to send to a casual acquaintance. And maybe . . . just maybe . . . the woman knew why Jim feared he was being followed.

She needed to find that woman.

In addition to the mysterious girlfriend, she puzzled over the missing lab book and the black car Mrs. Mahoney saw following Jim.

With any luck, one of Aunt Ginny's friends at the DMV could figure out a way to trace the car's license plate without doing anything illegal. As for the lab book . . . its absence probably had nothing to do with Jim's death or the attacks on Grandpa. The men who ransacked Jim's lab might have scooped it up along with the computer. Still, until Grandpa could tell her what happened, Kim hated to dismiss any oddity outright.

She turned onto the gravel alley. She now had more questions than when the day started. However, she was certain of one thing: Tonight she was not going to be alone when she met Jason.

She'd seen Jason in dating mode. He'd spend the evening flexing his muscles, trying to woo her. She needed him focused on the jewelry industry, on the gossip that might reveal clues to why someone was stalking Grandpa.

She'd considered asking Scott to come on the "date." But that would stir too much testosterone. Jason would spend the evening trying to one-up Scott and she still wouldn't get her answers.

Bringing Aunt Ginny, however, would solve both problems. Her aunt's presence would cool Jason's ardor. Given that Aunt Ginny was now staying at Grandpa's, Jason couldn't object to her presence. Plus Ginny could help direct the conversation to industry gossip.

Now Kim just needed to convince her aunt to agree to the plan.

She pulled into Grandpa's driveway, grabbed her heavy purse and the book Scott gave her, locked the car and climbed the back steps to Grandpa's office. The room was dim, lit only from the store lights beyond. She could hear voices in the storefront. But no wiggling black dog greeted her. Was Rory so caught up in schmoozing customers that he'd ignored the sound of her entry? So much for the watch dog.

She crossed the room and stood at the entry to the store. Aunt Ginny and a white-haired woman leaned over the sapphire display. Even from the back, the stranger oozed elegance, from her cream-colored shirt through the deeper cream trousers and kitten-heel sandals.

"Where's Rory?" Kim said.

The two women jumped and turned around, the white-haired woman bringing a hand to her throat. Kim froze.

The short woman wasn't Ginny.

Though she wore similar salt-and-pepper short curls, untucked t-shirt and flowered skirt, her blue eye shadow, pink lipstick and oh-goody grin screamed aging cheerleader.

What . . .

"You must be Kim." The taller woman stepped forward and offered her hand. "I'm Maureen Cloud and the woman drooling over the sapphires is Doris White. Ginny asked us to help in the store."

"Oh? Oh!" Kim's tired brain finally made the connection. "Aunt Ginny's friends!" When Kim left to meet Scott, Aunt Ginny's friends were just pulling into Grandpa's driveway. There hadn't been time to actually meet them.

Shifting her purse to the left shoulder, she shook Maureen's hand. "Thank you so much for helping."

"How could we resist spending time with all this?" Maureen swept an arm towards the sparkling displays.

Before Kim could respond, Doris pushed forward, offered her own hand, then posed like a fashion model.

"Don't you think I need pink sapphires to match my outfit?"

"Oh, Doris, don't be so greedy." Maureen reached behind the counter and removed a cream purse with a Chanel label. "You can buy them tomorrow if you still want them."

Doris lifted an enormous pink hobo bag onto her small shoulder. "See what I have to put up with? Do you need help closing up?"

"Thank you, but no I can handle it. Ah, is Aunt Ginny upstairs or . . ."

Maureen's eyes shifted. "She said she needed to pick up something at home."

"Don't worry," Doris added. "She's got Rorschach with her. No one will mess with them."

Kim closed her eyes and breathed deeply. Oh, yeah, an old lady and a poodle. No one's going to mess with them. Although, she did know a woman in Oregon . . .

She jumped as a hand touched her arm. Opening her eyes she gazed down at Doris.

"Will you be all right alone? We could stay longer if you're nervous . . ."

Kim smiled and touched the woman's soft hand. "No, I'm fine. I've got a dinner appointment at seven."

"Then we'd better leave and allow you to get ready." Maureen headed towards the door. "We'll be back tomorrow morning."

Kim locked the door behind them and turned the sign to indicate Grandpa's store was closed. A glance at the clock told her she had only half an hour to prepare for Jason. Quickly dismantling the displays, she returned the jewelry to the safe, set the store alarm and hurried upstairs to shower.

As the grandfather clock chimed the hour, Jason knocked on the kitchen door. Hmm . . . exactly on time. Trying to impress her?

She snatched her purse and keys, opened the door and blocked Jason's entry.

"Wow, right on time." She stepped outside and pulled the door closed. Turning her back to Jason, she slipped the key into the lock.

"Afraid to be alone with me?" Jason's breath was hot on her neck.

He stood so close she couldn't help breathing in the expensive cologne he'd worn in high school. Locking the door, she stepped away.

"Nope. Just very hungry."

Jason's arm shot out, trapping her between the house and the stairs. His blue eyes glinted in the dusky light, his smile looked wolfish. "I'm pretty hungry myself."

Kim bit her lip. Now she remembered why she'd fluctuated between attraction and terror in high school.

She also remembered how to interrupt his libido.

She forced herself to laugh. "Quit clowning around. I'm starving."

Pushing his now limp arm aside, she hurried down the stairs.

"Hey, aren't you going to set your alarm?"

"Can't," she called over her shoulder. "Aunt Ginny's not here. She has a key but doesn't know the alarm code." Safely at the bottom, she turned to look back.

Jason hesitated at the top of the stairs. For the first time she noticed he'd dressed for the occasion: Lightweight sport coat, pastel colored shirt, contrasting tie, crisply pressed trousers. The confident wardrobe, however, didn't hide the slight hunch to his shoulders or the dip of his chin. He started down the stairs, his smile tentative.

"Uh, Kim, I know I was a real ass when I stood you up for the prom. But, honestly, I've changed." He reached the bottom, but stayed outside of her comfort zone. "I wanted to call to apologize but . . ."

"But you didn't have the nerve." Kim crossed her arms. "Although I guess it would have been difficult to explain that you were breaking our date -- after I'd spent time and money making a gown, thank you very much -- because someone better came along."

"Is that what you think?" Jason blew air through pursed lips and ran a hand through his wind-tousled hair. "That's not what happened."

She gaped. "Did you or did you not stand me up so you could take Cindy McMann to the prom?"

"Well, yeah, but I never, ever thought she was better than you."

She dropped her arms. "Then why did you stand me up?"

Jason sighed. "Cindy called me, all in a panic because Rod -- you remember Rod Darling, the quarterback Cindy was dating? The day of the prom he came down with mono. Cindy needed a date because as the queen of the prom she couldn't go unescorted . . ."

"And you couldn't tell her 'Gee, Cindy, I already have a date?'"

"I know, I know, it was a shitty thing to do. And I'm sorry. I'm sorry I agreed to take her and I'm sorry I didn't have the nerve to call you and I'm sorry you ever thought I found Cindy more attractive." He started towards her but stopped when Kim stepped back. "I know it's years too late, but won't you please accept my apology and, well, let me try to make it up to you?"

He looked so hangdog that Kim felt the anger dissipate. As a psychologist she better understood the testosterone laden minds of high school boys. Speeding, drinking, vandalizing and other forms of acting out could all be attributed to hormone saturation. For most boys the out of control behavior was quickly followed by guilt -- one of the most difficult emotions to handle. Some responded by adopting an I-don't-care swagger. Others blocked the offending behavior from their minds, pretending it never happened.

Hormones had led Jason to dump Kim in favor of the more sexually active Cindy; guilt prevented him from apologizing.

Until now.

"Apology accepted."

She stepped off the concrete stair landing, her rubber-soled Mary Janes sinking into the grass. To reach the boardwalk from Grandpa's backyard, they needed to follow the narrow side yard to the front gate. She cast a longing look at the iron table and chairs Grandpa had arranged beneath the apple tree. Oh, for just a few minutes to sit in the twilight, listen to the seagulls and enjoy the evening breeze!

Sighing, she turned towards the left, skirted Jason's black Jaguar and rounded the corner of the house.

The setting sun illuminated the narrow strip of grass, picket fence and honey-scented white roses that separated Grandpa's house from his next-door neighbor's. Her gingerbread-trimmed house looked sad and lonely without its vivacious tenant. Apparently, Grandpa's not-so-secret admirer was away on one of her frequent trips.

The overgrown roses forced them to walk single file. Even so, an occasional rose cane snagged Kim's jeans. One more thing to put on her to-do list.

Out on the boardwalk, she accepted the arm Jason extended. "To make up for all of your high school transgressions," she said, "you can catch me up on the industry gossip."

An hour later, however, she'd listened to Jason's account of store openings and closings, the debate over labeling lab-made diamonds "cultured," the struggles to survive the recession, the impact of new trade regulations, the spike in gold prices, the arrest of a famous rare-jewels dealer for fraud. But Jason still hadn't mentioned any rumors of a new Colorado diamond mine.

Kim stared out the restaurant window at the darkening water, fighting back irritation. She'd worked so hard to steer the conversation away from "us" to the jewelry business. To end up with nothing to show for her efforts was maddening.

It'd even been hard to enjoy her barbecued chicken. Normally she adored the casual atmosphere of Doni's restaurant, especially the sepia toned prints of the Three Beaches that decorated the walls. The one across from their booth depicted a summer day on the boardwalk, the men jaunty in their straw hats, the women uncomfortable but resolute in bustled dresses. When she was little, Grandpa encouraged her to spin stories about the people in the photos.

The presence of the wealthy, debonair Jason White, however, made the restaurant seem a bit tawdry. How in the world had the man consumed an entire rack of barbecued ribs without getting any on his tie? Though she'd repeatedly swiped at her knit top with a wet napkin, she still looked like she'd stood too close to a gunshot victim.

"You are so lucky to have Max as your grandfather," Jason interrupted her thoughts. "I always envied the way he supported you."

She frowned and wiped her fingers. "But your grandfather always defended you. Remember when Miss Jackson accused you of stealing potassium nitrate from chem lab?"

She could still picture Bradford White, the bane of Grandpa's childhood, sweeping into chemistry class to berate poor Miss Jackson. Red faced, he'd towered over the woman and threatened to have her fired if she didn't retract her accusation and apologize. His grandson would never, ever steal.

Never mind the fact that Braddford's neighbors were reporting odd explosions in the woods behind the White's home.

Jason shrugged and reached for his water glass. "Telling everyone you're innocent is not the same thing as believing in you. I couldn't sit down for a week after the whopping Grandfather gave me."

Kim grinned. "And were you innocent?"

Jason laughed. "Of course not. But all I wanted to do was make fireworks. Grandfather acted as if I'd robbed the mint or something. Your grandfather thinks you're so perfect that even if the police told him you'd massacred a bunch of school children, Max would ask what the children did to deserve it."

Kim laughed. "Maybe because I am perfect."

"Actually, you've grown into a pretty perfect woman." All traces of humor were gone, replaced by . . . what? Longing?

Whatever it was, she wanted no parts of it. "Hey, how 'bout them Redskins?"

Jason chuckled. "You really shouldn't flaunt your football ignorance to someone who played wide receiver."

The arrival of the waitress eliminated the need to respond. Though Kim really shouldn't order dessert, she needed time to steer the conversation back to diamonds. Besides, Doni's apple pie was heavenly. And the calories didn't count since apples are a fruit.

While Jason ordered, she frantically searched for a way to bring up the Colorado diamond field. Ask directly or try a sneaky approach? Scott's warning tripped through her mind. Sneaky it is.

"I've heard an interesting rumor," she said. "Someone said the Kelsey Mine might reopen."

"Really? I hadn't heard that." Jason lifted his coffee cup.

"Too bad. I really like the idea of selling diamonds that are mined in the U.S."

Jason nodded. "Boy, if I thought I could make a go at mining in Colorado, I'd jump at the chance."

"I thought you enjoyed working in the store."

Jason snorted. Before he could respond, the waitress set the pies in front of them.

Kim bit into a sweet/tart apple heavily seasoned in cinnamon. "You were saying?"

"Oh, yeah. The store." Jason took a bite of pie, chewed and swallowed. "I probably would enjoy the store if Dad and Grandfather would leave me alone. But they're always hovering, telling me what to do. I'm a damn good manager; it's my work that brought the Annapolis store into the 21st Century. So what do they do? Switch me to the boondocks. Dad was doing just fine in Frederick. But Mom wanted to move to Annapolis and Dad didn't want to commute. Instead I'm the one commuting to Frederick. It's just not fair."

"Maybe not, but managing a diamond mine is risky." Kim took another bite of pie.

"Yeah, but at least any money I made would be mine, not the family's." Correctly reading the surprise on her face, he continued, "I get paid a salary. I should get a percentage of sales or at least a commission. But whenever I mention that, Grandfather and Dad brush me off. They're afraid I'll break out on my own. Like you did."

"Me?"

"Of course you." He pushed his half-eaten pie away. "My family freaked when they heard how you'd moved to the other side of the world."

"Oregon is not the other side of the world." She grinned. "Although it was as far west as I could go without getting my feet wet."

The joke didn't seem to register. Instead, Jason shrugged. "Whatever." He leaned forward. "The point is you had the nerve to stand up to your family, not let them smother you."

She resisted the urge to roll her eyes. Jason had no idea how hard she'd struggled against the family madness. Bad enough that everyone had been named after a gemstone, famous jeweler or, in her case, diamond mine. And that weekly family gatherings always ended with someone buying earrings or a bracelet or pendant. Grandma furthered the jewelry obsession by, on each girl's tenth birthday, bestowing a silver charm set with an imitation birthstone. If they cared properly for the charm, on their sixteenth birthday they could exchange the imitation stone for the real thing.

Kim was the only one who didn't make the exchange. She'd claimed she lost the charm, though in truth it rested in its original box, tucked beneath her underwear.

No, Jason had no idea what it meant to be smothered by family. Compared to hers, his family looked normal.

Still, the way Jason leaned towards her indicated a need for some comment. Reassurance?

"You've never struck me as a pushover." She smiled. "I'm sure your family respects you."

Jason frowned, but didn't respond. They struggled over the bill, Kim wanting to pay half, Jason refusing. She finally let him win.

Tossing his napkin onto that poor piece of uneaten pie, he said "Ready?"

Kim suddenly envisioned the dark boardwalk, the empty house, Jason's earlier hints. Better make sure Aunt Ginny is home.

"Uh, I need to hit the bathroom first." She stood. "Do you want to wait here or meet me outside?"

"Outside is fine."

In the bathroom, Kim washed her hands, then dug through her purse -- darn it, she'd forgotten to remove the travel stuff -- for her cell phone. Aunt Ginny's welcoming voice answered.

"Where are you?" Kim said.

"Just turned onto Bayside. Why?"

"Jason and I are just leaving the restaurant and I don't want to be alone with him."

"I'll get there as soon as I can, but your geese have stopped traffic in both directions. Rory keeps saying he can clear them."

"Don't let him out of the car; once he starts chasing those darn birds, you'll never catch him."

Ginny assured her she wouldn't release Rory from his seatbelt. Kim closed the phone and frowned, tapping her foot. She'd planned for Aunt Ginny to greet her when they arrived home, effectively stopping any of Jason's amorous intentions. Now it looked like they would beat Ginny home.

Well, she'd just have to improvise. She tucked the phone into a jeans pocket and swung the heavy bag onto a shoulder. Tonight she'd remove the flashlight, AAA guide and maps. The purse would still weigh a ton -- it more resembled a doggie version of a baby bag than a handbag -- but at this point she'd welcome any weight relief.

While they'd eaten, the sky had turned inky. The evening breeze carried the scent of wet sand, crushed seashells and honeysuckle. She spotted Jason leaning against the boardwalk railing, cell phone pressed to one ear. As she approached, he disconnected.

"You didn't tell me Max is actually in the hospital."

Kim frowned. "How did . . ."

Jason held up his phone. "Dad just found out, wanted me to send his best. So why didn't you tell me?"

"It . . . it's hard to talk about, you know?"

He looked away, probably embarrassed by her candor. She turned and started back towards Grandpa's.

Jason fell into step beside her. "Is he going to be okay?"

"I hope so." Their shoulders brushed. Kim stepped closer to the railing, feigning interest in the lapping waves. "I'll feel better when they catch the guy who attacked him."

"Can Max identify the person?"

Kim had a sudden inspiration. "Doubt it. The guy was wearing a ski mask. Besides, Grandpa lost a lot of blood. He probably won't even remember the attack let alone be able to describe the creep who stabbed him."

There, let Jason the gossip tell everyone Grandpa couldn't identify the thief. If she was right and someone in the industry was involved, maybe he'd stop seeing Grandpa as a threat and leave him alone.

They walked in silence, Jason occasionally brushing her shoulder. Shadows deepened as they left the lighted commercial section and entered the strip of houses or house/shop combination buildings. Feeling trapped between Jason and the railing, Kim scurried across the boardwalk to admire a narrow, all-white garden someone had planted beside their picket fence. Trumpet-shaped Datura flowers cast sweet vanilla and honey fragrance into the night air. Silver Dusty Miller and white snow-in-the-summer growing at the Datura's feet created an otherworldly atmosphere.

As Jason joined her, Kim opened her mouth to comment. But the words caught in her throat. She leaned closer to the blooming bush, squinting. What she'd assumed were small Datura blossoms were, in fact, white Morning Glory flowers. The vine had twined itself round the Datura's branches, strangling it.

With a shiver, she turned and headed towards Grandpa's, sneakers slapping the hardwood planks.

"So," Jason said as he caught up, "Where was your attack dog when I picked you up?"

Be nice, Grandpa's voice cautioned.

"With Aunt Ginny." She slowed her pace, suddenly remembering she needed to give Ginny time to reach the house. "Rory and Aunt Ginny should be home before us, so you won't need to walk me to the door." There, that should discourage any amorous feelings Jason might harbor.

"Oh, I'm not afraid of pouf dogs. He just surprised me."

Kim clenched her teeth. "Rory is not a pouf dog." She was tired of people dissing poodles because of the stupid haircuts they were required to wear in the show ring.

Turning, she faced Jason, legs spread, hands on her hips. "Standard poodles were bred for hunting and water retrieving. They were used as fishing dogs in Germany; helped set nets and retrieve tackle. Folks still hunt with them on the Eastern Shore."

"Sure looks like a pouf dog."

Too late she spotted the grin on Jason's face. The grin he'd worn in high school whenever he'd baited her so he could say "you're pretty when you're mad."

Well, she wasn't a high school kid any more. Dropping her hands to her sides, she faked a nonchalant shrug. The story she'd half-remembered earlier flashed through her mind.

"Don't let the curls fool you," she said. "I knew an elderly woman in Oregon -- lived in a former logging town with her Standard Poodle. Anyway, one night they were walking down the street when some hoodlum tried to steal her purse. Helen attempted to step away from him, but he lunged at her. Shaina, the poodle, knocked him over and then grabbed his pant leg. Guy started kicking and screaming, punching out at Shaina."

Kim grinned, remembering. "Helen was so incensed that the man hit Shaina that . . . well, by the time the police arrived, they found Shaina sitting on the man's legs and Helen straddling his shoulders. She was banging the man's head into the ground while saying 'Don't you hurt my dog.' When word got around that the guy was beat up by an old lady and her poodle, he had to leave town."

"You're making this up."

"Nope." She held up her fingers in the Boy Scout sign. "I'm sure the newspapers reported the story. You can look it up."

Jason's cocky grin disappeared. Good. Maybe next time he'd treat Rory with respect.

Turning, she started walking, this time staying away from the railing so Jason couldn't crowd her. Surely Aunt Ginny was home now.

Both houses on either side of Grandpa's were dark, the one neighbor visiting a daughter, the other who-knew-where. The only illumination came from the lamp she'd left burning in the living room, three floors above the boardwalk. Thank goodness Grandpa had installed outside motion-sensor lights.

She opened the garden gate and stepped aside to allow Jason to enter first before closing the gate behind her.

"Maybe you'd better lead the way," Jason said, peering into the gloom.

Kim stepped between the house and rose-lined fence. But the motion light failed. She stopped and stared up at the side of the house, searching for the telltale red dot that indicated the light was active. The dot was lit. So why didn't the light come on? Had she walked too close to the house to set it off?

Retracing her steps, she raised her arms and waved them around, trying to activate the motion sensor. Nothing.

Dropping her arms, she sighed. The bulb must be burned out. Thank goodness she still carried that flashlight.

She reached for the purse zipper, turning towards Jason. Behind him, a shadow moved. Jason whirled around. A fist swung out, into Jason's stomach. She heard the whoosh of Jason's expelled breath, saw the hand raise again, heard the thump of fist against flesh.

She inhaled to scream. A rough hand closed over her mouth, smothering her.

CHAPTER 19

A second arm snaked around her waist. Kim clawed at the hand that covered her mouth, inhaling the stench of oil, cigarettes and something putrid. The man's breath was overpowering, reminiscent of a sewer. No, a dead rat. She raked fingernails across his hand. Cursing, the man tightened both hands and . . . She couldn't breathe. Above the roaring in her ears she heard Jason struggling with the second man.

She stomped her right foot backwards, connecting with something firm. Rat Man cursed. The hand around her mouth eased and she could inhale. She drew in dead rat air, then bit down. Hard. She tasted blood. Her attacker yelled. She held on. She felt his arm release her waist. Spinning towards him, she raised her elbows. Her right elbow jabbed something soft and a whoosh of air told her the blow had struck near the diaphragm.

Now she could see the dark shape, doubled over, blocking her path to safety. She aimed a knee toward the groin, but a beefy hand deflected the blow, tripping her. As she fell backwards, she lashed out with both legs. The man tried to dodge, leaning away from the blow. She caught his side and his weight carried him into the rose bushes.

Kim scrambled away on hands and knees, clawing at the grass, toes propelling her forward. Regaining her feet, she raced through the side yard, around the corner of the house, her feet slapping asphalt, her mind processing the absence of Aunt Ginny's car. She'd lost her purse somewhere. No keys. She veered away from the house. A sliver of moonlight illuminated the yard gate, impossibly far away.

Behind her, Rat Man's cursing was joined by a second voice. The only intelligible words were "find her."

No time, no time. Again changing direction, she aimed for the apple tree. A leap carried her onto a wrought iron chair. Chair, table, tree. Her hands snagged the lowest branch and she pulled, sneakered toes scrabbling on bark, up, up, onto the branch, reaching for the next branch, bark scraping knees and hands, higher, higher.

Around the corner of the house, a light materialized. Kim froze mid-climb. The beam from the flashlight swept towards the house, illuminating the back stairs, raising higher, the door to Grandpa's office, across the landing, higher still, the kitchen door. Now the light lowered and started a slow sweep across the yard.

Kim wrapped her arms and legs around the tree trunk, koala bear style, and closed her eyes, waiting for the flashlight to find her.

Instead, she heard words.

"Frankie?"

Kim opened her eyes in time to see a second flashlight illuminate Rat Man. His sharp, pig-eyed face was covered in scratches from the rose thorns.

A muscled arm batted the light away. "Get that out of my face." The light pointed at the ground. "Where's the boyfriend?" It came out "Whar's the b'frien'." Baltimore accent.

"Out. Let's get outahere."

"Gotta find her first," Rat Man said.

"Jeez, we don't even know she has it."

It? Kim bit her lip. The diamond. They must be after the blue diamond.

"Well, someone's got it," Rat Man said.

The two men started arguing. Using the noise for camouflage, Kim eased back onto a branch and assessed her options. The houses on either side of Grandpa's remained dark. Across the alley, long backyards led to more houses. She could see lights in several rooms, but the homeowners were too far away for someone to hear her scream. She turned towards the boardwalk, straining for the sound of late-night strollers. Water lapped the shore, a bullfrog crooned its fog-horn croak. From nearby, a toad began its rat-tat-tat clucking, but stopped abruptly when the men moved.

One man shined the flashlight into her van. The second stepped onto the grass, sweeping the light left and right as he walked.

Kim's throat tightened. She fought the panic. Think! They had flashlights, brute strength and probably some sort of weapon. To beat them, she had . . . what? With her purse laying who-knew-where, she had no cell phone, no flashlight, nothing she could turn into a weapon. On the plus side, she knew her surroundings well. If she could devise a weapon, she'd also have the element of surprise.

Forcing herself to look away from the attacker below her in the grass, she studied the nearby branches. A branch would make a dandy weapon, but she had no way to cut one loose. Just as well since the crack of a breaking branch would attract attention. As long as the men didn't have guns, she could just stay in the tree, maybe climb higher. If they came after her, the height would give her an advantage.

But what would happen when Aunt Ginny arrived? She needed a weapon.

Her eyes lit on a round shape. Apples. She cupped one with her hand and twisted until it broke free. She hefted it. Not as good as a rock, but hurled from above, the pull of gravity would increase its weight. A lap full of apples might buy her time until Jason recovered or a car drove down the alley or . . .

Working as quickly and soundlessly as possible, she plucked apples from the tree, piling them in her lap. Across the driveway, Rat Man was now searching Jason's car. To her left, the second man . . . She froze as light swept the lawn furniture, chair, table, second chair, back to the table, searching beneath . . . don't look up, please don't look up.

From the far end of the alley, gravel rattled against metal. Kim turned towards the sound. The distinctive round headlights of a Mustang convertible pierced the dark. Aunt Ginny.

The man below her stiffened. The flashlight clicked off. In the driveway, Rat Man lay on his stomach, his light sweeping underneath Jason's car, then her van. He still hadn't heard Aunt Ginny.

How soon before Ginny could hear a scream over the clattering of the gravel?

"Car comin'" the man beneath her yelled.

Rat Man's light switched off. She heard him scramble to his feet. Then nothing.

What was he doing? Did he think the car would drive past? Was he planning to ambush Aunt

Ginny? Or was he even now creeping towards the tree where she hid?

The headlights drew closer, closer . . . She could see Ginny's face illuminated by the dash lights. The black blur beside her must be Rory. She opened her mouth to scream.

"Kim?" Jason's voice carried in the clear air. A shadow appeared near the corner of the house.

Feet slapped asphalt as Rat Man rushed Jason. Kim screamed and hurled apples at the man beneath her. Several thumped harmlessly in the grass, but a few thuds followed by cursing told her she'd hit her mark.

A sudden light -- Rat Man's flashlight -- blinded Jason. Rat Man ducked, his shoulder connecting with Jason's stomach with a sickening splat. Jason fell, Rat Man disappeared down the side yard.

The second man stumbled after him, Kim's apples now little more than added incentive to keep moving.

Ginny's car slammed to a stop. Rory jumped out, charged across the alley and leaped the four-foot fence with ease.

"Call the police," Kim yelled. "Rory, come!"

But adrenaline clouded the big poodle's mind. He disappeared around the side of the house.

With a glance at Aunt Ginny -- good, she had the cell phone to her ear -- Kim shimmied down the tree and ran after Rory. As she turned the corner of the house, a hand snagged her arm.

Kim screamed and kicked out.

"Ouch! Damn it, Kim, it's me." A flashlight flicked on; Kim batted it away, out of her eyes.

Even as she identified Jason, Rory tore back towards them.

"Rory, no. Stay."

Rory froze several feet away. The flashlight illuminated the hairs on his back, standing straight up. Feet planted, tail erect, head down, Rory growled at Jason.

"What's wrong with your dog?"

"Better let go of my arm." Kim rubbed her now sore arm -- Jason had grabbed just above the elbow she'd jabbed Rat Man with. As she stepped away from Jason, the hairs on Rory's back smoothed out. But his stance never changed.

"It's okay, sweetie." Kim stroked his neck, trying to ease the tight muscles.

"Are you okay?" Aunt Ginny rounded the corner, aiming a flashlight at her feet.

"I'm just scraped up a bit. But, Jason, they said you were unconscious."

"Not for long."

Snagging Jason's flashlight, she aimed it at the side of his head. "Turn around."

"I'm telling you, Kim, it's not serious."

"Don't argue with me. Turn around."

With a dramatic sigh, Jason turned. Kim winced as the flashlight illuminated what was developing into a vicious bump.

"You need to get that checked out." Kim returned the light. "Knocks to the head are serious."

"I told you I'm fine. I was only out a few minutes, I don't see stars, don't have double vision and I can think just fine."

Kim ground her teeth. "Fine." Turning to Aunt Ginny, she said "Are the police on the way?"

As Ginny nodded, Jason yelped "Police?" He took a step towards his car. "I'm not talking to police."

"But we have to report this . . ."

"You report it. My dad'll kill me if I talk to police."

"But you're a victim!"

"Doesn't matter. My family doesn't deal with cops." Turning, he strode towards his car. "I'll call you tomorrow, okay?"

Kim didn't bother answering. She gripped Rory's collar until Jason's car disappeared down the alley.

"Are you really okay?" Aunt Ginny's hand trembled as she touched Kim's arm.

Kim laid a hand over her aunt's. "Actually, I'm kinda proud of myself. I..."

From somewhere in the yard, the Indiana Jones "Raider's March" sounded. Her purse! Snatching Ginny's flashlight, she aimed at the sound. Was that...? Yes, under the rose bush. With a squeal of relief, she yanked the purse out, located the phone and flipped it open.

Scott didn't give her time to say hello. "Are you okay?"

Kim froze. "How'd you know?"

"They robbed me, too. Trashed my office and stole my computer."

Kim winced, imagining Rat Man throwing files around.

"Did they get the diamonds?" Scott said.

"No. They chased me up a tree, but Aunt Ginny . . ."

"They chased you?... Hang on." In the background, Kim could hear a door pounding. Voices, then Scott returned. "The police are here, so I gotta run. Do you want me to come down, spend the night? I can sleep on the couch."

"No, no, that's okay. I doubt the thugs will be back tonight. I just wish the police would get here so I can call it a night. Hope they're faster than the ones up your way."

"Faster?" Scott sounded puzzled. "I only called the police ten minutes ago."

"Why did you wait so long?"

"Kim, the break-in only occurred a few minutes ago, when I was taking Al for his night-time walk. We were only gone thirty minutes..."

Kim gripped the phone and tuned out Scott's voice. Rat Man wasn't the one who broke into Scott's home. But if not Rat Man, who?

Two hours later, Kim stood in the shower, scrubbing away the touch and smell of Frankie, the Rat Man. Turning her back to the spray, she allowed the hot pulse to ease her aching muscles. The cleansing ritual, however, did little to clear her jumbled mind.

The two young officers who answered Aunt Ginny's 9-1-1 call were useful for one thing only: They'd converted any lingering fear into anger.

She'd been so certain that once she revealed the overheard conversation, the police would agree that the men who attacked her were not part of the local burglary ring. She'd patiently described the thugs' reference to "it" and how "it" could only refer to the rare gemstone (diamond was too volatile a word) that Grandpa brought back from New York. Only a jewelry insider, she told them, would know Grandpa possessed it. Therefore, the police needed to investigate the people who'd known the purpose of Grandpa's New York trip.

"Are you saying a jeweler attacked you, ma'am," the female cop had asked.

"Well, no. I'm assuming they hired someone."

The officer had nodded, then summarized Kim's "theory": A jeweler -- someone who had every-day access to valuable gemstones -- had hired a couple of thugs to steal this rare gemstone from Mr. Hershey. Said jeweler trusted these common criminals to return the gemstone in exchange for, what? Money? More money than the thieves could get by selling the gemstone themselves? And the jeweler trusted these guys because...?

Kim turned off the shower and reached for a towel.

Put in flat cop words, she thought, her theory sounded ludicrous. Yet the police theory that members of a burglary ring would pursue an escaped victim or try to kill Grandpa in the hospital made no sense. According to every mystery book she'd ever read, thieves were thieves. If they murdered someone, it was in the heat of the moment, not days later.

Wrapping the towel around her hair, she donned a clean sleep tee and opened the bathroom door. The bedside light she'd left burning illuminated one side of the queen bed, the oak dresser she and Grandpa had refinished and, perched atop, Fluffy.

Chest tightening, she crossed to the dresser and brushed her hand over the toy's thin, scraggly curls, remembering the day her parents insisted she discard her life-long companion. She'd been thirteen, "a young lady now," and young ladies don't sleep with smelly toys.

During the altercation that followed, Grandpa arrived. In hindsight, he must have known her parents' intentions and decided to "visit" at the right moment. He'd brushed the tears from her eyes, slipped Fluffy from her arms and, with a wink her parents couldn't see, said he'd take care of it.

Which was how Fluffy came to live in Grandpa's house. Kim fingered the red satin bow tied around Fluffy's neck. Somehow Grandpa had cleaned the toy without destroying what remained of the worn fabric. The next time Kim visited, she'd found an almost white Fluffy sporting a brand new bow.

She lifted the toy and sniffed, smiling as she detected the faint odor of Grandpa. The urge to bring Fluffy to bed was almost overwhelming. But, no, she had a real poodle now to cuddle.

A real poodle who was sprawled across the middle of the bed.

Smiling, she replaced Fluffy and crossed the room.

"Scooch over."

Rory opened one eye, grinned and rolled onto his back.

Shaking her head, she leaned over to rub his belly. "This is blackmail, you know." When she withdrew her hand, Rory rolled to his side of the bed.

As she climbed between the cool sheets, the bedside alarm clock ticked over to midnight. She could hear the bonging from the grandfather clock in the living room and, farther away, the chimes from the store's wall clocks.

With each gong, her shoulders grew more rigid. In eight hours, Grandpa would lose his police protection. The only way to keep him safe was to convince the police someone outside of the local burglary ring was involved. Outlining her theory hadn't worked. She needed evidence.

First, however, she needed to ensure her loved ones were safe. She shivered, imagining tonight's scenario if Aunt Ginny had pulled into the driveway before Kim and Jason arrived. A fifty-five pound poodle could only do so much to protect someone against two determined brutes. Though she hadn't seen any weapons, she didn't doubt Frankie and his pal carried them and wouldn't have hesitated to use them. Aunt Ginny could have been injured and Rory . . .

She reached a hand towards him, stroking his side.

She had no choice. Tomorrow she needed to force Aunt Ginny to return to Annapolis, away from the danger. She'd close the store, go to the police station and find Frankie the Rat in the thug books. Maybe knowing who he was would help her identify who might have hired him.

She'd spend the day investigating and tomorrow night she'd guard Grandpa. She cast a guilty look at Rory. As much as she'd love to have him with her, the police would probably not allow him into the building and the hospital would definitely veto his presence. And, with Frankie prowling around, Rory could be in danger if left here alone.

Maybe she could send him with Aunt Ginny . . . She shook her head, imagining her tiny aunt trying to walk the rambunctious youngster. Rory was too much dog for Ginny.

Maybe she could talk Scott into taking him for a few days. Not that Scott's place was any safer than Grandpa's given the break-in there.

And what the heck was that all about? Surely anyone after the diamond would assume Grandpa had it. Of course, Scott had found a small blue diamond in Jim's safe. If they were correct and Jim knew about a new mine in Colorado . . .

She needed to stop her whirring brain, get some sleep so she'd have a clear head tomorrow.

She reached for the mystery she'd been reading, then remembered the book Scott gave her. Swinging her feet from the bed, she pulled the book from her purse, returned to the bed and snuggled beside Rory.

The cover pronounced this book as The first authentic account of the sensational diamond hoax chicanery. Beneath the title an illustration featured two bearded miners and a mule.

She grinned, suddenly six again, snuggled beneath a down comforter, listening to Grandpa's bedtime story.

"It all began in 1870 on a chilly November day when a pair of scruffy prospectors trudged into San Francisco."

Grandpa would bend over and shuffle forward, yanking at the reins of an imaginary mule. His arms jerked upward and for a moment he played tug-of-war with the mule while Kim squealed with laughter. Finally, with an exaggerated whoosh of relief, Grandpa tied the reins to a hitching post and mimed knocking on a door.

She grinned and stared at the book's cover. Grandpa had so thoroughly perfected the story that two years ago, when she'd begged him to share the tale with his new friend, Jim Hampton, he'd told it word for word. At the time, her intent had been to divert the scheming old men from their matchmaking plans. But Grandpa had held them both enthralled, now playing the role of a con man, now the not-so-innocent "mark."

She opened the book. Jim must have bought it after hearing Grandpa's version of the story. Wondering how much was real, she flipped through the pages, stopping to read key passages.

As she scanned, her breath quickened. It was true. All of it.

A couple of prospectors really did salt a Wyoming mountain with industrial diamonds, convinced investors, a geologist and even Charles Lewis Tiffany that the claim was real and walked away with today's equivalent of $8 million.

She'd stumbled across references to The Great Diamond Hoax while researching her thesis. The tale was pretty famous in the industry.

But her thesis focused on diamond advertising gimmicks of the 20th Century. So she'd never given the story much thought. She'd assumed Grandpa's rendition was based in fact with a lot of exaggeration thrown in to entertain a small child. It seemed unlikely that someone as knowledgeable as Charles Tiffany had been sucked into the hoax. But, according to this book, he'd succumbed along with the others.

How in the world did two con men scam some of the world's foremost authorities on diamonds?

Turning back to the book's beginning, she scanned now for an explanation. Slowly, an image began to form.

The timing of the swindle had been perfect. The California Gold Rush petered out mid-century, leaving thousands of hungry prospectors searching for the next get-rich-quick opportunity.

It came in the form of diamonds.

In the late 1860s the discovery of a diamond field near Kimberley, South Africa, sent thousands of diamond hunters pouring into Africa. What made the African find unique, however, wasn't the size of the field. It was the geological location.

Until the Kimberley discovery, diamonds had been found only in the riverbeds of India and Brazil. That the rare gems could be found outside of those two countries excited the imagination. Even more astounding, however, was the absence of a nearby river or stream. The African diamonds had been found in mountains. Mountains that looked awfully similar to the ranges in the American southwest.

Did that mean there were diamonds right here in the good ol' U S of A?

Once the question was posed, no one could ignore it. Prospectors who couldn't afford passage to Africa boarded trains for Denver and, from there, hired mules to pack into the mountains of Colorado, Wyoming and Utah. Those too timid to brave the rugged terrain offered to finance the explorers' efforts in exchange for a percentage of profits.

Of all of the would-be financiers, George Roberts, a San Francisco banker, was among the most fervent. After backing a failed diamond hunt in Utah, he let it be known he was looking for new opportunities.

Which is probably why it was his hitching post the con artists tied their mule to on that fateful day.

The swindlers played Roberts like a whore showing a bit of ankle:

"No, no, we don't want a backer. We couldn't possibly take your money . . . well, alright . . ."

"Look what we found this week. We had more, but the boat overturned and we lost a sack full of diamonds."

"Remember, this is our secret."

The scheme almost fell apart when Roberts sent a sample of the diamonds to Charles Tiffany for appraisal. Tiffany, however, had never seen rough diamonds; his expertise was with cut gems. So he based his appraisal on quantity and size, pronouncing the samples worth several hundred thousand.

The staggering amount cemented Roberts' commitment. He demanded the "prospectors" allow a geologist and a select group of potential investors to view the diamond field.

The con artists led the men on a merry chase. They boarded a train for Denver, hired horses, then traveled for four days through the dusty hills. By the time they arrived at the supposed diamond field, even the geologist couldn't pinpoint their location. The dry, brown land looked no different from the land they'd already traveled through.

The prospectors, however, insisted this was the place. Handing a shovel to one of the businessmen, they pointed to a small mound, saying the formation resembled places where they'd found earlier diamonds. After a few minutes with the shovel, the first diamond appeared. The others grabbed shovels and began digging.

As they unearthed more and more diamonds, even the geologist grew starry eyed.

Kim smiled, remembering Grandpa rushing around her bedroom, pretending to dig for diamonds. Grandpa's wide eyes, open mouth and squeals of delight whenever he "found" one perfectly captured the feeding frenzy that had overtaken the men.

Hmm. . . she flipped a few more pages. Did Grandpa actually read this book or did his story originate from local gossip? She'd have to ask him when he came out of his coma . . .

The tears came suddenly and no amount of gulping or teeth clenching would stop them.

She wrapped her arms around bent knees and buried her face. The question she'd been avoiding pushed to the surface: What if Grandpa never came out of the coma?

She jumped as a hand touched her shoulder. Looking up into Aunt Ginny's tender face, she felt herself unfold, spreading her arms wide. As she melted into Aunt Ginny's warmth, she focused on her aunt's croons.

"He'll be okay. Shhh. . . He really will be okay. He's too tough to leave us now. Shhh . . ."

A cold nose wormed its way under Kim's arm, snuffled, then a bright pink tongue lapped across her glasses. Kim choked, giggled and leaned back to gaze at her aunt through tongue-washed glasses.

"You really think he'll be okay?"

"I know he will." Ginny reached over, snagged a box of tissues and passed it to Kim. "When you were in the hospital, you didn't imagine Max gripping your hand. He's not going to leave you."

Kim blew her nose, then tried to wipe her glasses, smearing the tears.

With a shake of her head, Aunt Ginny removed the glasses, whipped a handkerchief from her robe pocket and began polishing.

Kim stroked Rory's head then reached for another tissue. "Kind of like old times, huh?"

"You never cried much. Always worried me."

Snorting, Kim accepted the glasses and put them on. "Why, 'cause I wasn't a crybaby like Tiffany?"

Aunt Ginny shook her head. "Because you tried to hold the world on your shoulders."

"Rough job, but someone's gotta do it."

As Ginny grinned, Kim leaned forward and grasped her hand. "You need to go home. It's too dangerous here. I'll close the store and set the alarm; it should be okay during the day . . ."

But Ginny was already shaking her head. "You really think I'm going to leave you here alone? Unless you'll come back to Annapolis with me . . ."

Kim shook her head. "Can't. The police aren't going to find these guys, so I need to do something. Otherwise, Grandpa remains in danger." As Ginny opened her mouth, Kim held up her hand. "I'm not going to do anything stupid. Just talk to people. When I find something, I'll turn it over to Lieutenant Brockley."

"It's not the daytime I'm worried about."

"I'll be spending nights in the hospital."

"And sleep when? Look at you. The bags under your eyes are drooping to your knees. And those cuts and scrapes aren't going to heal if you don't take care of yourself."

"I'll be all right."

Aunt Ginny folded her arms, her jaw muscles clenched, her eyes bright, a homeroom teacher going to battle rowdy students.

Or "student" singular.

Kim sighed, running fingers through her hair. "How 'bout we try this: I'll ask Tiffany to do the hospital night shift. She doesn't work, so she can rest during the day."

Ginny rolled her eyes. "You really want to trust fluff-for-brains?"

"But she's the only one who doesn't work . . ."

"None of my friends work. And they don't sleep much. Don't argue. They'll look at it as an adventure." She produced a leer. "Besides, Max is quite a catch. My friends will jump at the chance to earn Brownie points."

Kim protested, but her aunt brushed aside her concerns. They argued for fifteen minutes before reaching a compromise. Kim agreed to allow Aunt Ginny's friends to help in the store or to stay with Grandpa at night. However, everyone would work in pairs, keep their cell phones close and call the police at any hint of trouble.

As for Aunt Ginny, she'd either stick with Kim or pair up with one of the others and Rory.

Satisfied that the plan would keep everyone safe, Kim kissed Ginny's soft cheek.

"You'd better get some sleep," she said. "I'd like to get an early start tomorrow."

Aunt Ginny nodded and, with a yawn, wished her goodnight.

Kim, however, was still wide-awake. Opening Diamonds in the Salt, she flipped through the book. After a few minutes, however, her feet began twitching.

Darn it, she needed to do something. Not sit around waiting for morning.

But what she'd told Aunt Ginny was also true for her: If she didn't sleep, she'd be useless tomorrow. Setting the book on the bedside table, she removed her glasses and clicked off the light. Turning onto her side, she stroked Rory's back. Her mind immediately went to the scientist who'd bought the book.

"Do you remember Jim? You were just a baby when you met him." Rory slapped a paw onto her shoulder. She grinned, remembering Rory as a fluffy puppy trying to "help" Grandpa tell the diamond story by mimicking Grandpa's movements, then running to Jim for approval . . .

She sat up, heart racing. Images flashed through her mind. Jim applauding the con artists' cleverness. Scott describing Jim's anger at the diamond industry. The Torvosaurus etched onto a rare blue diamond.

Jim's movie collection.

The Sting: Robert Redford and Paul Newman planning a scam. The Music Man: Con man skips town with money intended for band instruments.

Ocean's Eleven: Eleven hustlers steal millions. The Flim Flam Man: More hustlers. Butch Cassidy and the Sundance Kid: Redford and Newman again, this time as bank robbers.

The letter hidden in Jim's bookcase: I won't watch you die. Quote from Butch Cassidy.

Grandpa's phone call: A friend just poked a hornet's nest and I'm supposed to keep him from getting stung.

Her fists clenched. Was Jim Hampton -- Grandpa's friend and Scott's uncle -- planning to use the blue diamond to con someone?

CHAPTER 20

The next morning, Kim rose before the sun. A long, exhausting day awaited her and she wanted to treat herself to a stroll on the boardwalk before returning to business. Maybe see what the resident ospreys were doing.

Donning shorts, t-shirt and walking shoes, she tucked dog treats and a training clicker into a pocket and set off down the boardwalk. Rory trotted ahead, puffy tail waving.

Her aching muscles loosened with each step and she breathed in the smell of brackish water and damp sand. Grandpa smells. The sky lightened along with her mood, the Chesapeake Bay changing from Oregon gray to blue-gray to greenish blue. Despite the early hour, the heavy summer air pressed onto her shoulders. A gentle breeze skimmed the water, providing just enough cooling to make walking possible.

As her feet slapped a steady rhythm, she reviewed the upcoming day. She needed to make a detailed list of things to do, prepare the store for opening, give the license plate number to Aunt Ginny, wait for Ginny's friends to arrive, look at mug books. Decide what, if anything, to tell Scott about her suspicions about his uncle.

In the daylight, the idea that Scott's mild-mannered uncle planned to scam someone seemed ludicrous. She ticked off her "evidence": Grandpa's sudden trip to New York to help a friend. The rare blue diamond Grandpa said to hide. A hidden note written in a woman's hand. Jim's collection of books and movies about scams. She snorted. Most likely none of these were even connected.

"Mmmpff." At Rory's alert, Kim refocused on her surroundings. Mrs. Jennings, the woman who owned the souvenir shop, power-walked towards them. Though the woman's shop was several doors away from Grandpa's, Mrs. Jennings was a known gossip. Maybe she saw last night's attackers hanging around the boardwalk.

Calling a greeting, Kim turned and fell into step beside her.

"Heard your grandfather's in the hospital," Mrs. Jennings said. "How's he doing?"

"He's in a medically induced coma to keep his brain from swelling." My goodness this woman moved fast! Kim had to trot to keep up with her. "We had some trouble last night. Did you notice a couple of big guys hanging around in the evening?"

"Wasn't home."

No one had been home. Where do these people go?

Still, Mrs. Jennings might have seen something during the day. "Hope you haven't had any trouble at your store."

"Only the usual shoplifters," Mrs. Jennings said. "We don't have anything to interest professional thieves."

"Just your cash register." Kim winced as a sharp pain stabbed her side. Darn, she was out of shape.

"We empty the till every evening. And believe you me we're careful about who's around when that happens."

"So . . . gasp . . . you haven't . . . gasp . . . seen any suspicious characters hanging around the boardwalk?"

Mrs. Jennings snorted. "All tourists are suspicious."

Kim trotted along a few more steps to be polite, then peeled away. Leaning against the railing, she stopped to catch her breath.

Rory, however, had other ideas. As a family of mallards started across the boardwalk, the big poodle charged.

"Slow down," she called.

But the young dog ignored her warning, reached the end of the leash with a jolt, then strained at the leash. Kim planted her feet. Reaching into her pocket, she removed the dog clicker, felt around for the clicking mechanism, placed her thumb over it and waited.

Overhead an osprey screamed. Rory tugged. Kim resisted.

Finally . . . Finally! . . . Rory looked back. As his eyes met hers, Kim thumbed the little metal box. Click. Grinning, Rory trotted to her. She handed him a small treat.

"Yes, remember me? This is loose-leash walking, not pull your human down the boardwalk."

Rory cocked his head.

"Shall we try again?"

She turned back the way she'd originally been walking. For a few steps, Rory trotted beside her, looking up. She reached for the clicker to reward him, fumbled it and clicked just as he looked away.

"Arghh!" Great, she just rewarded him for looking away. She needed to buy one of those new-fangled clickers, the ones with the easy-push buttons that could be worn on the wrist.

The osprey screed again and plunged into the bay. Its great wings flapped, straining, as it rose with a fish clutched in its talons.

Rory continued to look at her, so she clicked and handed him a treat. She paused by the railing to watch the osprey circle the messy nest it'd built on top of a platform-outfitted pylon. Inside the nest, two juvenile birds screeched, pinfeathers flying as they waved their wings. The mother dropped into the nest and began tucking fish pieces into hungry mouths. To think DDT almost eliminated these majestic creatures . . .

Her arm jerked and she stumbled as Rory dashed after another group of ducks.

"Rory, no!"

The big poodle halted, but continued to strain at the leash. Kim groaned. This is what happened when you didn't train daily; the poor dog forgot what he'd learned. Somehow she needed to fit in short sessions with Rory while pursuing the man who attacked Grandpa.

Well, no time like the present. She could train while they walked and maybe talk to more locals. The man who attacked Grandpa didn't suddenly materialize; he must have studied Grandpa's habits, known when he was traveling to New York. Surely someone saw him hanging around.

But training an overgrown puppy while quizzing the few locals she encountered proved futile. Every time she stopped to talk to someone, Rory searched for birds. She had to keep half her mind on Rory while listening to Grandpa's neighbors. No one had noticed strangers acting suspicious. And why should they? The beach was crowded with tourists;

it took all of their focus to control their own customers.

By the time she returned to Grandpa's, Rory finally trotted along with a loose leash. Kim, however, smelled like she'd been to war. Her damp t-shirt clung to her skin, her left hand was bleeding and her knees were grimy and sore from falling into a planter box.

She opened the side yard gate, unclipped Rory's leash and followed him around back. A strange blue car -- a Prius -- perched on the right side of the driveway. Frowning, she followed Rory up the outside stairs to the kitchen.

Aunt Ginny and Scott sat at the kitchen table, sheets of papers spread between them. At Kim's entrance they both turned and stared.

"Were you attacked again?" Aunt Ginny started to rise.

Kim quickly reassured her. "Rory caught a goose."

"A goose?" Her aunt thumped back into her chair.

"Well, yeah, he is a bird dog you know." Kim glanced at Scott. He'd been staring at her bloody knees. Catching her eye, his mouth quirked. A glare prevented the full on grin.

Aunt Ginny turned to Rory. "I don't see any blood on him."

"Of course not. He's got a soft mouth. He just wanted to carry it."

Scott kept a straight face. "I take it the goose didn't approve?"

Kim glanced at the cut on her hand. "Stupid goose." Looking back, her eyes again met Scott's. A jolt of electricity shot up her spine.

Sliding her eyes to the left, she spotted a box on the table.

"Are those Krispy Kremes?" She'd become addicted to the hot-from-the-oven donuts while finishing her thesis.

"Wasn't sure you'd be awake this early, so I brought a bribe." Scott nodded towards the papers. "I think I found a handwriting match to that note in Uncle Jim's office."

A clue? Suddenly the day seemed a little brighter.

"Let me get cleaned up. Then I want to hear all about it." She pointed at the box. "And there'd better be some donuts left when I get back."

Upstairs, she turned on the shower. While waiting for the water to warm, she called the hospital.

"Mr. Hershey is resting quietly," Grandpa's nurse said.

"Do you have any idea when the doctors will bring him out of the coma?"

"I'm really not supposed to . . ."

"Please." Kim's voice sounded child-like, but right now she didn't care. "I understand the medical terms." Mostly. "And I'm not going to freak out or anything." She swallowed. "I just need to know. He's my Grandpa."

"Well . . ." The woman's voice softened. "This morning Doctor said the swelling is going down. And Mr. Hershey is responding to external stimulus."

Kim's breath caught. Grandpa was getting better!

"Remember, though, he's still at risk," the nurse added.

"I understand." Kim thanked the woman, then did a little jig. Grandpa was getting better!

Stepping into the shower, she winced when the hot water splashed against her knees. The sting, however, couldn't wipe the smile from her face.

Okay, now she could admit it. She'd been terrified her aunts were right, that Grandpa wouldn't come out of the coma. Or he'd come out and wouldn't be Grandpa any more. Her college psychology courses had taught her just enough about the biology of the brain to envision all sorts of frightening scenarios.

But the nurse's report, coupled with the way Grandpa squeezed her hand the other night, indicated his brain was functioning just fine.

Fifteen minutes later, she burst into the kitchen announcing "Grandpa's getting better!"

As she described the conversation with the nurse, she snagged a donut, laid it onto a paper towel and popped it into the microwave. Ten seconds later, the fragrance of fresh pastry filled the room.

Pouring a glass of iced tea, she joined the others at the table.

"So," she said sitting across from Scott, "tell me about this handwriting."

"I found this in some of Uncle Jim's old reports from work." Scott pushed the pages across the table, pointing first at the message they'd found, then at the handwritten notes scattered across the typed reports.

Though the words on the hidden message were dark from pressing hard on the paper -- a sure sign of emotional turmoil -- the style matched the light, quick notes made on the typewritten reports.

"Looks the same to me." Kim set the papers aside. "Who wrote this?"

"Uncle Jim's secretary."

Huh. Secretaries often knew more about their bosses than even the boss's family. "What do you know about her?"

Scott shrugged. "I think she typed reports for everyone at the lab." He tapped the movie quote. "This, however, sure implies a closer relationship."

"Think she'll talk with us?"

"Only one way to find out." Scott pulled out his cell phone.

"Scott, it's only seven a.m.!"

"Old reporter's trick. At this hour, she'll still be home."

Sure enough, someone answered his call. Rather than eavesdrop, Kim reached into her purse for the license plate number Jim's neighbor had given her . . . was that only yesterday?

"Do you still have friends at the DMV who could look up this number?" She handed the paper to Aunt Ginny.

"Donovan owes me a favor or two." Aunt Ginny frowned at the numbers. "Where'd this come from?"

"We haven't compared notes from yesterday, have we?" Kim tapped the paper. "Before Jim died, his neighbor saw a black car -- BMW, Mercedes, something like that -- following him. She was able to get the license. And the police refuse to do anything about it."

Aunt Ginny nodded and tucked the paper in a pocket. "I'll call Donovan."

"What about here? How'd things go in the store yesterday?"

Aunt Ginny shrugged. "Not much to tell. We sold those pink sapphire earrings Doris wanted. Good thing you're keeping the store open; we had a lot of foot traffic. And before you ask, when I call the girls today, I'll make sure they know to stay in pairs and keep their phones nearby.

"Oh, and speaking of yesterday, a fax came in for you. I didn't understand it, but I put it on Max's desk."

The report on the blue diamond.

Excusing herself, Kim trotted downstairs to Grandpa's office.

The report lay exactly in the center of Grandpa's desk. She smiled, shaking her head. Aunt Ginny could be so meticulous sometimes.

Lifting the report, she casually glanced through it. Well, well, well. She'd correctly guessed the size: 4.68 carats. A nice chunk of rock. Polish: very good. Symmetry: Very good. Clarity: IF . . . Internally flawless? Wow, no wonder Grandpa paid to have the diamond tested; internally flawless diamonds were extremely scarce. Color Grade: Fancy intense blue. Better than the Hope, which was classed as gray-blue. Color origin: ...

The paper crinkled as her hand tightened. No. No way.

She pulled the report closer and read again. Color origin: Natural.

Natural. Not heated or irradiated. Natural.

She sank into the desk chair.

The diamond in the safe was large, intensely colored and natural. The rarest of the rare.

Grandpa's diamond was worth millions.

CHAPTER 21

Three hours later, Kim stared out the passenger window as Scott expertly steered the Prius onto Constitution Avenue. Tourists in rental cars crawled along the wide avenue, knuckles white on steering wheels, trying to make sense of the one-way streets. On the sidewalk beside Kim black-suited government workers wove through families dressed in loud t-shirts and shorts. Scott slammed on the brakes, cursing a tourist who'd suddenly cut in front of him. Welcome to Washington, D.C.

Too cowardly to drive in the city, Kim preferred the subway system. But Scott had worked as a reporter in D.C. Not only was he not intimidated, he knew every shortcut. Despite the fact it'd taken well over two hours to look through police mug photos, they would reach the Smithsonian in time for their noon appointment.

She just hoped Jim Hampton's former secretary could explain why the mild-mannered scientist had attracted the attention of Baltimore hit men.

Earlier, at the police station, she hadn't really expected to find last night's attackers in the mug shots. She'd read enough mysteries to believe that many thugs were never apprehended. But she'd dutifully perched in the uncomfortable chair and studied photo after photo of vacant-eyed criminals.

Rat Man's photo was easy to spot. Even among his peers, he excelled at appearing menacing.

When she pointed to his photo, the police officer frowned, clearly skeptical. But then Scott surprised both of them by claiming Rat Man was one of the thugs who'd robbed and killed Jim.

The officer left the room, returning a few minutes later with six photos. Scott shuffled through the bunch. Pulling one from the stack, he set it on the table, saying this was the second man he'd seen in his uncle's lab.

Turns out the two men were cousins: Frankie "Rat Man" Roberts and Alan Miles. Both had done time for assault and burglary. Frankie had been charged with several muggings but never convicted because his victims never materialized to testify.

Recently, Frankie had been the prime suspect in the execution-style deaths of several Baltimore drug dealers. The two men worked out of Baltimore and, according to the officer, never left the city.

So why leave Baltimore to rob Jim and attack her?

Throughout the drive to Washington, Kim fit puzzle pieces together, tore them apart and rearranged them. None of the patterns, however, made any sense.

"Okay, let's talk this out from the beginning." At Scott's nod, she continued. "We know that Grandpa took the blue diamond to New York for testing. He was also there to help a friend who'd gotten into trouble."

"But we don't know the friend was Uncle Jim," Scott protested.

"True. But we do know Jim tried to warn Grandpa about being followed. And after he was attacked, he called to tell Grandpa to hide something."

Scott's hands tightened on the steering wheel.

Kim plowed on. "Then Grandpa gave me the blue diamond to hide."

"And I found a small diamond in Uncle Jim's safe. . . Damn!" Scott smacked the steering wheel. "Why didn't he tell me what was going on?"

"You had no idea he was being followed or anything?"

Scott shook his head. "Nothing. He seemed a bit agitated, but he gets that way when working."

"At first," Kim continued, "I thought Jim might have wanted to reproduce that old diamond scam . . ."

"Salt a diamond field?" Scott grinned. "Yeah, I could see Uncle Jim enjoying that. Maybe selling shares in it to Alex White."

Kim bit her lip and studied Scott, remembering his almost violent reaction the one time she'd mentioned the Whites. But the idea of his uncle conning the Whites seemed to amuse him. She could see no tension in the muscles in his face or shoulders.

"You've mentioned the Whites before," she said. "What did Jim have against them?"

Scott sighed. "I told you Jim's father died while moonlighting to pay off a diamond, right? Grandfather bought the diamond from Bradford White."

"So?" Sheesh, if Grandpa made enemies every time a customer purchased a diamond with rent money . . . "He surely didn't blame Bradford for his father's death?"

"Of course not. But after grandfather's death, my grandmother sold their house and all valuables just to survive. But she refused to sell the diamond." He shrugged. "Mom, Uncle Jim and Aunt Cary blamed the diamond for everything that went wrong in their lives."

"Natural reaction. When someone dies, people often search for something or someone to blame."

Scott nodded. "So ten years later, when grandmother died, they decided to sell their mother's diamond. Figured it'd pay everyone's way through college."

"Oh, no." Kim's teeth ground. "The idea that diamonds increase in value is a myth, you know. Prices are so inflated that even at Grandpa's low costs, it'd take years of economic inflation before you could recover your initial investment. Even Elizabeth Taylor lost money on a diamond."

"Well, Uncle Jim never got a chance to find out." Scott suddenly clicked his turn signal and stopped to allow a car to vacate one of the rare parking spaces near the National Mall.

Kim glanced around, surprised. She hadn't noticed the series of turns that brought them here.

"When Uncle Jim brought the ring back to White Family Jewelers," Scot continued, "Alex White told him the diamond was fake." Scott parallel parked, but left the engine running. "Uncle Jim and Alex got into a fight and Bradford White had to break it up."

Kim's mouth dropped open. "Are you saying Bradford sold your grandfather a fake diamond?"

Scott shook his head. "Oh, the original stone was real. Bradford had a copy of the diamond report to prove it. But somewhere along the way, probably when grandmother had the ring cleaned, someone substituted a cubic zirconia for the diamond. Grandmother only took the ring to one place for cleaning: White Family Jewelers."

He turned off the car and they stepped into the hot, humid air. Kim's glasses immediately fogged.

"Are you sure Jim's mother didn't simply sell the diamond?" Kim wiped the glasses on her t-shirt. "If they were so strapped for money . . ."

"Mom, Uncle Jim and Aunt Cary all swear their mother never sold the diamond."

"On what basis?" Replacing her glasses, Kim fell in step with Scott.

"Never enough money. Even if, as you say, grandmother couldn't recover the initial investment, reselling should have brought in enough that the kids would have noticed."

They walked for a few moments in silence.

"Okay," Kim said. "Say someone really did substitute stones. Why'd Jim assume it was Alex and not Bradford?"

"Jim said the old man seemed shocked. Plus he offered to refund the original price."

"Generous. The resale value of the original diamond probably wasn't as high as what Jim's father paid for it. And Bradford had no proof that your grandparents hadn't replaced the diamond with a CZ."

Scott nodded. "Uncle Jim figured the only reason the owner would make such an offer was if he suspected his own son had made the switch."

Kim slammed to a halt. Jason's father . . . a thief?

As if on cue, her cell phone rang. Jason.

Let it go to voice mail? No, he'd just call back. Jason could be persistent. He'd probably spent last night stewing over his inability to "protect" her and now needed reassurance. Better to just get it over with.

"I'd better take this," she told Scott. "Go ahead, I'll catch up."

She flipped the phone open, her eyes on Scott as he climbed the stone stairs that led to the Smithsonian's National Museum of Natural History. She smiled. Scott might not be as handsome as Jason, but his personality oozed charm.

"Just wanted to see how you're doing," Jason said.

"A little sore, but fine. How 'bout you?" Since you didn't bother sticking around to talk to the police, you jerk.

"Same. Uh, what did the police say?"

Knowing it was childish, Kim gave in to the impulse to conceal she'd identified the attackers. "Not much. Look, I'm kind of busy so . . ."

"This will just take a minute," Jason interrupted. "I had an idea. Why don't I come help you in the store until Max gets out of the hospital? My assistant can take over the Frederick store while I'm away."

Jason offering to help? Now there was a first. "That's very nice of you, but I've got plenty of help."

"You're not letting your money grubbing aunts in the store, are you?"

Money grubbing! Kim's hand tightened on the phone and for a moment her throat was so tight she couldn't breathe. Her skin burned as guilt washed over her. When she dated Jason, had she been dumb enough to complain about her aunts? She must have. Otherwise, why Jason's comment?

Still, he had no right to throw that into her face. After all, she'd never called his father a pompous ass. Or a thief.

She unclenched her teeth. "I've got other people helping. But thanks for calling."

"Kim . . ."

She snapped the phone shut. Inhaling deeply, she started up the steps, her mind furiously searching her memories. What had she told Jason about her aunts? Surely, she hadn't called them "money grubbing." That would require a degree of brashness she'd never possessed as a teen. Especially talking to the rich guy who starred in all the school plays and led the football team to a state championship. All she'd done in high school was study like crazy, join the geology club and worry about cellulite. Which was why she'd been so surprised when Jason invited her to the prom.

Up until that invitation -- and Jason's failure to appear -- the only times they'd crossed paths had been at Grandpa's jewelry shows . . .

She slammed to a stop. Behind her, footsteps stumbled and a male voice cursed. Glancing to the side, she apologized to the scowling guy rubbing his shin.

She resumed her climb, the memory now hot and humiliating. It had been at one of the jewelry shows. The aloof, sophisticated Jason, bored by the show, had sidled over and begun complaining. Trying to copy his cool, Kim had joined him in a one-upmanship game of whose family was the strangest. She'd called her aunts greedy.

Stupid. Stupid, stupid, stupid.

Her phone rang. Jason again. She turned the phone off without answering and followed a small group into the museum's Rotunda.

The sight of Henry, the museum's thirteen-foot bull elephant, restored her humor. Trumpet raised, ears flapping, Henry had been charging toward visitors since he was first unveiled in 1959. Grandpa said it took more than 10,000 pounds of clay to shape Henry's body.

She'd just entered kindergarten when Grandpa first introduced her to Henry. In the following years, they'd explored every inch of the museum, Grandpa chuckling as she imitated the pounce of the spotted leopard, christened the Arctic fox "Homer," created stories about T. Rex "Rexy" and Triceratops "Topper." Grandpa's own tales grew more elaborate told among the displays of rough gemstones, volcanic rock and fossils.

Kim's chest tightened. Today was the first time she'd come here without Grandpa.

Still, some traditions must be followed.

"Hey, Henry," she whispered. Turning to her right, she passed the entry to the dinosaur exhibit -- Rexy and Topper would have to wait for another day -- and stepped on the escalator.

At the top, she scowled at the masses of people. Not surprising, considering this floor housed Egyptian mummies, a live butterfly exhibit and the Hall of Gems and Minerals. Her heart beat faster. She hated crowds.

But if she wanted to quiz Jim's secretary, she needed to deal with it. Taking a deep breath, she plunged in, weaving her way through knots of children, her eyes glued to the sign for the Henry Winston Gallery. Maybe Scott had already interviewed Carole and they could flee this madhouse.

The line to see the Hope Diamond was ten feet deep. Off to the side, Scott huddled with a bedraggled 60-something woman. Her rose-colored pantsuit might have started the day crisply ironed, but right now the linen resembled Henry's wrinkled legs. In one hand she gripped a red-faced boy, in the other a slightly older girl. A second girl, maybe eight or nine, stared into the distance, shoulders hunched.

"I wanna see the dinosaurs!" The four-year-old's wail sliced through the cacophony.

As Kim approached, Carole shot a pleading look at Scott before kneeling in front of her grandson.

"Honey, you saw the dinosaurs. It's Tina's turn to pick."

"Yeah, my turn." The younger girl bounced up and down, squealing "Diamonds, diamonds, diamonds."

Kim halted, one foot turned back towards the exit. Her breath caught, her face flushed, the back of her neck tingled. She resisted the urge to cover her ears as the chant pitched her back in time.

Same museum, different voices.

Tiffany, Opal and Coral chanted and bounced to the monotonous rhythm of "diamonds, diamonds, diamonds." Her older cousins -- Goldie, Pearl, Beryl and Amber -- rolled their eyes. Her three aunts beamed.

Grandpa whispered "Be nice."

But she hadn't wanted to be nice. Up to that day, the Smithsonian's Museum of Natural History had been her special place. Hers and Grandpa's.

As her oldest cousins neared puberty, however, her aunts decided it was time to show their daughters the museum's gem collection. They timed the visit to coincide with a teachers' in-service day. While the children didn't have to attend school, Mom and Dad couldn't take time off from work. Normally, Kim would have spent the day with Grandpa. But her aunts drafted Grandpa into going with them to play museum tour guide leaving Kim no choice but to tag along.

It was worse than anything she could have imagined.

In their rush to reach Gem Hall, her family snubbed Henry and raced past the entrance to Rexy and Topper's home. Grandpa and Kim brought up the rear, Kim muttering under her breath, Grandpa promising they'd visit Henry before leaving the museum. They climbed to the second floor to find the others standing at the back of a long line straining to see the Hope Diamond.

Unable to see over the top of the people in front, Tiffany suddenly bounced up and down, chanting "Diamond, diamond, diamond." Opal and Coral joined in.

All around, people winced. Some stepped out of line, away from the noise. Others fixed glares on the aunts.

Amber, always the rebel, noticed the crowd's reaction and joined in the chant.

Her cousins had ignored Aunt Ruby's hiss, Aunt Sapphire's admonishment to "channel your inner calm." Aunt Emerald spotted Grandpa and waved him over.

Kim held back. "Can't I wait . . ." She had gestured vaguely towards a wall.

Grandpa surveyed the crowd, then shook his head. "It's too crowded, monkey. I don't want you to get lost."

And so she'd joined the brats, eyes cast down, face hot, helpless.

A stern "enough" from Grandpa stopped the chanting, but the damage was done. The people who'd remained in line scowled and glared. At her aunts. At her cousins. At her.

Not even Grandpa's gift of a stuffed Henry elephant could erase the nightmare from her mind.

Well, she was an adult now. No longer helpless. She didn't have to tolerate screaming children, at least not kindly. And Jim's former secretary had clearly lost control of her grandchildren.

Crossing to the children, Kim pitched her voice low. "Enough."

The boy and girl froze, eyes wide, mouths open.

"Very good." Turning to Carole, she introduced herself.

Carole ignored Kim's outstretched hand, her eyes icy. Lifting her chin, she turned back to Scott. "As I was saying, I don't know how I can help you, but before we talk I need to show my grandchildren the world's largest diamond."

"Actually, it's only 45 and a half carats. Not the world's largest."

Carole's eyes narrowed. "Then it's the largest blue diamond."

Blue-gray. The stone was actually rated blue-gray. But under Carole's scrutiny, Kim remained silent.

"Well, let's go see the largest blue diamond," Scott said. "C'mon, buddy." He swung the little boy onto his shoulders.

Gripping the younger girl's hand, Carole
followed Scott and her now happy grandson to the
back of the line. Good, maybe Scott can get
something out of the woman.

"What makes it blue?" a small voice asked.

Kim glanced down at the remaining child. Unlike
her sister, who'd been dolled up in a pouf-skirted
dress and Mary Jane shoes, this child sported t-
shirt, torn jeans and scuffed Reeboks. A kindred
spirit?

"It's got boron in it," Kim answered. The girl
tipped her head, her eyes questioning. Kim smiled,
the claustrophobia receding. "Sometimes when
diamonds form, other minerals get trapped in the
crystals. Boron will make diamonds blue. Nitrogen
makes them yellow. There are also pink, green and
red diamonds."

The girl's eyes widened. "Can I see pink
diamonds?"

Kim turned towards Carole, easy to find standing
next to Scott and his small passenger. Waving her
hand, she caught the woman's eye, then pointed to
the little girl and then the doorway to the Hall of
Gems. Carole nodded and the little girl -- Liz not
Lizzie -- slipped her hand in Kim's. Together they
entered the next room and paused by a display case
holding a collection of colored diamonds.

Blue, pink, yellow, champagne, the stones
glistened beneath the museum's specially-designed

lighting. Liz stood transfixed, her eyes darting one to another.

Kim pointed to the heart-shaped stone. "This diamond is smaller than the Hope, but it actually has better color. The Hope has a gray tinge to it. This is a brighter blue. I like it better."

"Me, too." When Kim raised her eyebrows, Liz continued, "I saw the Hope Diamond when Grandma brought me here before." She grimaced. "Alone."

Kim stifled a smile. Definitely a fellow traveler.

"But we never saw these diamonds." Liz pointed to the marquise-cut stone. "The pink's pretty, isn't it?"

"Is that your favorite color?"

Liz shuffled her feet. "No. I just wanted to, you know . . ." She waved back the way they'd come.

Kim grinned. "So what's your favorite color?"

"Blue. But I've already seen . . ."

"Don't worry, I won't drag you back there. Let me show you some other pretty blue stones." She led her to a display case containing an egg-sized sapphire surrounded by brilliant-cut diamonds.

"Wow!"

"That one's from Sri Lanka. And over here are sapphires from Montana. See how the color is more of a cornflower blue instead of deep blue? But sapphires come in other colors, too." They walked to a display of pink, orange, yellow, purple and green sapphires.

"But I don't see any red." Liz leaned closer to the case.

"When sapphires are red, we call them rubies." As Kim started to explain the chemical composition of sapphires and rubies, Carole and Scott joined them.

"Lizzie, take your brother and sister to see the other diamonds," Carole said.

With a roll of her eyes, Liz thanked Kim for "the talk", gripped her siblings' hands and led them away.

"Wonderful little girl," Kim said.

Carole's eyes warmed. "She is, isn't she? Though she's been kind of cranky today."

"Oh, I think she just wants time alone with Grandma," Kim said.

But instead of accepting Kim's comment as a compliment, Carole stiffened. "I'm a good grandmother!"

"Of course you are." Kim's fingers clenched, but she kept her voice light. "That was a compliment."

Carole sniffed and turned to Scott. "We probably have three minutes before they get bored."

Kim took a step back. Best to let Scott handle the prickly woman.

Scott flashed his half smile and when he spoke his voice was gentle. "I know you and Uncle Jim were close."

The muscles in Carole's face softened and for a moment Kim could see the resemblance to Liz.

"I wondered if Jim told you about us." Her smile was wistful. "Such a cliché, isn't it? Boss and secretary?"

Ah, so they were romantically involved.

Scott didn't miss a beat. "You had nothing to hide," he said. "You were both consenting adults and neither of you was married."

Kim studied Scott as he expertly coaxed the story from Carole. He started by asking easy questions, relaxing the woman before leading her into the more important topics. His body language was perfect for interviewing: His warm eyes focused on Carole's face, the corners of his mouth slightly tipped upward and he occasionally nodded.

Carole responded by leaning towards him, arms at her side, open and accepting. Every time she mentioned Jim's name, her right hand touched the small, heart-shaped pendant around her neck. Looked like white gold. In the center of the heart, a brilliant-cut blue stone -- maybe three mm in size -- caught the light.

Kim squinted, trying to get a better view of the stone. The color resembled the diamond Grandpa gave her. Her breath caught. Another diamond? Was this further proof Jim had discovered a Colorado diamond field?

She tuned back in as Scott brought the conversation around to the important topics.

"We're trying to trace Uncle Jim's movements for the past month."

Carole's shoulders stiffened, her hand closed over the pendant.

"I wouldn't know," Carole said. "We broke up six weeks ago."

"I'm really sorry to hear that. Uncle Jim spoke highly of you. Did he tell you about his trips to Colorado?"

Carole tugged at the pendant, jerking it back and forth. "Only that he was visiting a friend, going fishing."

"He didn't mention finding diamonds?"

The necklace twitched faster. "Diamonds? Why would Jim be interested in diamonds?" Carole snorted. "Don't forget he worked for decades trying to coat joints with the darn things. Should have been sick of diamonds."

"Nah, Uncle Jim loved challenges. Like when he tried to grow a diamond hip joint."

"Pie in the sky stuff." Carole's eyes darted left, then right.

Was the woman impatient? Or nervous?

Up ahead the children huddled around a display case. The little boy, however, cast anxious eyes their way. Better move this along before the children reclaimed Carole's attention. Maybe girl talk would calm her.

"Pretty necklace."

At Kim's words, Carole's hand stilled.

"Is it a blue diamond?" Kim produced her best please-the-customer smile. "My Grandpa is a jeweler."

"Diamond?" Carole's voice climbed an octave. "My goodness, whatever gave you that idea? How could I afford a diamond? On a secretary's salary?"

"I thought it might have been a gift," Kim said. "Looks like something a man might buy a favored lady?"

Carole didn't take the bait. "No, no, this is just an old CZ I found. I love diamonds, but . . ."

So much for girl talk. Kim hastened to reassure Carole that the pendant was lovely no matter what material it was made of.

"Yes, well . . ." Carole's eyes rested on her grandchildren. "If there's nothing else . . ."

Forget the small talk.

"Carole, we found the note you left Jim," Kim said. "The one where you quote from the Butch Cassidy movie."

"So?" Carole crossed her arms.

"So we were wondering what Uncle Jim was doing to make you worry for his safety." Scott leaned towards Carole, his face earnest.

"What makes you think I was worried?" Carole said.

Why are you answering questions with questions? But Kim didn't dare express the thought aloud; Carole was already defensive and antagonizing her further wouldn't help.

"That movie quote," Kim said. "It said you wouldn't watch him die. Then you broke up."

"Oh, for heaven's sake, that was just a movie quote. To settle an argument." Carole's face flushed and she again gripped her necklace. "We were, er, trying to list the best movie quotes, things other than, ah, 'Play it again, Sam.'" She twitched the necklace back and forth, back and forth.

Anger? Or embarrassment because she was lying?

"But, Carole," Scott said. "Uncle Jim did die." Though his voice was gentle, his eyes were hard. "Did he tell you he was being followed?"

"What?" Carole gulped.

"He called Max," Scott nodded in Kim's direction, "Kim's grandfather, and said he was being followed."

"And before he died, he told Grandpa to hide something," Kim said. "Hide what?"

For a moment, it looked like the barrage of questions would break through Carole's defenses. But then her mouth thinned and her throat muscles tightened.

"How should I know?" Carole lifted her chin. "I haven't talked to him in weeks."

Something flashed through the woman's eyes, too fast for Kim to identify. Then Carole turned towards Scott. "Jim just wasn't the same after the cancer returned."

"Cancer?" The color drained from Scott's face. "What cancer?"

CHAPTER 22

Kim picked at her fast-food lunch salad and studied Scott from under her lashes. His complexion had regained some of its color since Carole's seemingly off-hand reference to his uncle's cancer. But the hamburger Scott ordered was still wrapped in its greasy paper, the fries growing limp and soggy.

Darn that Carole. The woman knew Jim hadn't told his family he'd been diagnosed with cancer, that the revelation would render Scott speechless and end the questioning.

But that was the point, wasn't it?

During Scott's stunned silence, Carole had collected her grandchildren and hurried away. As they'd turned the corner, Liz had stopped to wave.

Kim wanted to snatch up the little girl and protect her from scheming grandmothers.

Instead, she'd ushered Scott from the museum, loaded him into the car's passenger side and settled behind the wheel. With Scott navigating, they made the white-knuckled trip out of the city and pulled into the first fast-food restaurant they found. The only words Scott spoke for the entire thirty minutes were variations of "turn here."

Kim bit into a morsel of iceberg lettuce. Problem was, she perfectly understood Scott's depression. She'd be devastated if she discovered Grandpa hadn't shared something as important as a cancer diagnosis.

Reaching across the table, she covered Scott's hand with her own. Though he continued to stare into the distance, his fingers tightened around hers. A minute passed, two. Finally, Scott's eyes met hers.

"Thank you." He squeezed her hand and released it.

"For what?"

"For not trying to cheer me up." He dragged fingers through his hair. "That was a real shock."

"Try not to be too hard on Jim," she said. "Cancer is one of those diseases that's hard to discuss. Heck, during the Victorian era, people considered it a disease caused by uncleanliness."

"Yeah, I know. It's just . . . the idea of Jim keeping it secret . . ."

"Yeah. I'd feel the same way if Grandpa did that." Kim pushed her salad away.

Scott snorted. "On second thought, maybe you should try to cheer me."

Kim's shoulders relaxed. Jokes were good.

"You do realize Carole is hiding something." She sipped her diet cola.

Scott nodded. "I'm sorry I screwed up the questioning."

"We probably pushed her as far as we could today." She shrugged. "Besides whatever she's hiding might have nothing to do with the attacks. But you've got her contact information, so we can tackle her later? Good." She reached into her purse and pulled out a stenography pad and pen. Flipping the notebook open, she ticked off "Question Carole" on her "To-Do" list. After a moment's hesitated, she added "re-question Carole" to the bottom of the list.

"You want to call it a day or," Kim waved the notebook, "continue through the list?"

"Action would be nice."

Kim nodded, scanned the list and reached for her cell phone. "Let's see if Aunt Ginny had any luck tracking down that license plate."

Her aunt picked up on the first ring. "Car's registered to a private investigator named Decker Cunningham" she said.

Kim's heart sank. She'd hoped identifying the person who followed Jim would answer questions, not raise new ones. A regular person might be willing to talk; a private investigator, however . . .

Sighing, she gripped her pen. "Better give me the information." The car was registered to the detective's business, which was located in Greenbelt, one of the commuter communities just north of the Washington Beltway. Maybe forty minutes north of their current location.

Was there any way to trick the detective into revealing who'd hired him to follow Jim? Maybe Scott would have some ideas.

"How are things at the store?" Through the phone, she could hear the distinctive shushing of the refrigerator. "And where are you?"

"Upstairs making lunch."

"You left Doris downstairs alone?" Kim's pulse quickened.

"It's broad daylight and there's plenty of people around. We've been getting lots of tourists."

"Is Rory with her?"

"No, he was too much to handle. Kept trying to help. I trapped him in your bedroom."

Kim frowned. Rory couldn't protect the ladies if he was locked upstairs. "Please, Aunt Ginny, try to stick together. After last night ..."

"We'll be fine." Ginny hung up before Kim could respond.

Sighing, Kim closed her phone. She'd just have to trust her aunt's judgment.

Turning to Scott, she said, "Got any idea why someone would hire a detective to follow Jim?"

For a moment, Scott stared at her. Then his face closed and he stood. "Let's go ask him."

"He must be a lousy detective." Kim stood across the street from Cunningham's building, frowning at the neighborhood of run-down warehouses, apartments and office buildings. Not a single tree softened the expanse of gray. The mid-day sun illuminated every sidewalk crack, every broken streetlight, every squashed cigarette butt. The still, heavy air smelled of dirty socks and burned cabbage.

"Probably looking for a Sam Spade aura." Scott nodded towards the black BMW parked in front of the address Aunt Ginny had given them. "Looks like he's in."

Kim bit her lip, trying to calm the butterflies doing a conga in her stomach. On the drive here, she'd proposed and discarded one plan after another.

Theoretically, they should be able to wrestle information from Decker Cunningham. Ten years as a reporter gave Scott skill in quizzing the most recalcitrant subject. Kim's extensive coursework in body language enabled her to detect lies and evasions. Together the two should make a formidable team.

Even so, a professional investigator would have no reason to share information with them. They had no legal authority and, in any event, the detective was bound by some sort of code to protect the name of the person who hired him. Or, at least, that's the way PIs behaved in the mysteries she read.

But even if Cunningham wouldn't reveal the person who hired him, perhaps he'd share surveillance results. Knowing Jim's movements just before his death might reveal a clue to the person behind the attacks. Plus there'd be photos, maybe with Rat Man in the background skulking Jim.

This was assuming, of course, that Decker Cunningham had no connection to the two Baltimore hit men.

Therein lay the problem. If Cunningham was an honest investigator and innocent bystander, he might be willing to share information. However, if he was one of those sleazy PIs after a quick buck no matter what . . .

Kim kicked at a stray fast-food box. Decker Cunningham's decision to keep an office in this neighborhood did not bode well. Surely, if the man was good in his profession and actually earning a living, he'd move to a better location.

On the other hand, the BMW Cunningham drove glistened in the afternoon sun. Maybe Scott was right and the detective was intentionally channeling Sam Spade. She wouldn't know until she met the man.

She mentally reviewed the plan. Scott would interview Cunningham while she tried to read the man's body language. If she saw something indicating the need to change directions, she'd communicate to Scott via a series of signals. Her first goal would be to determine their overall approach: honesty or bribery.

She had one shot to get it right.

"Ready, babe?" Scott spoke from the side of his mouth.

Not the best Humphrey Bogart impersonation, but the attempt changed the butterfly conga to a waltz.

"Lead on, Macduff."

The front door opened into a narrow hall that smelled of dust, mold and urine. No sign of an elevator. A row of mailboxes indicated the detective's office was in 302. Three flights of stairs and a long, dingy hallway brought them to the man's door.

For a moment, Kim thought she'd stepped into a black-and-white movie. The overhead light barely illuminated the gray carpet, gray desk, gray man. Decker Cunningham perched in a thread-bare office chair, his back to them, staring out the window to the street below. To the right, a half-open door revealed an unmade single bed.

"Well, look again."

She jumped at the detective's words. The chair squeaked as he swiveled to face them. A cell phone pressed to his ear shattered the 1940s movie illusion.

Kim studied Cunningham. The detective was wiry and, unless he had long legs, probably only a few inches taller than her. Dark hair, dark eyes, the perfect nondescript investigator. The upward thrust of his chin and rigid shoulders, however, screamed banty rooster.

As he listened to whoever was on the phone, Cunningham's eyes roamed from her face to her toes and back up again, a slow climb that seemed to strip off each article of clothing. Kim's hands clenched and she resisted the urge to bash him with her purse. The man's knowing smirk indicated he'd correctly read her expression.

His eyes flicked to Scott. The two men stared at one another, assessing. Had they been in a jungle, they'd probably start thumping their chests. Cunningham clearly was the type to pick a fight with the largest guy in the bar.

At least the detective showed no sign of recognizing Scott. He may have followed Jim, but he'd clearly never seen Jim's nephew.

Cunningham broke the tension by waving towards two hard metal chairs.

Kim perched on the edge of the chair and, without hesitation, set her purse in her lap -- the sign to Scott to use the bribery approach. This detective was no amiable Archie Goodwin.

"Just get it done." Cunningham punched the phone off and tossed it on the desk. "Now, what brings you here?"

His voice was a low baritone, surprising for someone his size.

"My sources tell me you were recently hired to follow my uncle." Scott matched Cunningham's emotionless tone.

The detective shrugged. "Surveillance is one of the services I offer." He smirked, crossed his arms and leaned back. "You gotta know I can't tell you anything about the people who hire me. Gotta protect my client's interests."

"I understand." Scott pulled out his wallet, opened it and allowed Cunningham to see the wad of cash inside.

The detective's eyes widened.

"I don't need the client's name," Scott said. "But I'd like to buy the report you wrote."

"Why?"

"Does it matter?"

The two men stared at each other, the detective suspicious, Scott seemingly nonchalant. Kim, however, could see the muscle strain in Scott's jaw as he feigned casual interest.

The detective tried to copy Scott's cool. But he couldn't stop his eyes from flicking to the wallet and back to Scott's face. Kim gave it a minute before coughing a single time, the signal that their fish was hooked.

Scott shrugged, closed his wallet and began to tuck it into a pants pocket.

"Wait a minute, let's not be hasty." Cunningham dropped his arms. "How much is this report worth to you?"

"Couple hundred."

The detective's eyes narrowed. Kim could see the calculation run through his brain.

Cunningham forced a laugh. "Sheeet, I get that per hour. Surveillance ain't cheap, you know. You're probably talking a week's worth of work."

"Yeah, but you've already done the work, haven't you?" Scott said. "So this is just a little something extra. Your client will never know."

"Yeah, but two hundred bucks ain't much."

Kim stared at Cunningham, but the man had gotten his outward emotions under control. He sat stone-faced, hands clenched on the desk.

"I can go another fifty," Scott said.

Cunningham snorted. "Peanuts."

The man held his body so still she couldn't get a read on him. Darn it, if he made Scott bid against himself, Scott could lose the entire five hundred dollars they'd extracted from the ATM machine.

Unzipping her purse, she reached inside for a tissue. As she pulled it from a pocket, she dropped the bag onto the floor. Tissue, wallet, dog clicker, hairbrush, dog treats splattered.

Both men jumped.

"No, I'll get it." Kim waved away Scott's help and kneeled on the dirty carpet. From here, she could peer under the desk.

"So what would you consider your report worth?"

Good, Scott recognized the danger of continuing to up his offer.

Keeping an eye on Cunningham's feet, she slowly collected her stuff.

"Thousand would be a good start." Cunningham's feet started twitching, bouncing up and down furiously.

Kim coughed twice, telling Scott the man was lying, naming a pie in the sky figure.

Now it was Scott's turn to laugh. "Can't imagine a simple surveillance report would be worth even half that."

Cunningham's feet stilled. They could get the report for five hundred. But surely she hadn't misinterpreted the detective's interest when Scott mentioned two hundred.

She slipped the last of her belongings into her purse, but stayed on the floor.

"So what would you think it's worth?" the detective's voice oozed.

Don't do it, Scott. Don't bid against yourself.

"I wouldn't think the report would be worth more than three hundred," Scott said.

"Not enough." Cunningham's feet twitched wildly. He was lying again.

Time to put a stop to this.

Kim stood, sweeping her purse onto her shoulder. "C'mon, honey. This guy has no intention of helping us. Probably because he knows his surveillance reports are nothing but crap."

"Hey!" Cunningham rose, poker face now flushed. "My clients praise my reports."

"Yeah?" Kim lifted her chin. "Prove it."

The detective glared at her, shoulders so tense he had no neck. Kim retained eye contact, knowing if she glanced away, she'd not only lose but the beast might attack. This was one man who didn't tolerate a woman questioning his masculinity. Beside her, Scott stood.

Cunningham's eyes flicked to Scott, back to Kim. Finally, he sighed.

"Okay, you win," he said. "Three hundred it is."

They probably could have it for two, but Kim didn't want to press her luck.

The detective crossed to a four-drawer file cabinet. "What's your uncle's name?"

"Jim Hampton."

Cunningham froze. Then a hand smashed the cabinet. The detective wheeled around. Kim jumped backwards, her ears still ringing from the crash of fist on metal. Her knees connected with a chair.

Red-faced, breaths fast and shallow, Cunningham planted his feet and fixed them with a menacing glare. "Do you think I'm stupid?"

He clenched his fists. The muscles in his arms bulged. He took a step towards them. "Get out."

She felt a hand touch her shoulder, swivel her towards the open door. A slight push got her feet moving. She didn't need a second prompt.

As she rushed through the door, she glanced back over her shoulder. Cunningham shook a fist at her and growled "You haven't heard the last of this."

Wordlessly, they ran to the car, Scott keying the doors to unlock as they neared. Kim dove for the passenger seat, slammed the door shut and locked it. Their tires squealed as they pulled from the curb. Kim turned to stare behind them. The street remained empty.

But her pounding heart didn't slow until they turned onto Rt. 201 and headed south, blending into the slow-moving traffic.

"I hope he didn't get your license number," she said.

Before replying, Scott loosened his death grip on the steering wheel. "If he's any kind of detective, he shouldn't have trouble finding Jim Hampton's only nephew. Let's just hope he doesn't figure out your connection."

Kim silently cursed. They should have disguised Scott's relationship to Jim. But, darn it, if Cunningham had been an Elvis Cole type detective, the family relationship would have cemented his instinct to help them. Instead, they'd left tracks any fool could follow.

She should call the police, tell them Cunningham had threatened them. But then she'd have to reveal how she'd figured out the detective was following Jim.

Did they actually arrest people for using inside sources to track license plates?

Better not chance it. Besides, what could the police do? Cunningham hadn't actually assaulted them. If she'd learned nothing else in the last few days, she'd learned the limitations of the police.

The sight of a drive-through restaurant triggered awareness of her parched tongue. Scott pulled into line behind a van loaded with bouncing children.

"I hope you don't want to call it a day yet," she said. "I need to do something positive to remove the image of Cunningham."

Scott nodded. "I brought Uncle Jim's address book and phone bills. Figured we could track down the friend he visited in Colorado."

Kim glanced at the car's clock. Just after three. Which meant in Colorado, it'd be . . . what? One o'clock? Noon? Probably not a good idea to disturb someone at lunch time.

"Let's make the calls from Grandpa's. That way we can put the call on speaker phone." Kim pulled her to-do list from her purse, skimmed it and grimaced when she read apologize to Amber. Probably best to do that in person.

"On the way home, I'd like to swing by my cousin's apartment. Shouldn't take more than a couple of minutes." Assuming Amber even opened the door.

In front of them, the van with the children finally pulled away from the order speaker. Kim's stomach growled, reminding her of the uneaten salad. Screw health; she needed carbs.

Scott leaned towards the window to order their drinks.

"Uh, add a hamburger and fries to that." At least the cola was diet.

Scott added two hamburgers and fries to the order.

"Nothing like a little fear to stir the appetite," he said, waving away the money she held out and passing a twenty to the cashier. Accepting his change, he pulled forward. "By the way, you still owe me the opportunity to take you to dinner. This doesn't count."

Kim's feet tapped a happy dance in time with the bouncing children in the car ahead. Oops. She willed her feet to stop.

"I think on the way to Max's we'll pass the pet store where Uncle Jim buys Al's food," Scott said. "I'm almost out. And maybe, while we're there, you can help me pick out a new collar."

She grinned. "Something with studs on it instead of rhinestones? We'll need to bring Al with us to fit him."

"That'll take us out of our way. I live in Davidsonville."

Hmmm . . . Davidsonville was a sleepy farm community just outside of Annapolis. Quite a ways from the university where Scott taught.

Where she and Scott taught. A thrill coursed through her. With the packing, dealing with movers, travel cross-country and attacks on Grandpa, she hadn't had a chance to celebrate her new job. That'd been something she'd intended to do with Grandpa.

Maybe once they identified the man who attacked him, life would go back to normal. Grandpa would recover and the three of them could go to dinner to celebrate the University of Maryland's newest associate professor of psychology.

In the meantime, however, it'd be interesting to see where Scott lived. "I don't mind making a side trip if you don't."

When Scott concurred, she pulled a Maryland map from the door pocket and traced the most efficient route back to Grandpa's: First collect Al. Cut back to Rt. 301. Visit the pet store. Continue south to Amber's apartment building.

She accepted the diet cola from Scott and took a deep sip. Reaching for a fry, she realized the side trip for Al had an additional benefit: It postponed what might be another confrontation with Amber.

CHAPTER 23

Forty minutes later, as the car neared Davidsonville, they wove through gently rolling hills. Kim opened her window and inhaled the spicy-sweet aroma of wild honeysuckle. Goldfinches flitted among the black-eyed Susans that dotted the roadside. In the distance, a homeowner puttered on his lawn tractor. You'd never know Annapolis was only a few miles east.

She turned to Scott. "This is lovely. But isn't it a long commute to University Park?"

Scott shrugged. "I'm not much of a city boy. The university is only forty minutes away and, aside from faculty meetings, I only have to go in twice a week. It'd probably be too much if I had to commute daily. But this way I get the intellectual stimulation from the college community, plus the peace and quiet of the country."

"Huh." The drive from Osprey Beach to University Park was sixty minutes, not forty. Like Scott, however, she'd be teaching only two days a week. If she could schedule those days to coincide with faculty meetings . . . Maybe Grandpa wasn't so off base when he'd suggested she move in with him.

Of course, if she actually lived with him, he'd try to suck her into the store. No way would she let that happen. She'd been on her own for ten years; best to keep it that way.

Scott turned into a long, winding driveway and pulled up in front of a small, cottage-style farmhouse. Now this was something she could enjoy. The house's white siding and green shutters gave it a fairytale quality. Mature azaleas lined the foundation while the wide-spreading branches of a white oak shaded the gray shingle roof.

"I'm hoping the owners will sell me the place when I get a down payment together," Scott said, opening his car door.

Kim pushed back a flash of envy and climbed out. She could never afford a place in upscale Davidsonville, even if she got the asking price for her Oregon house.

"In case you're wondering, Uncle Jim left his house and everything to me." Scott climbed the front porch steps. "Once I sell Jim's house, this won't be as far out of my range as it used to be." He opened the front door and looked back over his shoulder. "Coming in?"

Go into an empty house with a disarmingly attractive man? Not if she wanted to get any work done this afternoon. "Uh, no, I'll just wait out here." Coward.

Scott's crooked grin told her he knew exactly why she'd chosen to remain outdoors.

Feigning nonchalance, she turned and buried her nose in a blooming rose. The fruity tea scent filled her nostrils. She heard the front door open and close. Lifting her head, she glanced towards the house. The porch was empty.

With a sigh, she cupped a pink rosebud and stroked its velvety petals. What she really wanted to do was stroke Scott's face, run fingers through his hair, find out how his lips tasted. But after a series of disastrous relationships, the thought of acting on her instincts terrified her.

Scott was so very different from the other men she'd dated. While the other men had been intelligent like Scott, they'd possessed that devil-may-care attitude that attracted her to Jason in high school. Bad boys may make good heroes in the mysteries she read, but their irresponsibility ultimately grew tiresome.

Once Kim had identified the self-destructive pattern in her dating habits, she'd sworn off men for a while and thrown herself into work. The job offer in Maryland made it easy to keep distance from the Oregon men who came courting.

So why was she even attracted to Scott? Until she answered that question, she didn't dare act on her feelings.

She turned towards the car. A rose thorn snagged her t-shirt. She gently disentangled it. After the role Grandpa's roses played in last night's escape, she'd never complain about thorns again.

The cottage door opened and Scott emerged with a bouncing Al straining at the end of a six-foot leash.

Kim bent to pet the enthusiastic dachshund. He reared onto his hind legs, begging her to lift him. Smiling, she scooped him up and carried him to the car.

The pet store where Jim bought Al's food was a family owned affair tucked at the end of a small strip mall that included a nail parlor, Starbucks and bait store.

"How did Jim ever find this place?" A blast of heat hit Kim in the face as she opened the car door.

"One of the best bait stores around. In his heart of hearts, he was an incurable fisherman." Scott took the end of Al's leash. "Plus there's coffee."

They crossed to the sidewalk and Kim fell into step with Scott. Al plunged ahead, pulling on the leash so hard his throat made hacking noises.

"Stop. I can't stand it." Kim dug through her purse until she found the clicker and dog treats she always carried. Grabbing Scott's hand, she turned it over and slapped clicker and treats into it. "Time to train this dog."

"What's this?" Scott examined the small, plastic rectangular box.

"Dog training tool. See that metal strip in the middle? When you press it, it makes a clicking sound."

Al wheeled around, clearly wondering about the strange noise. Kim gave him a treat.

"The clicker marks the behavior that you want. Now, whenever Al's leash is loose, you click and when he turns, give him a treat."

"Sort of like Pavlov, huh?"

"More like Skinner, but, yeah, same idea."

They started walking again, but Scott's big thumb hit the clicker just as Al slammed against the end of the leash.

"Uh, you just rewarded him for pulling. Here, give me that thing. You keep the treats, give him one whenever I click."

Despite her scolding, Kim admitted the timing was tricky. Every time they took a step, Al charged ahead, giving her only a few seconds before the leash tightened.

But dachshunds were known for both their feral intelligence and their obsession with food. After only two trips up and down the sidewalk, Al figured out staying close to Scott produced a click and treat. They could finally walk into the store without the little dog choking himself.

Kim passed the clicker to Scott and watched to make sure he used it correctly. "Keep it," she said. "I need to get one with a wrist band, anyway."

"Wrist band?"

"Kind of like a bracelet with a clicker attached. Makes it easier to find when I need it. Maybe they've got one here."

First, however, came the collar selection. Kim laughed when she saw dachshund-sized collars with macho studs protruding.

"I had no idea they made these things so tiny," she said.

"That's almost as bad as the rhinestones," Scott said.

As she opened her mouth to reply, Al slipped his head from the offending collar and dashed down the aisle.

"Al, come!"

The little dog ignored Scott's call, careening around a corner. Scott set off in pursuit. Figuring they'd trap the dog between them, Kim trotted the opposite way, turning into the neighboring aisle at the same time as Scott. She slammed to a stop.

A plump, middle-aged woman stood by the squeaky toys, cuddling Al like a baby and crooning nonsense to him. Her eyes lifted to Scott's, traveled to the leash he still carried and the empty collar at the end. Her mouth spread into a huge smile.

"This is Cuddles!" she said. "I mean Almas." She stepped towards Scott, right arm extended. "You must be Mr. Hampton's nephew. I'm Tricia Gershman. Owner of this store."

Scott shook her hand. "Scott Wilson. And, yeah, I'm Jim's nephew." He waved Kim over and introduced her. "Uh, how do you know Al?"

Mrs. Gershman kissed the dog's muzzle. "Oh, we're old friends, aren't we, fella? Al's original owner died when this little guy was only a year old. Of course, he was named Cuddles then. Anyway, no one in the owner's family could take Al, so they brought him here." She swept her hand to encompass the squeaky toys and rawhides, the fish tanks along the wall, the display of dog treats. "As you can see, I don't sell puppies. Occasionally, though, I will try to place a pet for someone."

Scott frowned. "So how did Uncle Jim end up with him?"

Mrs. Gershman beamed. "Oh, it was the most amazing thing, almost like it was fated. Mr. Hampton was passing by on the way to the bait shop when he spotted our new display of dog collars. That one . . ." She pointed at the rhinestone collar Scott now held. "He said that collar was

identical to the one worn by the dog he grew up
with."

"Huh. I didn't know Uncle Jim ever had a dog."

"Oh my, yes. I forget the dog's name, but your
poor uncle was devastated when it was run over by
a car. He said he kept the dog collar for years, but
lost it somewhere along the way.

"Well, as we were talking, Al here was batting at
Mr. Hampton's leg. I couldn't resist scooping him
up and trying on the collar. It was a perfect fit. Mr.
Hampton bought both right on the spot."

Scott's mouth hung open. Kim, however, had no
problem finding words.

"That has got to be the weirdest dog-buying story
I've heard," Kim said. "And believe me, I've heard
many."

Mrs. Gershman turned to her. "Oh, but don't you
see? The timing couldn't have been more perfect. Al
needed a home. The sight of the collar reminded
Mr. Hampton of his childhood friend and viola`
instant harmony."

Kim resisted the urge to roll her eyes. She should
introduce this woman to Aunt Sapphire.

Naturally, Mrs. Gershman asked about Jim.
While Scott recounted the story of his uncle's death,
Kim extracted Al from Mrs. Gershman's arms and
returned to the collar display. Selecting a bright red
one, she slipped it over Al's head. Perfect fit.

She looked up as Scott approached, his mouth set
in a grim line.

"Must be awful having to explain Jim's death over and over." She gently took the leash, removed the rhinestone collar and clipped the leash to Al's new collar.

Scott offered a rueful smile. "At least Mrs. Gershman was happy to hear Uncle Jim's final words were 'Al.'"

Kim shook her head. She definitely needed to introduce the woman to Aunt Sapphire.

"Why did she originally call him Almas?"

Scott rolled his eyes. "Uncle Jim didn't think Al was a grandiose enough name for him. So he went looking on the internet."

"But why Almas? Why not Albert or Alfred or . . ." She stopped, unable to think of another name.

"He wouldn't answer that question. So I looked up Almas on the web. It's another name for Bigfoot." Scott tickled Al's feet. "When I told Uncle Jim what I found, he just laughed."

Kim lifted a paw. Well, yeah, it was large compared to the length of his legs. Probably because dachshunds were bred to dig.

Still, it seemed insulting to name the poor fellow Bigfoot.

She kissed Al's nose. "I like your feet." Setting Al on the floor, she held out the rhinestone collar. "Maybe your mom or your aunt would want this."

His eyes crinkled with the first real smile she'd seen since Jim's secretary dropped her bombshell. "I've got a better idea." Taking the collar, he unbuckled it and gently re-buckled it over Kim's left wrist.

Though large, the collar was surprisingly comfortable. As she turned her wrist, the blue, red, yellow and green rhinestones caught the light. Her aunts would freak if they saw it. All the more reason to wear it.

Besides, if she got tired of it, it would probably fit Fluffy.

They separated to finish their shopping. Kim found an enormous, American made rawhide for Rory, a seatbelt to fit Al and a box of Rory's favorite cookies. When they left the store, a new clicker dangled from her right wrist -- another gift from Scott.

As she climbed into the car, she realized for the first time that day, her shoulders weren't tense. Maybe now was the time to tackle Amber.

The drive from the pet store to Amber's new apartment took only fifteen minutes. While dreading the inevitable confrontation with her cousin, Kim looked forward to seeing the luxury apartment complex that had caused a rift in the family.

A few years earlier, Amber the rebel had terrorized her parents by leaving Annapolis and moving to the notoriously crime-ridden Prince

Georges County. That Amber's apartment was located in upscale Bowie with access blocked by high fencing and gates did little to reassure Aunt Sapphire. During the ensuing family uproar, Kim was grateful to be living in Oregon, twenty-eight hundred miles away.

Now, however, she wished Amber's apartment wasn't quite so protected. If she could simply appear on Amber's doorstep, confronted her face-to-face, her cousin might be willing to talk. The security added one more barrier between them. As Scott pushed the intercom button, she wondered if Amber would even open the gate.

"Hello, hello?"

Kim's mouth dropped open. Leaning across Scott, she yelled "Tiffany? What are you doing here?"

"You better come in." Tiffany's normal bouncy voice sounded flat and grim.

The gates swung open. Remembering Grandpa's description of the place, Kim directed Scott to the right, past the swimming pool and tennis court to the row of apartments facing a park-like square. Scott pulled into a spot marked "visitor."

Kim breathed deeply. "I guess I'd better do this alone."

"Good luck."

With a nod, Kim climbed from the car. Her glasses immediately fogged. Peering through the mist, she made her way into the building -- where the frigid temperature created a new layer of mist on her glasses. She stumbled into the elevator and pressed "three."

By the time she arrived at Amber's open door, Kim's glasses had cleared and she could see Tiffany's pursed lips and furrowed brow.

"She's not happy with you." Tiffany turned and led the way into a combination dining/living room. To the right, a half-wall revealed a galley kitchen. The hallway to the left led to three closed doors.

Sunlight streaming through sliding glass doors illuminated Amber hunched on one end of a blue couch. With her legs curled under her and bowed head, red-brown hair hid Amber's face.

As Kim approached, Amber lifted her head. Kim froze mid-stride. Amber was holding something to her eye . . . something . . .

"A pork chop?"

Tiffany shrugged. "She didn't have steak in the freezer."

Kim rushed to Amber's side. Pulling her cousin's hand from her face, she gawked at the swelling, blackening eye.

Amber wrenched her hand from Kim's grasp, slapped the chop back onto her eye and again leaned over to stare at the floor.

Kneeling in front of her cousin, Kim opened her mouth, closed it, her mind racing through all of the battered-spouse approaches taught in her psychology classes. But those were theoretical scenarios. This was real.

"Who did this to you?" She'd attempted a gentle voice, but couldn't mask her anger.

Amber's head shot up, her good eye glaring. "You."

Kim jerked back onto her heels. For a moment, she couldn't breathe.

Amber's eyes filled with tears. "You told me to ask Darin if he told anyone about Grandpa's New York trips." She waved a shaking hand at her face. "This is his response."

"Did you call the police?"

The tears dried up and Amber aimed another glare at her. "I called Tiff."

Kim looked up at Tiffany. "Did you call the police?"

"She wouldn't let me," Tiffany said. "I was about to call you."

Oh, great. She was back in Maryland for less than a week and already her younger cousins were relying on her to straighten their messes.

Knowing it was futile, she asked the question anyway. "Do you want me to call the police?"

Amber grabbed Kim's hand. "No! Please, Kim, it'll just make it worse."

"Worse than being someone's punching bag?" Even as the words left her mouth, Kim grimaced. That wasn't in the psychology rule books.

Releasing her hand, Amber flopped back onto the sofa. "You don't understand. He's never done this before."

Kim glanced at Tiffany, who shrugged and looked away. If Amber was lying, Tiffany wouldn't betray her. The two had always been partners in crime.

Kim assessed her options. First step was to keep Amber safe. She glanced around the living room, searching for the telltale signs of a resident male primate: dirty socks, recliner with multiple television controls, little mounds of coins removed from pants pockets. But the room was as pristine as Amber's former Annapolis apartment.

"Does Darin live here?"

Amber shook her head. Good. One obstacle she didn't have to hurdle. And maybe Amber was telling the truth when she said Darin never hit her before.

"Does he have a key?"

"Yeah," Amber muttered.

"We need to get the locks changed." Kim studied Amber. "Unless you're planning to let him back in."

"I'm not a masochist," Amber said.

Kim released the breath she'd been holding. "You have an apartment manger here, right? Where do you keep the number?" Surely the apartment complex employed locksmiths. If not, the manager could recommend someone.

As Kim reached for the phone, Tiffany sat beside Amber and pulled her close. "See, I told you Kim would know what to do."

The manager did, indeed, have a locksmith on call. After Kim explained the urgency, he promised to send someone immediately.

Hanging up, Kim perched on the chair across from her cousins. "They're sending someone over. Tiff, can you stay until the man arrives?"

Tiffany nodded. Taking a deep breath, Kim continued. "Amber, I thought you said you didn't tell anyone about Grandpa's New York trips."

"I lied." Amber met Kim's eyes. "But Darin would never hurt Grandpa."

Any man who'd hit a woman wouldn't hesitate to stab an old man. But Darin's arms were free of Rory's teeth marks. Darin wasn't the man who'd attacked Grandpa.

Of course, Darin's friends might be more violent than Darin himself.

"Has Darin ever mentioned an Alan Miles or Frankie Roberts?" Kim said.

"Wasn't Frankie Roberts one of Mom's favorite singers?" Tiffany said.

Amber rolled her eyes. "That was Frankie Avalon, silly." She turned to Kim. "And, no, he never mentioned those guys."

Thank goodness for small favors. "Have you told any other boyfriends about what Grandpa carries in his briefcase?" As she asked the question, Kim studied her cousin, looking for signs of lying or discomfort.

Amber bit her lip, looked away, inhaled deeply, finally met Kim's eyes. "I might have told Bobby. And Michael. And maybe George. But they'd never hurt Grandpa. Would they?"

Kim leaped to her feet. "You told four of your thug friends?" All of the worry and fears of the last few days came rushing back. "Don't you understand that every time you tell someone Grandpa's carrying jewels, you put his life in danger? Someone wanted that damn briefcase bad enough to kill for it, bad enough to attack Grandpa in the hospital . . ."

Her cousins gasped and their eyes widened, reminding Kim they knew nothing about the fake doctor. But she couldn't stop to inform them now because the image of Grandpa in the hospital swam to the surface, Grandpa attached to all of those machines, Grandpa pale and helpless.

Tears streaming down her face, she snatched her purse and stormed outside. Behind her, Tiffany's voice begged her to return. But Kim had had enough. Too impatient to wait for the elevator, she charged down the stairs, marched across the lobby and pushed outside.

Where her glasses immediately misted over. Tears of frustration blinded her. She groped for a wall, leaned against it and sobbed.

Strong arms enveloped her and she smelled the Irish Spring soap Scott used.

"I'm gonna kill her, I'm gonna kill her." Her hand gripped Scott's shirt in a fist.

Scott stroked her back. "You've been through a lot in the past few days."

"Give me a minute." Pushing away, Kim dug in her purse, searching for something to clean her glasses.

Something soft pressed into her hand. She looked down at the white handkerchief.

"Thanks." She scrubbed at the glasses, returned them to her nose, then held out the handkerchief.

"Can you walk?" Scott tucked the cloth into a pocket. "I left the air on for Al, but we'd better get back." He grinned. "No telling what he's getting into."

Kim accepted the arm he offered, but her body still trembled. The anger started to recede, replaced by guilt.

They returned to the car in silence. Al greeted her with a joyful yip and face washing. Grateful for the little dog's warmth, she lifted him into her lap.

Scott pulled onto Route 301 and headed south. At the first stoplight, he gave her his half smile. "I take it that didn't go real well."

Kim actually laughed. "Yeah, you could say that."

She filled him in, concluding "I'd like to tell Brockley, get him to ask Amber for a list of old boyfriends who knew about Grandpa. Problem is, I don't want to put her into further danger. Imagine how Darin would act if Brockley showed up at his door. And the others might be just as bad."

The light turned green. After a few blocks, Scott said, "How long ago were the other boyfriends?"

"Oh, Amber switches boyfriends every six months or so. But I see what you're getting at; it doesn't make sense for any of the old boyfriends to wait until now to rob Grandpa. Darin's the one who worries me. He knows where she lives."

"Wouldn't be hard to find out where you're staying, either."

Kim shivered. Surely there must be a way to reveal Darin's potential involvement without jeopardizing Amber. Or herself.

Her cell phone rang. Aunt Ginny. Kim flipped the phone open. "Everything okay?"

"We're fine" Aunt Ginny said. "How soon will you be home?"

"Why?"

"A Lieutenant Brockley just arrived. And he doesn't look happy."

CHAPTER 24

The evening rush hour delayed their trip south and by the time they arrived back in Osprey Beach, there was no sign of Lieutenant Brockley.

Just as well, Kim thought as she tossed her purse and packages onto the kitchen table. She still didn't know if she should tell Brockley about Amber's boyfriends.

Besides, judging by Rory's enthusiastic greeting of Al, she was going to need half her brain to keep the two young dogs from tearing around Grandpa's house. The new collar prevented Al from slipping his leash, but didn't stop him from batting his big paws at Rory's muzzle. Rory backed up, sending a kitchen chair sliding across the floor.

"Better keep him on leash until they settle down," she told Scott. "Aunt Ginny, we have company!" From the living room came the television noise of the evening news.

Reaching into the bag, she pulled out the new toy she'd bought for Rory. She removed the tags, held the yellow duck out and squeezed.

"Quack-quack-quack-quack-quack-quack."

Rory abandoned Al, ran to Kim and waved his paw, leaped into the air, spun in a circle and finally sat. Kim tossed him the toy, then headed for the refrigerator. Rory gripped the duck and pranced around the kitchen, his head up, tail wagging furiously.

"You spoil that dog," Aunt Ginny said from the doorway.

"What happened to Lieutenant Brockley?" Kim poured two glasses of iced tea, handed one to Scott and downed half of hers in a single gulp.

"Got called out on another case. Said he'd catch you later."

"Wanna help go through Jim's phone book, look for Colorado area codes?" Kim refilled her glass. "We're trying to figure out who he visited."

Aunt Ginny grinned and lead the way back into the living. Scott settled in a chair across from Ginny and began arranging Jim's phone bills and address book on the coffee table. Al watched for a moment before curling onto Scott's lap.

Kim crossed to the television, prepared to turn it off.

As she reached for the remote, the blond anchor said "And in local news, two people were arrested when an orderly protest outside of an esteemed Annapolis jewelry store turned into a brawl between two senior citizens. Monica Sherman has more."

Kim's hand froze as the reporter's face disappeared and a video began to play. She recognized the facade of Jason's family's Annapolis store.

On the sidewalk out front, an elderly woman, dolled up in an expensive-looking dress, matching wide-brimmed hat and pumps, pushed flyers at people walking by. The camera zoomed in to a face Kim recognized.

"That's Mrs. Johnstone." Kim flopped onto the couch. "Grandpa's best customer," she added for Scott's benefit.

Ginny leaned forward. "Isn't that the woman who asked you to appraise a diamond ring?"

"Not appraise. She wanted me to look for flaws . . ."

Kim broke off as a photo appeared on the screen. In bright red letters, the flyer's headline proclaimed "White Family Jewelers Deceive Customers."

"Mrs. Johnstone was distributing this flyer to passersby," the anchor's voice said. "She claims the store uses deceptive -- but legal -- sales tactics."

The view switched to Mrs. Johnstone being interviewed by a twenty-something, brown-haired woman.

"Mrs. Johnstone," the reporter said, "why are you here today?"

"A week ago, Alex White sold my niece and her finance a diamond engagement ring." Mrs. Johnstone's chin lifted. "He didn't tell them about the numerous inclusions any idiot could see through a loupe."

The reporter widened her eyes. "Isn't that illegal?"

"Darlene and Jeffrey were so overcome with the romance of it all, they never asked about inclusions, never looked at the diamond's grading report, never looked through a loupe. So, illegal, no. Immoral, yes."

The reporter tapped the stack of flyers Mrs. Johnstone held. "But you've got a list of questionable items here."

Nodding, Mrs. Johnstone held up an open ring box. "A few days ago, Alex White sold me this ring." The camera zoomed in on the ring Mrs. Johnstone held.

Kim groaned. It was the same ring she'd examined.

"I was never told that this ring has flaws that were filled with clear glass or plastic to make them invisible."

"How did you discover the problem?" the reporter said

"I took it to a jeweler I trust," Mrs. Johnstone said.

Don't say it, Kim thought. Don't say it, please don't . . .

"Osprey Beach Jewelry," Mrs. Johnstone continued.

She'd said it. Grandpa's gonna kill me.

"The owner's granddaughter was kind enough to examine the ring," Mrs. Johnstone said. "She found the fracture filling."

Maybe Jason wasn't watching television . . .

As if on cue, her cell phone rang. She ignored it.

"Surely, that's illegal?" the reporter said.

"Only if the jeweler doesn't tell you," Mrs. Johnstone said. "And, despite what Mr. Hotshot Alex White now claims, he never told me about the fracture filling."

"So it's your word against his?"

Mrs. Johnstone's shoulders thrust back. "My word -- as a good citizen -- against a man who inflates prices so he can hold phony fifty percent off sales. Who identifies carat weight in fractions instead of decimal points so he can round up to the nearest fraction and charge more. And who inflates a diamond's clarity grade just enough to stay within the law." She waved a flyer. "It's all right here."

Kim winced. Though she agreed with every word Mrs. Johnstone spoke -- Grandpa preached against such practices -- she couldn't help feeling a tinge of sympathy for Alex White. When a customer accuses a jeweler of any wrong doing, the jeweler loses even if he's innocent.

Grandpa once told her about a jeweler who'd been wrongly accused of switching a diamond with a lesser quality one when he cleaned an engagement ring. Though the small claims court ruled in the jeweler's favor, his business never recovered from the negative publicity.

The camera cut back to the anchorwoman, who spoke solemnly to her audience. "A few minutes after this interview, as our news team prepared to leave, Alexander White stormed from the store."

More footage in front of the jewelry store. The camera wobbled, twirled, focused on Alex White as he reached Emily Johnstone. Towering over her, the red-faced man waved his hands in the air. Mrs. Johnstone shook her head, turned and held the flyer out to a young couple. Alex snatched the paper and ripped it in half, growled something at Mrs. Johnstone. She slapped his face.

The muscles around Alex's mouth tightened. He grabbed Mrs. Johnstone's arm and attempted to drag her away. She responded with a kick to his shins.

"You go, girl," Aunt Ginny said.

As sirens wailed in the distance, Alex snarled and pushed. Kim gasped as the woman toppled backwards, high heels slipping out from under her, papers flying into the air.

The camera zoomed in on Alex's enraged face.

The anchorwoman's face replaced Alex's. "Police arrested both combatants, who were later released," she said. "Mr. White was unavailable for comment. In other news . . ."

Kim turned off the television, but continued to stare at the screen, her brain a scrambled mix of emotions. On the one hand, she couldn't help but applaud Mrs. Johnstone's efforts to educate jewelry buyers. On the other hand, all jewelers suffered when one was accused of dishonesty.

She also wondered how local jewelers would react. Grandpa's colleagues well knew the dispute between Grandpa and Alex White.

At a recent jewelry conference, the two men had participated in a panel discussion on ethics. Alex White insisted any marketing practice approved by the FTC was fair game. Grandpa argued for total openness with customers, that FTC accepted or not, some business practices bordered on immoral.

Given the past animosity, would Grandpa's colleagues assume Kim or Grandpa instigated Mrs. Johnstone's protest march?

Surely any thinking person would realize the altercation between Mrs. Johnstone and Alex White had escalated too quickly for a mere dispute. Alex White was known for his cool demeanor and aloof superiority. Though sneaky, none of his business practices were illegal. If he'd ignored the single protestor, the media would have quickly lost interest.

Instead, he'd called the police, pushed into Mrs. Johnstone's personal space and said something that made her flush and slap his face. Whatever was going on, Kim would bet money its roots were personal.

Too bad the camera hadn't picked up the heated exchange.

"Thought we were going to do some investigating," Aunt Ginny's voice cut through Kim's thoughts.

Kim focused on the woman sitting beside her. Color had returned to her aunt's face and all evidence of exhaustion had vanished. Nothing like a little mystery to perk a person up.

Grinning, Kim said, "Okay, we're working on the assumption that Jim or a friend of Jim's discovered a new diamond field in Colorado, a field that produces blue diamonds." She waved her hand at the papers Scott had spread on the coffee table. "We're looking for phone numbers with Colorado area codes."

"Actually," Scott cut in, "I found someone in Uncle Jim's address book, a Claude Monroe, who lives in Denver."

Kim pushed Grandpa's phone towards Scott. "Please use the speaker phone. This I want to hear."

The male voice that answered the phone in Colorado sounded elderly and tired. As soon as Scott identified himself, however, Claude Monroe grew animated.

"Well I'll be danged," Mr. Monroe chirped. "Jim's little Scotty."

Scott winced. Kim made a note to tease him about the nickname later.

"I haven't seen you," Mr. Monroe continued, "since you were planning to become the next Indiana Jones."

The confusion on Scott's face suddenly lifted.

"And if I remember correctly," Scott said, "You and Uncle Jim were the only adults who didn't discourage me."

A wheezy chuckle filled the room. "Yeah, well, Jim and I've always been big on adventures." A phlegmy cough. "Good for young'uns to have something to look forward to. How is the old fart? Haven't heard from him since our diamond hunting trip."

At the words "diamond hunting," Kim's heart rate increased. Did Jim and his friend actually find blue diamonds in Colorado?

As Scott told Mr. Monroe about Jim's death, Kim let her mind wander, imagining the implications of blue diamonds in Colorado. The Kelsey Lake diamond mine had closed because it hadn't produced enough diamonds to support the cost of mining. Blue diamonds, however, commanded a much higher per-carat cost. And if the diamonds were as high quality as the one Grandpa told her to hide . . .

She tuned back in to hear Scott saying, "I've got a couple of friends with me. We're on speaker phone because I'd like them to hear this. Is that okay?"

When Mr. Monroe agreed, Kim introduced herself. Aunt Ginny remained silent, apparently content to allow Kim and Scott to do the interviewing.

"Tell me about hunting for diamonds," Scott said.

Mr. Monroe snorted. "Well, it wasn't supposed to be a diamond hunting trip. We rented a cabin in Red Feather Lakes -- that's in the Rockies, two, three hours north of here. Real pioneer sorta place. Nothin' but cabins, a place to pump gas and a general store. Good fishin', though.

"Anyways, since there was nothin' else to do at night, we sat around a campfire and told tall tales. You know how it is: My story can top yours.

"So the next thing I know, Jim starts describin' these old prospectors pullin' some sorta scam on some banker . . ."

Kim leaned forward as she recognized Grandpa's diamond hoax story.

"And Jim says there really are diamonds in Colorado," Mr. Monroe said. "Well, that got us thinkin' and, after four days of fishin' and tall tale-in, we packed the car, bought buckets and gold-prospecting screens and headed deeper into the mountains. Spent the next ten days pokin' around the rivers and lakes near that closed mine."

"Kelsey Lake?" Kim said.

"Yeah, I think that's what Jim called it."

"Find any diamonds?" Kim said.

"Sure did." By the tone of his voice, Kim could picture the old man puffing out his chest. "At least Jim swore they were diamonds. Said a buddy of his was a jeweler and had shown him what rough diamonds look like."

"That'd be my Grandpa," Kim said. "When I was a kid, he bought some small rough gemstones so I could see what they looked like. He must have shown them to Jim. Ah, were any of the diamonds you found blue?"

"Blue? Don't think so. Everything looked white to me. Why don't you ask your grandfather? Jim brought everything back to show him."

There it was. The connection between Grandpa, a friend in trouble and diamonds.

She took a deep breath. "Grandpa's in the hospital. There was an attempted robbery." Not wanting to answer questions about Grandpa's condition, she quickly added, "Mr. Monroe, could you show us on a map where you found these diamonds?"

"I wish." The old man chuckled. "We must've tramped a couple hundred miles. My old knees still ache. I might be able to find the rivers and streams on a map. Although . . ." He paused.

As the pause dragged on, Kim bit her tongue, sensing Mr. Monroe needed a few minutes to collect his thoughts.

Finally, Mr. Monroe said "You might want to check that cabin Jim was gonna buy."

"What cabin?" Scott's voice was an octave higher than normal.

"He didn't tell you?" Mr. Monroe said. "Huh. Maybe he was gonna surprise you."

Scott opened his mouth, closed it. Laying a hand over Scott's, Kim leaned towards the phone. "Mr. Monroe, maybe you could tell us about the cabin."

"Oh, it's a dandy," Mr. Monroe said. "Lotsa acreage, streams and a river for fishin', cabin in pretty good shape, been on the market awhile so he hoped he could get a good price."

"Let's back up a minute," Kim said. "When did Jim decide to buy this cabin?"

"Well, it took me a couple of months to find the one that suited all of Jim's requirements . . ."

"Better back up even farther," Kim interrupted. "When did he even decide to buy a cabin? And why?"

Mr. Monroe answered the why question first. "He said we were getting too old for all of that drivin' and prospectin', that land was always a good investment, so he might as well buy some where we could fish and prospect in comfort."

"When was this?"

"Oh, let's see, maybe a month or so after our trip."

Long enough to show Grandpa the stones he'd collected, have them cut.

But even if the gorgeous blue diamond in Grandpa's safe and the smaller one Scott found were cut from those rough gems, that didn't necessarily mean the men had discovered a diamond pipe. Surely Grandpa told Jim how difficult it was to trace surface diamonds back to the original pipe.

"When he asked you to look for cabins," Kim said, "did Jim say anything about a diamond pipe?" she said.

"Nope. Just gave me some map coordinates, asked me to find a realtor and go look at property in that area."

Scott glanced at Kim, then leaned towards the speaker. "I didn't find anything about a cabin in Uncle Jim's papers. Did he actually buy one?"

"Don't know. Once I found a place that suited Jim, he worked with the realtor directly."

"Do you have the realtor's name?"

"Justa minute. Let me pull out the yellow pages." A few minutes later, Mr. Monroe read off a name and phone number.

As Kim and Scott thanked Claude Monroe for his help and broke the connection, Aunt Ginny rose, pantomimed walking to the kitchen and disappeared down the hallway. She returned carrying the giant rawhide Kim had purchased for Rory.

"Who are you planning to club with this?" Aunt Ginny gripped the bone two-handed like a baseball bat.

With a muffled woof, Rory dropped his duck and raced to Ginny's side. When she ignored him, he repeated his repertoire of tricks, ending by slapping a big paw on Ginny's leg.

"Oh," Ginny said, widening her eyes as if she'd just noticed the big poodle. "Do you want this?"

Rory waved his paw again.

"Take the tag off first," Kim said. "Rory you can play with it, but just for an hour."

Rory lugged the large bone over, plopped onto Kim's feet and began gnawing.

Kim glanced at Scott, concerned that he hadn't responded to the commotion. Instead, he held Al and stared into space.

Aunt Ginny gave an exaggerated yawn and stretch. "Well, I think I'll turn in." Catching Kim's eye, she slid her eyes to Scott, back to Kim, and waggled her eyebrows.

Scott tossed Ginny a smile that didn't reach his eyes and wished her goodnight.

As Ginny left the room, Kim studied Scott. His furrowed brow and hunched shoulders indicated his thoughts were focused on something other than romance. Al licked Scott's hand. Scott didn't seem to notice.

Sensing Scott needed to work something out, she tucked her legs under her and waited.

"Every time I turn around," he finally said, "I find some other secret Uncle Jim kept from me. I thought he trusted me."

"Of course he trusted you. Maybe Mr. Monroe was right and Jim wanted to surprise you." She waved the notebook where she'd written the number of the real estate agent. "We don't even know if Jim bought the cabin."

When Scott didn't answer, she pushed the notebook towards him. "Call the agent. Find out what he knows." With any luck, the agent would say the sale fell through and Scott wouldn't feel like his uncle was sneaking around behind his back.

The call, however, went straight to an answering machine. Scott left a message and hung up.

"We should probably call it a night." Kim stood. Though she'd love to spend more time with Scott, he clearly needed some alone time. The grateful half-smile Scott gave her confirmed her instincts.

Standing, she led the way to the kitchen door and turned on the outside light.

"Talk tomorrow?"

When Kim nodded, Scott leaned towards her. She tilted her chin. Just as their lips were about to meet, Al pushed his head between them and licked Kim's mouth.

Wrinkling her nose, Kim swiped a hand across her mouth.

Scott frowned down at the little dog. Al responded by leaning back against Scott's arm and waggling his feet. "Next time, buddy, you're staying home."

With a crooked grin, Scott tweaked Kim's nose and disappeared down the outside stairs.

Kim closed and locked the door, sighing. Something thumped against her foot. Rory's bone. He grinned up at her.

"Tell you what, let's save this for tomorrow, okay?" She lifted the heavy rawhide and set it on a counter. "Go get Quack."

Rory raced into the living room, returning in time to follow her up the stairs to bed. As she turned off the bedside light, Kim frowned.

What other secrets had Jim Hampton been hiding?

CHAPTER 25

Early the next morning, Kim trotted downstairs to prepare the store for opening. Rory accompanied her, his new toy duck clutched in his mouth. The toy's quacking serenaded her as she opened Grandpa's safe.

Thank goodness she'd drawn sketches of the display case arrangements she'd created . . . was that only three days ago? She sure didn't have creative energy now to design new jewelry groupings. She needed to focus all of her brain cells on identifying Grandpa's attackers.

First, however . . . Her hand hovered over a tray of bracelets. Yesterday Aunt Ginny sold the citrine bracelet in the window display. Since it was part of the fireworks design, she needed to replace it with something similar. . .

From the storefront, Rory began barking.

Kim glanced at the clock. 8:30. Still half an hour till opening time. Surely whoever was at the front door would see the sign and go away. She reached for a yellow bracelet. The barking continued and now someone pounded on the store door.

Sighing, Kim replaced the bracelet, pushed to her feet and trudged into the store.

The silhouette of a man loomed from the front porch. She froze. The shape moved, a face appeared. Kim let out the breath she'd been holding, then crossed to open the door for Lieutenant Brockley.

"Sorry to startle you," he said. "Yes, hello there." Rory leaned against Brockley, duck again between his teeth. "You're a ferocious watchdog." In response, Rory went into a frenzy of prancing and quacking, bringing a smile to the officer's fatigued countenance.

Kim took in Lieutenant Brockley's day-old beard, rumpled t-shirt and jeans and the purple bruising under his eyes.

"You look like you didn't sleep last night," she said.

His eyes met hers. "We need to talk."

She nodded and locked the front door. "Coffee?" Turning, she started towards the stairs, then veered off and entered the elevator instead. No way was she going to climb the stairs and give Brockley a good view of her butt.

But she'd forgotten how tiny the elevator was. Even with Rory crowded between them, she could feel the heat that oozed from the man. He lounged against the far wall, studying her. The day-old beard only increased the dangerous image. And the attraction.

When the doors opened, Kim stumbled over Rory trying to escape. Brockley followed more leisurely.

As the lieutenant greeted Aunt Ginny, Kim crossed to the cupboard. "You'd better sit down before you fall down." She poured coffee and set it before Brockley. "Milk? Sugar?" Brockley shook his head, his face already buried in the mug.

Kim returned to the counter, popped bread into the toaster and set butter and jam on the table. Aunt Ginny, bless her heart, had brewed a pot of tea for her. Kim set the pot on the table, refilled Brockley's cup and laid a plate of toast in front of him.

"Eat."

Brockley's mouth twitched, but he did as he was told. In the meantime, Kim fixed toast for Aunt Ginny and herself.

As she was taking her first bite of toast slathered with strawberry preserves, Brockley explained the reason behind his visit.

"Spent the night in Laurel," he said. "Someone found a body behind a Safeway store."

"Isn't Laurel out of your jurisdiction?" Laurel was smack dab in the middle of Prince Georges County.

"We had an APB out for the two men who attacked you." Brockley laid a photo on the table. "This one of them?"

Kim swallowed the last of her toast, wiped her fingers and reached for the photo. It was Rat Man's partner and he was clearly dead. Mercifully, only the head showed, the body draped in some sort of sheet.

"What killed him?" She allowed Aunt Ginny to remove the photo from her hand.

"Single shot to the heart, close range, " Brockley said. "He was killed somewhere else and dumped at the Safeway. And before you ask, I checked his arms for marks from Mr. Curly here. Arms were clean. We're still looking for his partner."

His eyes met hers. "So. You wanna tell me why a couple of Baltimore hit men were after you?"

Kim took a deep breath before plunging in. "We think Grandpa's friend -- the scientist who was killed in a robbery?" She waited for Brockley to nod before continuing. "We think Jim Hampton found a source of blue diamonds in Colorado and that someone in the jewelry industry learned about it and hired a detective and maybe the two hit men to steal a map of the location."

"You think they're looking for a treasure map." Brockley's emotionless tone made the words sound ridiculous.

Kim fixed him with her best don't-mess-with-me glare. "A Colorado diamond pipe that produces high quality blue diamonds could be worth billions. So call it a treasure map, call it whatever. The point is to some people the location of the pipe would be worth killing for."

If she'd convinced him, Brockley gave no sign.

"What makes you think someone hired a private investigator?" he said.

Not wanting to get Aunt Ginny in trouble, she sidestepped the question. "His name is Decker Cunningham. He was going to sell us his surveillance report of Jim Hampton but freaked out when he heard Jim's name . . .

"You contacted Decker?" Brockley exploded.

Kim shrank back in her chair. "Well, yeah, I mean, there wasn't any harm . . ." She broke off when Brockley held out his palm.

"Decker Cunningham was a crooked cop," he said between clenched teeth. "He was thrown off the force because he couldn't control his temper. He beat up one too many suspects. Last one was a twelve-year-old trying to break into a car. Kid'll never walk again."

Brockley glared at her. "Decker may be a PI but you can be sure he hasn't changed. And now he knows you're involved."

Kim lifted her chin. "If he's the one who hired these guys . . ." She waved at the dead man's photo . . . "Then he already knew I was involved."

"Or maybe he just suspected and now he knows for sure." Brockley fixed her with cold eyes. "Or maybe he was operating on his own and now you've put yourself in his sights."

Kim felt the blood drain from her face. Aunt Ginny reached across the table to grip her cold hand.

"What gives you the right to terrify my niece?" Ginny said.

Brockley turned steel eyes towards Ginny. "It's my job to serve and protect. I can't protect people who intentionally put themselves in harm's way."

He looked back at Kim. "This isn't a game."

Kim opened her mouth to protest, but Brockley silenced her with a look.

"I don't know how Decker and a couple of hit men fit in with our rash of thefts," he said. "But I'm almost certain there's at least one cop involved."

"A cop helping the thieves?" Kim's voice came out a squeak.

Brockley nodded. "Can't give you specifics. But you need to understand: Whatever is going on is dangerous. Stay out of it."

He studied her face. "Did you hear me?"

Dry-mouthed, Kim nodded.

Brockley rose and pulled a business card from his wallet. "Here's my cell number," he said, scribbling on the back. "If you need me, try the station first. If I'm not there, call this number." He handed Kim the card. "Until we know who's involved, don't talk to anyone else."

He crossed to the kitchen door. With a hand on the knob, he looked over his shoulder. "And no more Nancy Drew."

"Actually, I preferred Frank Hardy," Kim muttered as the door closed behind him. With a sigh, she stood and crossed to the microwave. Her tea had long gone cold.

"Do you need a warm-up?" She lifted the coffeepot.

But Aunt Ginny waved the refill away. "It'll just make me run to the bathroom."

The microwave dinged. Kim removed the mug and carried it back to the table. "Guess we'd better cancel your friends. Looks like I'll be here to run the store."

Aunt Ginny glanced at the kitchen clock and shook her head. "Doris should be here any minute. Besides, she enjoys working in the store."

"Who's been watching Grandpa?"

"Wilma and Maureen have been taking turns with a couple of women from their church. Why?"

"I want to spend tonight with him." Kim snorted. "Since I'm not allowed to play Frank Hardy. Can you alert the ladies they aren't needed tonight?"

"Who's going to help you?" When Kim hesitated, Ginny frowned. "Remember, we're trying to stick together."

"Okay, I'll ask Scott." The thought of spending the night with the sexy reporter turned professor --

even if they were surrounded by nurses and aides --
made her smile.

Gulping the last of her tea, she reached for the
phone.

Scott said he'd be happy to spend the night
watching Grandpa.

"But let me take you to dinner first," he said.
"Some place quiet where we can actually relax."

"Do you like crab cakes? There's a nice place that
juts out over the water. With outside seating. We
can walk from here."

"Sounds perfect. Pick you up at seven?"

That settled, Kim returned to the store to finish
setting up. She carried a stack of jewelry trays into
the showroom, reflecting that with the help of Aunt
Ginny and Doris she should have time to study her
to-do list. Maybe if she locked herself in Grandpa's
office for a few hours, she'd see something in her
notes that she'd missed.

Brockley might be able to stop her sleuthing, but
couldn't stop her mind.

CHAPTER 26

Aunt Ginny's friend Doris arrived just as Kim placed the last ring in the front window. To Kim's surprise, the tiny woman rushed over and embraced her.

"Thank you so much for letting me help in the store," Doris gushed into Kim's shoulder. Stepping back, she beamed. "Selling jewelry is much more fun than volunteering in a smelly old consignment shop. Did Ginny tell you I sold a garnet ring yesterday?"

Doris's enthusiasm eased the tension caused by Lieutenant Brockley's revelations.

"I'm impressed," Kim said. "Took me months before I made my first sale." That wasn't entirely true; she'd had more success selling semi-precious jewelry than Girl Scout cookies. Grandpa's customers had been amazingly responsive to a ten-year-old's comparison of ruby and red spinel.

"I can't tell you how much I appreciate your help," Kim added. "Without you and Aunt Ginny, I'd be lost." Now that was totally and completely true.

Aunt Ginny walked over to give her friend a hug. "Doris is a good egg," she said.

With the two women standing side-by-side, Kim was again struck by the resemblance. They were the same height and build, their hair color and style were similar. Today they both wore flowered skirts and knit t-shirts.

Smiling, she wished the ladies good luck and carried her notebook into Grandpa's office. Settling in the chair behind Grandpa's workbench, she gazed through the interior window into the storefront. Aunt Ginny waved at her, then turned towards the front door as it opened to admit their first customers.

Satisfied that the ladies had everything under control, Kim opened her notebook and began reading.

Unfortunately, the window between Grandpa's office and store worked two ways: She could monitor the store. But customers could also see her.

Seemed like every time she started to make sense of her notes, someone tapped on the window to inquire about Grandpa's health. How in the world did Grandpa get any work done in this fishbowl?

She'd once suggested replacing the glass with a two-way mirror. Grandpa had chuckled and explained he wanted customers to see him at work. Women who gave Grandpa their rings for cleaning and prong-tightening could observe the tender care Grandpa gave to their cherished diamonds. This increased their trust in Grandpa, which often led to more sales or referrals.

The window also protected Grandpa from accusations that he'd substituted a lesser-quality diamond for the stone brought in for cleaning. Grandpa and whatever ring he was cleaning never left the customer's sight.

Right now, however, the window proved too inviting for well wishers. Maybe she should hang a blanket over the glass . . . No, then she couldn't see Aunt Ginny, which would defeat her reason for sitting in Grandpa's chair instead of retiring to the upstairs apartment: She wanted to be easily available to help.

Sighing, she studied the to-do list she'd made yesterday. She'd checked off all but two things: Contact the realtor who was selling Jim the Colorado property. Decide whether or not to tell Brockley about Amber's thug boyfriends.

The first item was half-way complete. Yesterday, Scott had left a message for the realtor, so maybe he'd hear back today. If not, they could call the man tonight after dinner.

As for Amber's boyfriends . . . She tapped her pen against Grandpa's workbench. She really had no evidence that Amber's friends were involved in the attacks on Grandpa. Telling Brockley might accomplish nothing more than angering some pretty scary guys.

She crossed that note off of her to-do list.

Flipping to a clean sheet of paper, she jotted down the information Brockley had given her this morning. The revelation that a cop might be involved in the local thefts was chilling. Was there a connection with that cop and the cop-turned-private-investigator who'd been following Jim?

Darn it, everything she learned raised more questions than it answered.

Maybe if she started over, listing everything they knew in some sort of timeline ...

But the timeline, while interesting, didn't trigger revelations. She probably needed to allow her subconscious to work on the questions. Setting the timeline aside, she reached for the telephone. Time to return some of the earlier messages.

Four hours later, her rumbling stomach reminded her she'd eaten only a single slice of toast for breakfast. She looked through the office window in time to see a family of four exit the store, probably on the way to one of the waterside restaurants.

Pushing back her chair, she stretched and joined Aunt Ginny and Doris.

"Maybe we should close for lunch," she said.

The words were barely out of her mouth when a young couple entered the store. They couldn't be more than twenty or twenty-one, the boy tall and gawky, the girl perky-nosed and blond. There was something familiar about the girl. The nose perhaps?

The young woman offered her a tentative smile. "Is Mr. Hershey in? I'm Jennifer Tyson. My Mom -- Dorothy Tyson? -- said he could help us." She reached for the young man's hand, took it and squeezed. "We just got engaged."

Aunt Ginny and Doris immediately surrounded the girl, asking for details about the engagement, coo-ing and aah-ing as Jennifer described Allen proposing as they strolled the beach.

The distraction gave Kim a minute to search her brain for an image of Dorothy Tyson. The name sounded so familiar . . .

When she made the connection, Kim had to stifle a groan. Dorothy Tyson was Grandpa's most fastidious customer. Descended from a line of wealthy socialites, Mrs. Tyson demanded Grandpa's immediate attention when she stepped into the store.

Kim had been ten years old when she first encountered the woman. She remembered the day clearly.

It'd been a warm Friday afternoon and Grandpa had promised to take Kim fossil hunting after work.

Two minutes before closing, a woman with a blond-beehive, blue eye shadow and Jennifer's turned-up nose swept into the store and announced she needed a diamond necklace. Grandpa pointed out the time and gently suggested she come back tomorrow.

Dorothy Tyson refused. She said she needed every minute tomorrow to prepare for the benefit ball being held that night. And she must have a new diamond necklace to wear to the ball.

With an apologetic glance at Kim, Grandpa had closed the store and begun gathering diamond necklaces for Mrs. Tyson's inspection.

Kim, dressed in her water-repellant fossil-hunting sneakers, perched on a stool by the cash register. As the minutes ticked by, she clenched the edge of her stool and banged her heels against the stool legs.

Mrs. Tyson pronounced the diamonds on the first necklace too small, the design of the second too common, the shape of the third too gaudy. With each rejection, the woman's comments grew increasingly scathing. She all but accused Grandpa of stocking inferior merchandise.

"Perhaps," he said, "You should look somewhere else."

"No time," the woman snorted. "Let's see that one. At least the diamonds are a proper size."

The back of Grandpa's neck grew red.

Dorothy Tyson pointed to a platinum sweep of one carat diamonds too delicate for the woman's structure.

As Grandpa removed the necklace from the showcase, Kim leaped from her stool.

"Oh, no, Grandpa, you can't sell that one," she said. "Mrs. Haggerty wants to buy that."

Before Grandpa could inquire who Mrs. Haggerty might be, Kim turned her most innocent smile on Dorothy Tyson. "She's wearing it tomorrow at the ball."

The old crone straightened, her nostrils flared. "Did this Mrs. Haggerty give you a deposit?"

Kim widened her eyes, turned to Grandpa. "I'm sorry Grandpa, I forgot to ask for the deposit."

"Well." Dorothy Tyson plopped her heavy purse onto the display case. "Then you can sell it to me."

"Oh, but then Mrs. Haggerty won't have anything to wear to the ball!"

Grandpa opened his mouth -- probably to question Kim about the existence of Mrs. Haggerty -- but changed his mind when he saw Mrs. Tyson's evil grin. He rang up the sale, escorted the woman to the door and locked it behind her.

As he turned around, Kim bit her lip. But above Grandpa's stern mouth, she could see the twinkle in his eyes.

"What am I going to do with you, you imp?" he said.

"Take me fossil hunting?"

She could still hear Grandpa's chuckle as she studied Dorothy Tyson's daughter. Despite the physical resemblance, Jennifer exhibited none of her mother's haughtiness or, for that matter, confidence. She clutched her fiancé's hand and beamed at the two women fawning over her.

"We saw the most gorgeous ring at White Jewelers in Annapolis," she told Aunt Ginny. "And the owner said it was on sale! But just for today. But we promised Mom we wouldn't buy anything until we'd talked to Mr. Hershey. So, ah . . ." Her eyes darted around the room. "Is he here?"

Kim sighed. No way would she allow this innocent young woman to fall for Alexander White's "on sale today only" schemes.

"Grandpa's not here today," she said stepping forward. "But since you've come all this way, why don't you let me show you what we have?"

Leaving Aunt Ginny and Doris in charge of entertaining the young people, Kim trotted into the office and kneeled in front of the safe. She pulled out a tray of loose diamonds, then hesitated. Though Dorothy Tyson seemed to have money to burn, Jennifer's fiancé looked like your average graduate student: Broke.

She reached back into the safe and pulled out several envelopes of sapphires and rubies. Locking the safe, she crossed back into the store and stood behind the u-shaped display cases. Laying a piece of black velvet on the case, she began to open gemstone envelopes: two .75 carat blue sapphires, a .68 carat yellow sapphire, a .56 carat pink sapphire, a .98 carat ruby, two .73 carat rubies.

Arranging the stones on the velvet, she called the engaged couple over. Aunt Ginny and Doris positioned themselves on either side of Jennifer and Allen, their eyes bright.

"If you'd like something unusual, you might consider a sapphire or ruby," Kim told Jennifer. "Princess Diana's engagement ring was a blue sapphire surrounded by diamonds. As you can see, sapphires come in just about every color. A ruby is basically a red sapphire. These stones are durable, as well as sparkly.

"You can get a rarer, better quality sapphire or ruby for less money than what you'd pay for an imperfect diamond."

For a moment, Jennifer gaped at the glistening stones. Her hand hovered over the largest ruby. Then she sighed and shook her head.

"Mom would be disappointed if I didn't get a diamond," she said.

Kim forced her face to remain neutral. Dorothy Tyson was probably also picking out the wedding dress, the flowers, the cake and the honeymoon destination.

Be nice, Grandpa's voice whispered.

Setting the sapphires aside, Kim reached for the diamond envelopes. Grandpa had five loose diamonds in stock. Thank goodness he'd written each stone's four Cs on its envelope. Kim removed them one at a time and arranged them on the velvet from smallest to largest.

"Tell me about the rings you've seen that you liked," she said.

Jennifer pulled a piece of paper from her purse and read aloud. "Mom said we should get a one-carat, brilliant cut, internally flawless, D color." She looked up at Kim. "But Mr. White said he didn't have any in stock, that he'd have to order one for us."

"What you've just described is very rare," Kim said. "And very expensive. Last time I looked, the price of internally flawless diamonds started at twenty-six thousand dollars per carat."

Jennifer's fiancé gasped. "I can't afford that!" Allen squeaked. "Jennifer, honey, I love you, but I can't . . ."

Kim held up a hand to silence him. "You shouldn't have to spend anywhere near that much to get a quality diamond. Without a microscope, most people can't tell the difference between an internally flawless diamond and, say, a very slightly included stone. And, frankly, the inclusions are what make each diamond unique. Diamonds are kind of like snowflakes; no two are exactly alike."

Reaching for a pair of locking tweezers, she lifted the smallest diamond and handed the tweezers to Jennifer.

"Look at this diamond and tell me what you see," she said.

Jennifer frowned at the stone, then passed the tweezers to her fiancé. "Looks perfect."

Kim nodded and handed a loupe to Jennifer. "Now hold the loupe at your eye. That's right. Take the tweezers and bring the diamond towards the loupe until the stone comes into focus. Yes, that's the right way. Now what do you see?"

"Oh! There's bubbles and . . . and scratches?"

"The bubbles are natural crystals. The scratches are actually grain lines caused when the carbon crystallized to form a diamond."

Kim accepted the tweezers and returned the diamond to the velvet. "This stone is graded 'included one' and is the lowest clarity grade I'd recommend for an engagement ring. The imperfections in this particular stone won't affect the durability and, because it's small, you can't see the imperfections with the naked eye. Even though its color is rated D -- that's the highest rate -- and the cut is excellent, it's the least expensive diamond in the store."

Kim picked up the largest diamond and handed it to the girl. "This is the most expensive diamond in the store."

"It's beautiful."

"Look at it through the loupe."

"It . . . it looks flawless."

"There are some tiny dots toward the center."

"I still don't see them." Jennifer handed the tweezers back to Kim.

"This stone is graded very slightly included one."

"But . . .that's four grades lower than what Mom recommended!"

Kim smiled and nodded. "That's one of the secrets of diamond buying. Though the grading system was designed to help you choose, you can't judge a diamond until you see it in person. The location of an inclusion, for instance, usually won't affect the clarity grading. But if it's in the center of the stone, a single inclusion could ruin a diamond's sparkle."

Allen suddenly smiled. "So what you're saying is that we don't need to buy one of those expensive perfect stones."

Kim smiled back. "Unless you're buying the diamond simply as an investment, you need to buy what you like."

Jennifer reached over and squeezed Allen's hand, then turned back to Kim. "What about color? Mom said I needed a D, but these all look the same."

Kim unlocked the display case and removed two rings set with marquise-cut diamonds.

"I can show you the color differences in the loose stones by laying them on white paper. But it won't mean anything until you see the diamond on your hand." She held up the two rings. "You may not like this style, but try on these two rings to see which color you prefer."

Obediently, the girl slipped on one ring and then the other. After a moment, she handed Kim the ring with the larger stone. "They both look clear to me. But I think I like this ring the best."

Kim smiled. "You picked the diamond with the lower color grade. Don't look worried! I'd have picked that diamond, too. It has more yellow it. That makes it a lower color grade but the hint of yellow gives the stone a warmer feel.

"I, personally, think the D colored stones are a bit harsh looking. But I'm like you; I have yellow skin tones. The warmth of this diamond matches your skin better." She pointed to three of the loose diamonds. "These would also look good on you."

Jennifer frowned and peered at the diamonds. Then she pointed at the ring she'd just removed. "May I see it again?"

Alexander White and probably every other jewelry salesman would have handed the ring to Allen, not Jennifer, so Allen could slip the ring onto Jennifer's finger. But, darn it, Dorothy Tyson was already yanking this poor woman around emotionally. Kim wanted to give the girl a chance to make a decision without emotional interference.

She removed the ring from its box and handed it to Jennifer.

Jennifer held her hand out, allowing the diamond to catch the light and send flashes across the room. The lines between her brows softened.

"Mom wanted me to get a round ring," she said softly. "But I really like this shape."

"The marquise is my favorite cut, too," Kim admitted. "The pointed ends and elongated shape make your hands look slimmer."

"Is . . . is this diamond as good as . . ." Jennifer waved at the loose stones.

"Absolutely. Let me show you the diamond certificate." A look at Aunt Ginny brought her to the sales side of the case. Kim checked the number on the ring's tag, then left the store in her aunt's care while she rummaged through Grandpa's files to find the diamond certificate.

Back in the store, she showed Jennifer and Allen how to read the certificate.

"No matter where you buy your engagement ring, be sure to look at the certificate before you hand over your money," she said. "See how the certificate maps all of the stone's inclusions? If possible, get the jeweler to show you how to find them in your diamond. That will help ensure that the certificate matches the diamond you buy."

Jennifer removed the ring so Kim could show her how to compare the stone to the diamond certificate.

While Allen studied the ring, Jennifer asked "It says here that the diamond in the ring is the same size as this one." She pointed to the largest of the loose diamonds. "But the one in the ring looks larger."

Kim nodded. "Marquise cuts do tend to look larger than brilliant cuts. But they're the same carat weight."

Jennifer hesitated. "It's not what Mom wanted me to get." But her eyes never left the ring.

Kim's fists clenched. Darn that Dorothy Tyson. She clearly bullied her daughter the same way she'd tried to bully Grandpa.

Well, not this time. "Pick the ring you like, not the one everyone expects you to buy," she said. "You'll be wearing it for the rest of your life."

Jennifer bit her lip, then pointed at the ring. "I . . . I really like this one. Allen?"

His hand closed over hers. "I like it, too." He turned to Kim. "The ring we saw in Annapolis was on sale. Can you give us a sale price?"

"Grandpa never has sales because he keeps his prices as low as possible." Kim took the ring and turned over the price tag so only Allen could see it.

With a wide grin, Allen handed Kim his credit card.

"Why don't you place it on Jennifer's finger?" she said, handing him the ring. Now that the couple had made a decision, the action seemed appropriate.

Jennifer giggled and held out her left hand. As Allen slid the ring on, Jennifer's eyes widened. Too bad Grandpa didn't have a way to play schmaltzy music, Kim thought as she rang up the sale.

She escorted the couple to the door.

Jennifer turned, tears in her eyes. "Thank you for helping me pick the perfect ring." She threw her arms around Kim, whispering "And for allowing me to stand up to Mom."

As the couple strolled down the boardwalk, Kim's own eyes teared. So this is why Grandpa loves selling jewelry.

After a quick lunch of grilled cheese and tomato sandwiches, Kim left the store in care of Aunt Ginny and Doris and trudged upstairs to the bedroom. The emotional roller-coaster that began with Brockley's early morning visit and peaked when she sold the engagement ring had left her psychologically -- if not physically -- exhausted. She wasn't sure she could actually nap, but she definitely needed quiet time to regroup before dinner with Scott.

Crossing to the balcony doors, she gazed down at the tourists strolling the boardwalk. Mothers pushed strollers, grandparents herded grandchildren, couples held hands.

Across from the store, one man had stopped to lean against the railing. Odd . . . Instead of looking out towards the Chesapeake Bay, his gazed fixed on the front door of the store. The straw fedora he wore cast a shadow over his face. Trying to get a better look, Kim leaned towards the doors.

Her movement must have caught his eye because the man suddenly glanced up at her. Gray eyes met hers, narrowed. Decker Cunningham turned and sauntered down the boardwalk.

Kim ran towards the bedroom door. By the time she reached the stairs, however, sanity returned. The private investigator had a substantial lead. She'd never overtake him before he reached the parking lot.

Besides, even if she did catch him, what would she do? Tackle him and demand he reveal the person who'd hired him?

Frustrated, she returned to the light-filled bedroom, flopped onto the bed and stared at the ceiling. She could call Lieutenant Brockley. Problem was she'd only gotten a glimpse of the fedora-clad man. Her impression was of Decker Cunningham. But Cunningham was just sort of average looking. The man outside could have been a tourist waiting for someone.

Which is exactly what Lieutenant Brockley would say. No, forget Brockley. However, she'd better warn Aunt Ginny. If the private investigator was indeed skulking around, everyone needed to be extra cautious.

Rather than tramp downstairs, she called her aunt on the phone, explained what she'd seen and described Decker Cunningham. Aunt Ginny promised to alert her if the man in the fedora reappeared.

"Now rest," Ginny said before hanging up.

Kim set the phone on the night stand. Now that her heart rate had slowed, she was suddenly aware of a heaviness in her arms and legs. Returning to the balcony doors, she peered out. No sign of the fedora-clad man. She pulled the drapes closed, then crawled into bed beside Rory. As the adrenaline faded, she drifted into sleep.

"Wake up, sleepyhead."

Aunt Ginny's soft voice penetrated Kim's slumber. Kim cracked an eye open. Her tongue felt thick and fuzzy and her muscles seemed disconnected from her body.

"What time is it?" Her voice sounded like a croak.

"Five thirty. Didn't you say your young man would be here at seven?"

Kim nodded and struggled into a sitting position. "Why do afternoon naps always make me feel worse?"

"You'll feel better after a shower. C'mon, Rorschach, let's give Kim time to make herself beautiful." As Aunt Ginny and Rory left the room, Ginny called, "And put on some makeup. Those under eye circles look awful."

A shower did, indeed, improve her mood and alertness. No amount of makeup, however, could hide the dark smudges under her eyes. Kim frowned into the mirror. The stress of the last few days showed not only in her tired eyes but in her pale skin and dull hair.

A light-pink blush brought some life to her ghostly complexion. Hair goo added some shine. She started to pull her hair into its traditional ponytail, frowned and reached for the curling iron. A bit of mascara, lip gloss . . . Well, at least she looked human now.

Crossing into the bedroom, she opened the closet to scan her minimal wardrobe. For the cross-country trip, she'd packed only essentials. All of her work and dressy clothes were stuffed in a hot moving van now somewhere in the Midwest. Which left her with jeans, shorts, t-shirts and . . . Kim reached for the emerald colored sundress she'd purchased specifically to wear to the celebration dinner with Grandpa.

She carried it into the light. The modest halter-style top was fitted to the waist. A flared skirt flowed gracefully to just below the knees. She'd chosen the dress for its classic style and the fact she could wear it with flat sandals. The dress was casual enough for the beach while dressy enough for a nice restaurant.

Pulling the dress over her head, she smoothed the skirt and glanced in the mirror.

"Well I'll be darned," she whispered. The blue-green color of the dress brought out the red highlights in her hair. Loose waves fell to her shoulders and softened her tired face. She reached for a pair of abalone shell dangle earrings; they added just the right touch of glitter.

As she reached for her oversized handbag, she spotted Al's collar sitting on her dresser. She shivered, remembering Scott's gentle touch as he'd buckled the thing onto her wrist. Impulsively, she strapped the collar onto her left wrist. She giggled. The leather strap with its gaudy jewels added just the right touch of individuality. *Tomboy has a date.*

Grinning, she headed downstairs.

She followed the murmur of voices into the living room. Scott stood near the balcony doors, head tilted toward a chattering Doris. He'd dressed for the occasion in khakis, light blue sport coat and tie. Aunt Ginny slouched on the couch, a glass of iced tea in her hands.

Rory was the first to notice Kim's entrance. Snatching the jumbo rawhide she'd bought him, he raced to her. Kim shuffled backward as he tossed the heavy bone in her direction; it landed with a thud, just missing her bare toes.

"Why don't we put this away until later?" She lifted the rawhide and set it on top of the grandfather clock.

She turned to find Scott studying her, his brown eyes warm, his mouth tilted in a half smile.

"You look lovely," he said.

Kim swallowed. "You clean up pretty good yourself." Her stomach grumbled.

Scott laughed. "Sounds like I need to feed you. I tried to get these ladies to join us, but they refused."

Aunt Ginny waved away the suggestion. "I'll fix us something here. You two go have fun." She waggled her eyebrows at Kim.

Rolling her eyes -- Aunt Ginny in matchmaking mode alternated between frightening and humorous -- Kim gestured to Scott and led the way to the boardwalk.

Fifteen minutes later, a waitress led them across the outdoor deck to a water-side table. Kim ignored the proffered menu; it'd been two years since she'd tasted the distinctive Maryland crab cakes -- thick chunks of sweet blue crab spiced with Old Bay. The fragrance of the flavorful seasoning hung in the air, making her mouth water.

Scott ordered the same. "Wine?"

Kim shook her head. "That'd just put me to sleep. Iced tea would be better."

"Make that two." Scott returned the menus to the waitress, then leaned across the table. "You really do look lovely."

Kim could feel her face flushing. Why hadn't she noticed the gold flecks in his soft brown eyes? She licked her lips, opened her mouth.

Scott silenced her with a grin and upraised hand. "And don't ask me about the Redskins; I'm not a football fan."

Kim smiled. The waitress deposited glasses and a pitcher of iced tea on the table.

"No football?" Kim reached for her glass. "Didn't Jim teach you the basics?"

Scott chuckled. "Uncle Jim's idea of masculine influence involved trips to the science center, archeological digs and fossil hunting. What about you? Your mom is the oldest of four girls, right?"

Kim sipped her tea and nodded. "Mom and Dad both teach at the high school. English and biology."

"That combination should generate interesting dinner conversations."

"I suppose, if you call frog dissections and verb conjugations interesting."

Scott laughed. "So how did you end up in psychology? Max said you originally studied geology. I got the impression he wanted you to join him in running the store."

Kim sighed and stared at the table. "Yeah. But I got turned off by the world's obsession with diamonds."

"You mean like the grandmother I never met."

"Your grandmother, my grandmother, Grandpa's customers, my aunts, my cousins. Everywhere I turned it was diamonds, diamonds, diamonds. I couldn't get away from it. Heck, astronomers even found a planet-sized diamond orbiting a pulsar. You should have heard the family reaction to that ... And if it wasn't diamonds, it was emeralds or rubies or pearls ..."

The waitress interrupted with their meals. Kim forked a bite of crab and moaned with pleasure. For a moment, they ate in silence.

"With my family background I can certainly understand your dislike of diamonds." Scott reached for a thick french fry. "But why did that stop you from working with Max?"

Kim set her fork down. "Disappointing Grandpa was one of the hardest things I've ever done. But the people around me acted like they were infected by some sort of bacteria that fed on jewelry. I was so afraid I'd become like them . . ."

Scott remained silent, his attention fully on her.

"When I was a kid we had a weekly family dinner," she said quietly. "Every Sunday all of my relatives congregated at my grandparents'. And after dinner, my aunts and cousins demanded Grandpa open the safe so they could pick something to buy. At Grandpa's cost, of course."

She snorted. "My cousins started wearing 14-karat gold when they were little more than toddlers. But Mom and Dad couldn't afford those things, not on a teacher's salary. Mom would watch her sisters buy stuff and she looked so sad . . .

"I saved babysitting money, but even with Grandpa's prices I never could afford more than one or two pieces. As I look back, I'm sure Grandpa supplemented those purchases."

Sighing, she ran fingers through her hair. "Thing is, even though I couldn't afford that stuff, I wanted it. Oh, god, how I wanted it. Helping in the store, looking at all the glitter, watching my aunts and

cousins stroll in and plop down a thousand bucks
for a bracelet. . .

"I got a scholarship to college, but it didn't cover
books. And geology books were expensive, two,
three hundred bucks a pop. I worked different jobs
to pay for them, but it was always a near thing."

She closed her eyes and sucked in air. After all
these years the memory still burned. She wanted to
push her thoughts back into her subconscious, lock
them in a sealed room labeled "Stupid things I've
done."

A warm hand closed over her fist. Kim opened
her eyes. The gentleness in Scott's gaze allowed her
to continue.

"When I was a senior," she whispered, "Grandpa
and I went to New York to select gemstones and
jewelry for the holiday season. There was this
bracelet." She swallowed. "Yogo sapphire. That's a
periwinkle blue stone from Montana. Usually,
sapphires are set in white gold, but yellow looks
better on me . . . This bracelet had these gorgeous
yellow-gold filigree twists interspersed with Yogo
sapphire. Grandpa's cost was a thousand dollars.

"I told Grandpa that I had the money, that I'd
been saving to buy myself something special. But
that wasn't true. I spent my book money on that
stupid bracelet."

Scott squeezed her hand. "You were young.
Young people do impulsive things."

Kim shook her head. "Not me. My cousins, yeah. But I was always the smart one." She sighed. "Anyway, by the time I came to my senses, it was too late to return the bracelet. I asked Grandpa to sell it. But the market for Yogo sapphire is very specialized and it took him months and months to find a buyer. In the meantime, I had to borrow book money from Grandpa."

She swallowed. "I'll never forget the disappointed expression on his face."

"You know he understood," Scott said.

"Yeah, but . . ." She bit her lip, looked away. With a sigh, she turned back. "Thing is, when I bought that stupid bracelet . . . It was scary. Like I was looking down from above, watching myself spend every penny I'd saved. Like I'd been possessed or something."

Scott's eyes suddenly widened. "Is that why you changed your major from geology to psychology?"

Kim tossed him a rueful smile. "Yeah. I finished my undergrad degree in geology. But I'd already been accepted into the grad school." She shrugged. "Switching to psychology just required a few extra classes."

"So did you figure out why you bought that bracelet?"

"Oh, that part was easy. Peer pressure, competing with the Jones's -- or in my case, all of my cousins. What I haven't figured out is how to prevent it from happening again." She gave a rueful laugh. "Let's talk about something happier."

"That I can do." Scott reached for the check. "You sound like a lady who needs to have a little fun."

"Oh, really?"

"Yep. Come with me."

He paid the bill, took her hand and led her from the restaurant. But instead of heading for the boardwalk, he took the stairs down to the beach.

"Scott, we can't go down here. We're dressed too nice for the sand."

Scott kicked off his loafers, tucked his socks inside and rolled up his pants cuffs. "That's the point of playing. You need to be able to do it on the spur of the moment. You probably want to take off those nice sandals."

Kim slipped out of her shoes, then accepted Scott's hand. The sand was still warm and she automatically scrunched her toes in it. As they neared the water, however, the damp sand made her shiver. Scott draped his jacket over her shoulders and wrapped his arm around her. She leaned into him, smelling Irish Spring soap and a musky aftershave. A gust of wind blew hair into her face. He gently brushed it aside, tilted her chin up and kissed her.

She was so startled that it was over before she could respond. She leaned into him, their mouths lingering a hair's breadth apart, then pressed closer for a second kiss. This time she opened her mouth and allowed his tongue inside. From somewhere nearby, a series of explosions snapped and popped.

Kim jumped, her hand flying over her heart, her mind racing.

"It was just firecrackers." Scott nibbled on her ear.

"And here I thought it was the kiss." Her voice sounded husky.

A gust of wind whipped her hair, smacking Scott in the face. He laughed. "Maybe this wasn't the best idea."

Kim lightly kissed his lips. "It was a great idea. But we should probably head to the hospital."

They mounted the nearest steps, dusted the sand from their feet and slipped into their shoes.

As they neared Grandpa's house, the boardwalk darkened. This time Kim had come prepared. Pulling a flashlight from her purse, she opened the garden gate and swept the side yard with the light. No one lurked in the shadows.

Even so, she breathed easier when they reached the driveway. Scott's Prius stood next to Doris's sporty little Camero. Kim grinned. Aunt Ginny drove a Mustang, Doris a Camero. Maybe when she turned sixty, she'd trade in her van for a sports car.

Aunt Ginny, dressed in pajamas, robe and bunny slippers, sat at the kitchen table sipping a cup of hot chocolate.

"Hot chocolate? In the summer?" Kim tossed her purse on the table.

Ginny shrugged. "Milk helps me sleep. You two have a good time?"

"Yep. Where's Doris?"

Aunt Ginny shrugged. "She left an hour ago."

"But her car . . ." As the implication crystallized, a hand squeezed her heart.

Scott beat her to the door. Grabbing the flashlight, Kim charged down the stairs after him. Oh, please, please, please, don't let it be a heart attack. She reached Doris's car and shined the light inside.

No elderly woman slumped in the driver's seat. Scott tried the door. Locked. Kim swept the light across the passenger seat, back seat, floor.

"Is she there?" Aunt Ginny stood at the top of the stairs.

"Not in the car." Kim swept the driveway. "Can you try calling her?"

Ginny disappeared into the house.

"She's not on this side." Scott stood between the two cars. "You suppose she went into the alley?"

Kim followed him to the back gate. But there was no sign of Doris there, either.

From behind Kim, "In the Mood" began playing. Whipping around, she scanned the yard. The sound seemed to be coming from Doris's car.

Aunt Ginny stepped outside. "Doris's phone is ringing now."

Kim trotted to the car and again swept the flashlight across the interior, this time searching for a purse. Nothing.

"May I?" Scott accepted the light, dropped to his knees and aimed the light beneath the car. With his free hand, he reached under and pulled out a black purse.

"Is she under . . ." Kim couldn't finish the sentence.

"No." Scott stood and handed the purse to Kim. The song was clearly coming from inside.

"I don't understand." Aunt Ginny joined them. "If she just dropped it, how'd it get under the car?"

"Someone must have kicked it." Kim leaned against the car, goose bumps forming on her arms. Rat Man. Had Rat Man returned, encountered Doris and . . .

And what? Invited her for pizza?

She pushed aside her paranoia. Rat Man wanted to get into Grandpa's safe. If he'd been lurking nearby, he'd have used Doris to force his way in.

So where was Doris?

The house phone started ringing. Doris?

Kim bounded up the stairs, counting each ring, begging the caller to hang on until she reached the phone.

Four, five, six . . ."Hello?"

At first, there was no sound. "Hello?"

Heavy breathing. And then a voice, low, male, full of menace.

"Missing something?"

CHAPTER 27

Missing something?

The hissed words sent spiders scurrying up Kim's spine.

"Who is this?"

"You've got something I want." Kim strained to hear the whispered growl. "Now I've got something you want."

Before Kim could protest, an elderly voice said "Kim?" The woman's voice trembled. "It's your Aunt Ginny."

Kim whipped around. Aunt Ginny and Scott stood beside the kitchen table watching her. Ginny's hands twisted the handle of a black purse.

The purse they'd found under the car.

Doris. The woman on the phone must be Doris.

"Are you all right?"

"I'm . . ." Doris screamed, a pain-filled wail that pierced Kim's heart.

The man's voice returned. "Put the disk and diamond into a plain brown envelope."

Disk? What disk?

Kim tried to interrupt, but the man plowed relentlessly ahead. "Wait for further instructions. No police. If you want to see your aunt alive."

The line went dead.

Kim gripped the phone and fought the rising panic. Someone -- Rat Man? -- had kidnapped Doris, mistaking her for Aunt Ginny. She bit her lip. Stay calm.

"What's going on?" Aunt Ginny's voice trembled.

Kim hung up the phone. "Doris has been kidnapped."

The color drained from Aunt Ginny's face. As her knees buckled, Kim and Scott surged forward, each catching an arm. They settled her in a chair.

"Put you head between your knees," Kim said.

Ginny shook her head. "I'm not going to faint. Is Doris all right?"

Kim inhaled deeply. "Yes. I talked with her." No need to mention the scream. "He wants the diamond. And . . . and a disk. I guess he means a map of the diamond field. He said no police."

"Of course he did." Scott's voice was icy. "He say where you're supposed to deliver these things?"

"Said he'd call later." Kim closed her eyes and willed her heart to slow. Fear sweat pasted her new dress to her back. She'd been breathing too rapidly ever since discovering Doris was missing . . .

Wait a minute. She opened her eyes and tried to bring a thought into focus. By the time she'd arrived home from dinner, Doris had been missing for well over an hour. The search lasted . . . Five minutes? Ten? But the kidnapper hadn't called until after they discovered Doris's purse. At the exact moment of absolute terror ...

Kim leaped from her chair, dashed to the kitchen door and swung it open. She stood on the stair landing, straining her ears, peering into the darkness. Silence. No frogs, no crickets. Total, absolute, unnatural silence.

Rory nuzzled her hand. A puff of wind ruffled his top knot. Rory suddenly stiffened, raised his nose and sniffed the air. He charged down the steps. Racing to the right corner of Grandpa's yard, he stood at the fence barking.

Aunt Ginny and Scott stepped outside.

"The kidnapper's out there," Kim whispered. "He's got some kind of listening device or night vision binoculars or maybe both." She turned to face them. "That's how he knew exactly when to call."

She needed Lieutenant Brockley's help. But how could she call him if the kidnapper was monitoring their every move?

Scott seemed to read her mind. "Stay here," he said, marching down the stairs. He climbed into his car and turned into the alley.

Kim slipped an arm around Aunt Ginny and listened to the ping of gravel on the car's undercarriage. Rory's barks slowed, then stopped. He stood at the fence, body quivering. With a final sniff, he turned from the fence. Pausing only to mark a bush, he trotted up the stairs.

Kim's shoulders relaxed. The kidnapper was gone.

But he'd be back. If she was going to call Brockley, she needed to do it now.

Aunt Ginny and Rory followed her back into the kitchen.

"I'm sorry, Lieutenant Brockley is unavailable," the police receptionist said. "Would you like to leave a message?"

Remembering Brockley's warning about crooked cops, Kim declined, hung up and dialed Brockley's cell phone. It cycled immediately to the answering machine.

"Uh, this is Kim West. You said to call this number if I had something important to tell you." Tell him about the kidnapping? No, best to do that in person. She had no way of knowing who would be standing nearby when Brockley picked up his messages. "I really need to talk to you as soon as possible. It's an emergency." She recited her cell phone number and hung up.

The kitchen door opened and Scott stepped inside. "I saw someone running through a neighbor's yard, but by the time I got out of the car, he'd disappeared."

"S'okay. You chased him off long enough for me to leave a message for Lieutenant Brockley. But we'd better make plans before the kidnapper returns."

"You're not going to meet this nut," Aunt Ginny said.

"Only if we don't have a choice. We don't know how long before we hear from Brockley. If the kidnapper calls first . . . " She suppressed a shiver, forced what she hoped was a confident smile. "That probably won't happen, but we need a backup plan.

"He wants a computer disk with information about the diamond field. Scott, can you call the Colorado realtor again? The one who was selling a cabin to Jim? Maybe the realtor's secretary can email us the property information. While you're doing that, I'll get the diamond ready."

"What about me?" Aunt Ginny said. "I'll go nuts if I don't do something."

Kim paused, trying to think through the immediate needs. Grandpa. What if this was a ruse to leave Grandpa unprotected?

"Do you think your friends would mind sitting with Grandpa tonight?"

In answer, Aunt Ginny reached for her cell phone.

While Ginny and Scott made their phone calls, Kim trotted downstairs to Grandpa's office. She opened the safe, reached into the deepest shelf and extracted the envelope containing the blue diamond. For a moment, she stared down at Grandpa's fluid, almost-feminine handwriting: "Will it pass DiamondView?" The nightmare of the last few days had all started with this stupid blue diamond.

But would relinquishing it really stop the attacks?

She fished around in the safe, searching for Grandpa's supply of unmounted, semi-precious stones. He'd placed them, still wrapped in their envelopes, onto a velvet-lined tray. Kim carried the tray to Grandpa's workbench and snapped on the task light.

She emptied the tray, then removed the diamond from its protective envelope and paper and placed it on the velvet. Next, she sorted through the envelopes of loose jewels. Amethyst, citrine, topaz, garnet . . . Huh. What was Grandpa doing with a package of CZs? He usually didn't stock man-made gemstones.

She weighed the envelope, considering. Cubic zirconias often served as cheap substitutes for diamond. But while they could be made in any color, Kim had never seen a blue CZ the same shade as the diamond Grandpa told her to hide. Besides, if the kidnapper was looking for a diamond substitute, he'd be expecting CZ.

What he wouldn't expect would be a natural zircon, another diamond look alike. Though softer than diamonds -- a sharp knock could damage a zircon's edges -- zircons' high refraction and fire made them darn near as pretty as diamonds. And a lot less expensive.

In their natural state, zircons were brown, yellow, green or red. They could be heat-treated, however, to create the most popular color, blue. But would Grandpa have a four-carat blue zircon in stock?

Kim found an envelope with zircons, opened it with trembling hands and sorted through the paper packets, each labeled with information about their contents. Brown, yellow, yellow, blue -- no, that one was too small. There. A four-carat blue.

As she removed the zircon from its wrapper, the gem caught the light and sent fiery rays across her hand. She reached for a loupe and examined the stone at ten times magnification. No inclusions were visible. Turning the gem, she studied the facet edges. Clean and sharp.

She set the zircon beside the diamond and studied the two stones. Side-by-side, the zircon's color more resembled an aquamarine than a diamond. Still, without the diamond for comparison, she doubted the kidnapper would notice.

Satisfied, she wrapped the blue zircon and tucked it into the diamond's envelope. The diamond went into the zircon's envelope. Returning the loose gems to the safe, she locked it and hurried upstairs to see how the others were doing.

"Maureen and Wilma are on the way to the hospital," Aunt Ginny said as Kim entered the kitchen. "Hope you didn't leave dirty clothes laying around; I sent Scott to your room to retrieve your laptop. The realtor is emailing details about the cabin Jim wanted to buy."

"Did Jim actually buy it?" Kim refilled her aunt's iced tea glass and poured one for herself.

"No, they never got that far." Scott crossed to the kitchen table and set down Kim's laptop. "Sorry for invading your privacy, but I didn't want Ginny climbing stairs."

Kim waved aside Scott's concern -- after all, a messy bedroom was the least of her worries. Sitting behind the computer, she booted it up, then turned it to Scott so he could check his email. The message from the realtor included a link to the cabin's web site. Scott immediately clicked on the map.

"Is this a logical place for a diamond field?"

Kim leaned into the screen. "This isn't even Colorado. May I?" She took the mouse and clicked the map to back up far enough to get some perspective. "Oh. My. Gosh." The property was located in Wyoming, midway between Casper and Rawlins.

She pointed at Rawlins. "This is where the fake prospectors once staged the Great Diamond Hoax." She traced her finger along Route 282 towards the

Granite Mountains. "There are kimberlite pipes here, right around the property Jim wanted." The property -- 116 acres -- included a rustic cabin and fifty miles of river and streams. Kim switched the view to overhead geology and zoomed in as tight as the satellite allowed. "See how there are no woody plants, only grass? That's a sign of possible kimberlite. At least in this part of the country."

"So he really found it." Scott's voice was soft. "Uncle Jim was going to become Diamond Jim."

"Maybe." Kim switched the view back to a regular map and saved it to her hard drive as a photo file. "Don't forget the expense of mining. Although, if the area produces blue diamonds like the one Grandpa gave me . . ." She didn't bother finishing the sentence. Exiting the internet, she opened the map in Photoshop.

"Giving our friend an X marks the spot?" The amusement in Scott's voice made her smile.

"Almost." She inserted a note with coordinates for the property, then scribbled some color on a couple of places near the stream to make it look as if Jim had marked where he'd found diamonds.

"Looks like a treasure map to me." Aunt Ginny peered over her shoulder.

"Let's hope it satisfies our friend." Kim saved the file, copied it to a disk and shut down the computer. "Let me put this with the diamond, change my clothes and then we'll be ready."

Now if only Lieutenant Brockley would call.

CHAPTER 28

But Lieutenant Brockley didn't call.

As the minutes passed, Kim, Aunt Ginny and Scott grew increasingly restless. What if Brockley never called? What if the kidnapper called first?

What if she had to actually meet the kidnapper?

Kim knew nothing about kidnapping, just what she'd read in books or seen in movies. The internet held little information. The notoriety of the Lindbergh baby led to laws making kidnapping a capital offense; this meant kidnapping for ransom in the United States was rare. When someone was kidnapped on U.S. soil, the culprit was usually a parent, boyfriend or husband.

In most instances, she read, victims were eventually released unharmed.

So. Assume the kidnapper was actually willing to release Doris when he got the diamond. To prepare, Kim needed to . . . She pulled a pad and pencil from her purse and began making a list:

One: Insist he bring Doris to the exchange.

Two: Arrange for back up so she wasn't going in alone.

She frowned. Not much of a list. And how the heck could she accomplish number two?

She tapped the pencil against the pad. Scott eased the pencil from her hand and wrote: Three: Take Scott.

Kim rolled her eyes. "You really think I'm gonna get away with that?"

Aunt Ginny snatched the paper and pencil from Scott and wrote "Take Ginny."

"Oh, for heaven's sake." Kim sighed. Probably no way to prevent Aunt Ginny from participating.

But maybe this could work.

Aware that the kidnapper might once again be outside with a listening device, Kim retrieved the writing implements. "Stay in touch with cell phones?" she wrote.

"Now you're talking." Scott pulled his phone from his pocket and handed it to Kim. It was one of those rectangular smart phones. Seemed a lot heavier than her clamshell style phone.

But why his cell instead of hers? Kim wrote "???" and passed the pencil to Scott.

"Keep it in your pocket," he wrote. "Yours will disconnect when you close it."

"I've got one, too." Aunt Ginny dropped another smart phone onto the table.

Hmmm . . . If she used Scott's phone to call her aunt and left the line open, maybe she could then hide Scott's phone in a pocket. That way Scott and Ginny could monitor the meeting with the kidnapper.

What a professor and an old lady would do if things turned nasty was a whole other matter. Adding Rory to the mix would help, but she'd really rather have a police force behind her.

Darn it, Brockley, why weren't you calling?

From the living room, the grandfather clock began chiming midnight. Where was Brockley? As the last chime died away, Grandpa's phone rang.

"Gimme your cell number," the kidnapper hissed.

Kim recited her number. The kidnapper hung up. Her cell phone rang.

"This is him," she said before opening her phone and pressing "talk."

"I'm not meeting you anywhere unless you bring my aunt" she said as a greeting.

"She's right here. Wanna hear her scream again?"

"Don't! I . . . I'll do what you say."

"That's better." The voice, little more than a whisper, seemed at once familiar and alien. "Do not disconnect this phone. Get in the car and drive north on 261. Leave the boyfriend and mutt at home."

Kim hurried to repeat the directions so the others could hear, then remembered: Her van and Aunt Ginny's convertible were trapped in the garage. "Uh, I can't get my car out of the garage. I'm blocked in."

"Then take one of the other cars. Tell your boyfriend to stay inside. If he tries to follow, I'll know."

He must be watching the driveway. But maybe there was another way.

"Give me a minute to get the car keys," she said.

No response, though she could hear the kidnapper's breathing.

"Scott, he wants me to use your car," she said loud enough for the kidnapper to hear. "I think you left the keys in the living room."

Scott's eyes widened, but he played along. "Let me get them."

But he remained in his seat. Kim scribbled as fast as she could: "K. can't see storefront from back. Disable store bell and use that door to leave. Take Rory. Access to another car?????"

Aunt Ginny grabbed the pencil and wrote "I'll text Maureen."

Kim shook her head, writing "Can't leave Grandpa alone."

"You're the one in danger," Aunt Ginny wrote. Whipping out her phone, she began typing.

"What's taking so long?" The voice from every terrifying movie she'd ever watched.

"I'm still waiting on the keys." Kim stood and motioned Scott to move away from the phone.

Scott retrieved his phone, accepted Aunt Ginny's and crossed to the hallway, his head bent over the two phones. Turning, he gave her a thumbs up.

"Did you know your dog is a key thief?" he said loudly, walking towards her. "Found them on the floor." He held up his phone; the screen indicated it was connected to Aunt Ginny's phone.

Scott handed Kim his phone and car keys. "Stay safe."

His kiss was warm and far too short. She lifted her purse, tucked the fake diamond and disk into a belly pack and slipped Scott's cell into a jeans pocket. After hugging Aunt Ginny, Kim stepped outside.

She'd never felt so alone.

CHAPTER 29

Scott's car started immediately. Kim adjusted mirrors and seats and studied the control panel. Bad enough meeting a kidnapper; worse driving an unfamiliar car.

Laying her open cell phone on the passenger seat, she steered with both hands as she backed out of Grandpa's narrow driveway. She navigated the dark alley, turned right onto Second Street. By the time she turned north on the two-lane that paralleled the Chesapeake Bay she felt comfortable enough with the car to ease her death grip on the wheel.

Steering with her left hand, she brought the phone to her ear. "Okay, I'm on two-sixty-one."

"'bout time," the kidnapper said. "Let me know when you reach the traffic light in Chesapeake Beach."

Kim switched the phone to her left hand so she could drive with her right. The ear piece that would allow her to talk while keeping both hands on the steering wheel was locked in her van in Grandpa's garage. In Maryland, it was illegal to drive while talking on a phone. She hoped a cop didn't stop her.

Aunt Ginny had apparently contacted Maureen and re-directed her to the beach instead of the hospital. But how soon would Maureen arrive? At this hour, there certainly wasn't any traffic. That was both good and bad. Good because nothing would slow Maureen. Bad because nothing slowed Kim: She was quickly pulling away from the only people who knew she was meeting a kidnapper.

The first light in Chesapeake beach appeared. Green. Why did it have to be green?

"I'm at the first light," she said, slowing. But the light stayed green. A car appeared behind her, honked and forced her through the light. The kidnapper?

"Turn left on 260." She strained to understand the whispered words.

As Kim neared the intersection of 260 and 261, the light turned red. Kim pulled into the left lane. The car behind her followed. Kim stared into the rearview mirror, but the driver of the other car was nothing but a silhouette. There was no one in the passenger seat.

Of course, if that was the kidnapper, he wouldn't allow Doris access to a window. She'd be laying on the back seat or . . . oh, dear God, please don't let Doris be in the trunk.

Kim tried to picture the roads ahead. Route 260 would take her away from the Bay, through a small section of Owings and across Route 2. If she continued on 260, she'd end up traveling north on Route 4. In the meantime, there'd be lots of side streets. Plenty of ways for the kidnapper to check for followers.

Assuming she had any.

The light changed and she made her turn. "Turning onto two-sixty." She hoped Scott and Ginny were still listening. She had no idea if they were even still connected. This part of Calvert County was notorious for dropped calls and the phone tucked in her pocket had been alarmingly silent.

Of course, Scott wouldn't dare say anything; the kidnapper might hear. Still, she'd better assume that wherever she was going, she'd be on her own for a while. She took stock of potential weapons. Her purse contained the heavy flashlight she'd used to search Grandpa's driveway for Doris. Other than that, she had stuff to clean her glasses, lip balm, hand lotion, dog treats and the new clicker.

Darn it, most women carried hairspray or some other aerosol that would temporarily blind an attacker. The eyeglass cleaner came in a spray bottle, but the liquid didn't travel far. Plus it probably wouldn't hurt someone. Just make him angry.

Surely Scott had a lug wrench and other tire-changing equipment in the trunk. But how would she reach it?

The four-lane narrowed, Route 260 veering right, a small country road heading left. The car behind her disappeared down the country road.

Now she could see a single streetlight illuminating the two-block business section of Owings.

"I'm coming into Owings," she said into the phone.

"Stay on 260."

Beyond the bank, the traffic light at Route 260 and 2 turned green. "You want me to cross over Route 2?"

"Stay on 260."

Kim slowed but the damn light stayed green. She crossed the wide intersection and entered a dark residential area. No street lights here. With the moon barely a slit, the only illumination came from her headlights.

Where was the kidnapper? Had he been in the car that turned off? Surely he'd want to monitor her progress. Unless . . .

Unless he'd put some kind of tracking device on Scott's car. He'd used some sort of sophisticated listening device to monitor their search for Doris, so he probably had access to a tracking device.

Even so, the kidnapper had no way of knowing which car she'd take for the rendezvous. No, a mechanical tracker didn't make sense. He had to be nearby.

Where was Lieutenant Brockley? She'd given his cell number to Aunt Ginny. As soon as her aunt connected with Maureen, she'd use Maureen's phone to call Brockley.

In the meantime, Kim's backup consisted of a senior citizen, a professor and a poodle.

Up ahead, the complex intersection with Route 4 appeared. Two one-way lanes brought traffic towards her. Her only option was to the right, a ramp that would force her onto Route 4 north.

Was the kidnapper taking her out of Calvert County?

"I'm coming to the dead end onto four north," she said into the phone.

"Make a U-turn onto four south."

Kim's fist tightened on the phone. As the only north/south highway in Calvert County, Route 4 was seldom empty no matter the hour. To turn south, she'd need to merge into traffic, whip into the left lane, make her U-turn, then ease into the south-flowing traffic.

"I need to lay the phone down." Without waiting for a reply, Kim set the phone onto the passenger seat and gripped the steering wheel with two hands.

She eased onto Route 4, her eyes darting from the windshield to the rear-view mirror to the side mirror. Slowing to allow a pickup to pass, she pulled into the left-turn lane. She waited for traffic to clear before making the u-turn.

She checked her rear-mirror, hoping to see Scott and Aunt Ginny following. But no other car made the turn.

She lifted her phone. "I'm heading south on Route 4," she said, hoping Scott could hear.

"At the next light, turn right."

Kim frowned, trying to remember when she'd next encounter a traffic light. Wasn't there one as she entered Dunkirk? With a shopping center and McDonald's on the left and . . .

"You want me to turn into Dunkirk Park?" She said it loud enough for the cell phone in her pocket. "It's closed at night."

"Just make the turn and park the damn car."

This was it. She swallowed and willed herself to breathe. She could do this.

I think I can, I think I can, I think . . . Grandpa's voice. Reading The Little Engine That Could.

"Turning into Dunkirk Park." Could Scott hear? She sent a prayer to the cell phone gods.

A metal gate appeared, blocking the entrance to the park. She aimed the car into the gravel pull-off on the left and shifted into park.

Hers was the only car. So where was the kidnapper?

"Step out of the car." Nothing but a whisper on the phone.

She clipped the belly pack to her waist and slung her heavy purse over a shoulder. Palming the car keys -- keys could be weapons, right? -- she opened the car door.

The change from the overly air-conditioned car to the humid outdoors fogged her glasses. She squinted, waiting for her glasses to clear. The car's headlights bit into the gloom. No movement, no sound, just an endless expanse of dark.

"Step out from behind the door, hold your hands out to your sides and turn around."

Where was he? Did the spare cell phone make a bulge in her pocket?

"Get rid of the keys."

How did he know she had the keys? Night vision binoculars?

"Get rid of them."

She tossed the keys onto the driver's seat.

"Now the purse."

Kim fought the panic. The kidnapper was systematically stripping her of weapons. She turned so that the open car door blocked the man's vision and eased the flashlight from the purse. She held the bag above her head so he could see it, then flung it into the car.

"There's a snack stand ahead and to your left. Meet me there. Now toss the phone and close the car door. You have three minutes before I make your aunt scream."

"Wait! I can't get there that fast." But the kidnapper had already hung up.

However, he'd be watching.

She tossed the phone into the car and, holding the flashlight close to her leg, slammed the door shut.

Stepping around the car, she tried to envision the park's layout. The gate blocked the road but not the grassy expanse on either side. Entering the park shouldn't be a problem.

She'd been here with Grandpa two years ago. They'd driven through the gate and . . . and turned left into a football field sized parking lot. The snack stand stood at the end of that lot.

Easily walked in daylight. At night, however, the only illumination came from tall, widely spaced lights that created more shadows than brightness.

Using the flashlight would alert the kidnapper that she had a potential weapon. But she'd never reach the snack shop in three minutes without the additional light.

She shuffled forward one step, two. The car's automatic timer extinguished the headlights. Another step and her toe connected with something hard. She clicked on the flashlight.

A boulder? A sweep of the light revealed a series of ornamental quartzite rocks spaced several feet apart. Kim moved towards the widest path.

The flashlight illuminated a sudden drop in the path, but she couldn't stop her forward momentum. Her right foot sank into the blackness down to her calf. Flailing to keep from falling, she dropped the light, heard the sickening crunch of metal striking rock. She landed on her butt and pain shot up her spine.

Biting her lip, she felt around on the ground beside her. Her hand closed on metal. She pushed the on button. Nothing.

She shook the light. "C'mon, c'mon."

A dim beam appeared. She swept it around her. She'd stepped into a gravel-lined culvert. The darn thing had been hidden between two boulders.

She aimed the light to her left. The paths between the other boulders were level.

The light winked out and no amount of shaking brought it back to life.

Pushing herself upright, she stepped to her left to avoid the culvert, skirted the boulders and finally reached the road beyond the gate. She picked up speed, her eyes on the first overhead light.

Heat rose from the asphalt road. Sweat dribbled down her neck onto her now damp t-shirt. The hand that clamped the flashlight felt clammy. She could hear nothing but the squeak of her tennis shoes and the beat of her heart.

As she moved deeper into the park, her ears searched for any sound, some sign that she wasn't alone. Where were the owls, the frogs, the crickets? It was as if the whole world was held in suspended animation.

The first overhead light dimly illuminated the entrance to the parking lot that led to the snack stand. This, too, had been blocked by a gate.

Kim picked her way between the gate's edge and an ornamental tree, her feet sinking into dew-dampened grass. She could see the snack building now, silhouetted by another overhead light. The distinctive shapes of picnic tables dotted the area around the building. If Kim remembered correctly, to the right a shrub-rose lined path led to a small playground.

Conscious of time ticking away, she stepped back onto pavement and covered the ground with long strides. As she moved, she scanned the ground for fallen branches or hand-sized rocks -- anything to use as a weapon. The grounds keepers, however, had done their job well. The asphalt was clear.

Squeak, squawk, squeak . . .

Kim froze. What was that sound?

Squawk, squeak . . .

She took a tentative step towards the rose-lined path. Metal on metal. A squeaky swing? Seesaw? Had the kidnapper arranged some diabolical horror for her to find?

"Stop that!" The kidnapper's voice came from a few feet ahead. That deep voice from her nightmares.

The sound stopped.

A shadow stepped from behind the building. A clicking sound was followed by a blinding white light.

"That's far enough," the man said.

Kim raised her hand, trying to shield her eyes from the light.

The kidnapper was only a few inches taller than her -- perhaps 5'10 to her 5'6. Not Rat Man. This guy was average build.

Except for his head. His head was enormous, unnaturally hug... What was wrong with his head?

He stepped forward and now she could make out the motorcycle helmet he wore.

"Toss the package over here."

"Where's my aunt?"

The kidnapper hesitated, then aimed his flashlight away, towards the playground. It illuminated one of the spring-based animal rides, a bright yellow seahorse. Doris was straddled across it, her arms wrapped around the neck, her hands tied together. More ties held her legs to the metal springs. Like the kidnapper, she also wore a motorcycle helmet.

"Are you okay?"

The springs squeaked as Doris bobbed her head. Squeak, squawk. But she didn't say anything.

Under that heavy helmet, the poor woman must have a gag over her mouth.

Kim's hands fisted. Jim dead. Grandpa fighting for his life. Doris kidnapped and humiliated. All because of this man and his thug buddies.

"How could you do this to an old woman?" She took a step towards him. "Don't you have a mother, a grandmother? Or were you hatched from an egg?"

The kidnapper moved his flashlight, illuminating the gun he held in his right hand.

Kim's throat constricted.

"Don't tempt me," he said.

Talk! She needed to warn the others about the gun.

"You don't need the gun." Her voice was unnaturally high pitched, but at least the words were clear. "I've got what you wanted. Just take it and leave us alone."

"Bring it over there." The flashlight pointed at a picnic table with something flat and silver sitting on it. A laptop computer.

"Put the disk into the drive."

Kim's hands trembled as she pulled the disk from her belly pack. Why did he need to check the map? Did he think she'd bring the wrong one?

"Open the file." The kidnapper leaned close enough she could smell his sweat.

Under the picnic table, she tightened her grip on the flashlight. The table's bench would limit her motion. But if she got the opportunity . . .

"What are you waiting for? Open it."

She clicked on the file. The document opened, the map appeared.

"What are you trying to pull . . ."

Kim swung the flashlight. The kidnapper leaped safely away. Unable to check her swing, Kim heard the sickening crunch as the flashlight smashed against the picnic bench. The impact ripped it from her hands. She heard it rolling away.

"I should kill you right here."

So why didn't he? Why hadn't he fired?

"Where's the disk? The real one?" he said.

"This . . . this is what we have. What Jim left us. It's what you wanted."

"Bullshit. Where's the formula?"

"Formula? What are you talking about?"

For a moment, the kidnapper studied her. Trying to gauge her honesty? Would he see anything in her face but fear?

He leveled the gun at her face. "Toss me the diamond."

Kim swallowed. "Will you let us go?"

The kidnapper stiffened. She knew that body language. Whatever he said next would be a lie.

"Of course. Now toss me the diamond."

Kim unstrapped the belly pack, held it out. As the man stepped forward, she pitched the diamond as far as she could. The pack landed in the roses.

"What the hell . . ." The kidnapper turned towards the bush.

Kim grabbed the laptop and hurled it at his exposed neck. This time her aim was true. The man staggered, lost his footing and tumbled into the roses. The gun went off, the bullet smashing into the grass.

In the distance, a dog barked furiously. Rory.

The kidnapper struggled, tangled in the thorny canes, his flashlight sending beams into the sky.

Kim ducked under the table, her hands scrabbling for her dropped flashlight.

Where was it, where was . . .

There!

Gripping the heavy flashlight, she wiggled out from under the table. Using a two-handed grip, Kim brought the flashlight onto the kidnapper's gun hand.

The man screamed, the gun fell into the thorns. He scrambled towards it. Don't let him get it, don't let . . . Kim swung again. The kidnapper twisted. The flashlight grazed his back as a hand whipped backwards, snagged Kim's ankle and jerked her feet out from under her.

As she tumbled to the ground, Rory appeared. Launching himself, he flew at the kidnapper, smacking the back of the man's knees. Dog and man crashed back into thorns.

The gun. Where was the gun?

Gripping the flashlight, Kim pushed to her feet. Rory yelped as the kidnapper flung him aside.

The kidnapper rose, the gun in his hand, aimed at Rory.

"Nooooo!" She was too far away, too far . . .

She threw the flashlight. Metal crunched against metal. The gun jerked away from Rory. But the kidnapper held on. Now the gun pointed at her.

Kim dove to the ground as Scott appeared. He tackled the kidnapper. The two men fell hard.

Kim rolled to her feet and stomped on the kidnapper's hand. Once. Twice. He dropped the gun.

She snatched it, the metal cold in her hand. She turned in time to see the kidnapper land a punch on Scott's diaphragm. Scott doubled over. The kidnapper kicked Scott's feet out from under him.

As Scott landed next to Rory, Kim raised the gun. It felt huge and awkward in her hands. She wrapped a finger around the trigger and pointed it at the kidnapper.

"Stop. Stop or I'll shoot." Even with two hands, the weapon trembled.

What was she thinking? She didn't know anything about guns.

"You really think you'll shoot me?" the kidnapper sneered. He took a step towards her. "You don't have the nerve." Another step.

Kim squeezed the trigger.

The blast echoed in the night. Her hands jerked back. She was falling, falling, her finger still on the trigger, two more blasts straight into the air. She landed hard on her tailbone. Pain pierced her spine.

Her ears rang with the sound of the shots. She sensed movement nearby. Rory licked her cheek. Scott bent over her, his face wrinkled with concern.

From somewhere nearby, Aunt Ginny called "Kim! Kim, are you okay?"

And then another sound, a rumble like a low flying airplane. Kim staggered to her feet and tried to pinpoint the sound's location. On the other side of the snack stand, a single headlight illuminated picnic tables. A motorcycle appeared.

"He's getting away."

"Let him go," Scott said.

But if the kidnapper got away, Grandpa would still be in danger. They'd all be in danger.

Could she get a license plate number?

Picnic tables and grass slowed the bike's progress. Kim jogged towards it. As the kidnapper began to navigate the last picnic tables, its headlights illuminated a running figure. Aunt Ginny.

And the heavy bike was aimed straight at her.

CHAPTER 30

The sight of the motorcycle bearing down on her froze Aunt Ginny in place. Eyes wide, she stared into the blinding light. The kidnapper corrected his course, but with picnic tables on both sides, he had little room to maneuver.

Kim charged towards Ginny. She and Scott reached her at the same time. Their combined momentum carried Ginny out of the bike's path.

The motorcycle grazed a picnic bench. Wood splinters pierced the air. The bike wobbled. For a second Kim thought it would topple. But the bike righted, skidded on the grass, then finally gained the asphalt.

Rory streaked after it.

"Rory, come!" The adrenaline-filled poodle ignored her.

Kim took a step in Rory's direction, stopped, looked at Aunt Ginny.

"I'm fine," Ginny said. "Go get your dog."

Kim tore after Rory, yelling every command that might possibly stop him. "Come. Sit. Stay. Leave it. Damn it."

If he followed the motorcycle onto the highway . .
.

The bike slowed to maneuver around the first set of gates. Rory closed the distance.

The kidnapper glanced back, spotted Rory. Gunning the engine, he aimed for the space between gate and tree. Front wheels dug into the sandy soil, throwing clods of grass into the air.

Rory slowed to dodge the flying debris.

"Rory, coooooome." A stitch jabbed Kim's side. Ignoring it, she pushed on. By the time she reached the first gate, motorcycle and poodle were nearing the intersection with the road that led from the park.

She could close the distance by cutting across the grass. But could she run across the uneven ground without twisting an ankle?

The motorcycle's headlights illuminated the exit road. No choice.

Kim veered right towards the grass. As she left the asphalt, the ground dipped. Momentum carried her forward faster than planned. She leaned back, slipped, but remained upright. At the bottom of the dip, she dug in her feet and pushed towards the exit gate.

The shortcut carried her within fifty feet of the gate. The motorcycle's headlight illuminated the boulders lining the park entrance. The bike turned to the right and, yes, yes, yes, aimed for the widest space between the rocks. The kidnapper didn't see the culvert until he was almost on top of it.

With no way to avoid the ditch, he leaned to the right, laying the bike on its side. The front tire smashed against the culvert opening.

Kim inhaled, then belted out the only command she hadn't tried: "Rory, no!"

Rory skidded to a stop.

"Come." No way was she or her dog going near the angry man now struggling to right his motorcycle.

"Rory, leave it. Come."

Rory ran to her. Cupping her fingers in his collar, she ran for Scott's car. Behind her, metal scraped against gravel. The kidnapper cursed.

Kim pulled open the passenger door. Rory hopped in. The motorcycle rumbled back to life. The keys were still on the driver's seat where she'd tossed them. Kim snagged the keys, flung herself inside and locked the doors. The bike's headlight illuminated the car's interior. Kim shoved the keys into the ignition.

The car started immediately. She backed across the road, blocking it.

The motorcycle swerved, crossed in front of the car's headlights. Kim caught a glimpse of the first letter on the license plate. B? Or was it an S? Darn her astigmatism.

Kim flipped the gear shift to drive and turned towards the exit. Yes. The first letter was definitely a B. B, T . . . V? Or U?

The kidnapper roared through the green light, Kim right behind him. It was a U. B, T, U, 1 . . . The bike leaned into the left turn. Kim followed.

She had maybe two miles of straightaway before the highway began a series of dips, twists and turns. The more maneuverable motorcycle would surely lose her on the turns.

Two miles to obtain the rest of the license . . .

She pressed the gas pedal. Scott's car shot forward. The speedometer read 75, 80, 85. The cycle drew nearer.

Her cell phone rang. She glanced at the phone laying next to her. Probably Scott or Aunt Ginny. At this speed, she didn't dare remove a hand from the steering wheel.

She peered ahead. B. T. U. 1. Was the next number a six? Or an eight?

The phone stopped ringing. The kidnapper glanced behind him, spotted her. The motorcycle roared and shot forward. Kim stayed with him.

Her phone rang again. They were probably worried.

The next number. Six or eight?

Her headlights illuminated a bend in the road. She'd run out of straightaway.

She tapped the brakes, threw out an arm to prevent Rory from sailing through the windshield.

"Down!"

Rory dropped to the floor.

The car slowed, but not enough. The back wheels slipped sideways. She used two hands to aim into the slide. The road curved the opposite way. Turn the wheel, turn the wheel . . . Rory whimpered. The road dipped, then rose. The slight hill helped slow the car. The speedometer read 65. Kim breathed deeply.

The motorcycle was nowhere in sight.

The cell phone sounded again, muffled. It'd slid under her right hip.

Kim retrieved the phone and flipped it open.

"I'm okay."

"Where are you?" Scott. She could hear sirens in the background.

"Trying to get the license plate. Got a pen? B as in boy, T as in Tom, U as in uncle, one. The next number is either a six or an eight. Is Doris okay?"

"Just shaken up. EMTs are working on her now. Cops are roping off the snack stand. Better get back here; you'll never catch a motorcycle."

"I know who the kidnapper is." Her subconscious had pieced together the baritone whisper, the angry growl. The banty rooster stance. "Decker Cunningham. The detective."

"Private investigators don't go around kidnapping people."

Kim envisioned the blue diamond tucked safely among the semi-precious gemstones in Grandpa's safe. "There are a million reasons this one might."

The road straightened. In the distance, a single tail light passed the exit to Route 301.

"Kim, he's a retired cop."

"A retired crooked cop. He'll know exactly how to manipulate the other cops, how to refute all the evidence."

Scott sighed. "Okay, I'll let them know you think you recognized Cunningham. How soon will you be back here?"

"Uh." The road curved and for a moment she lost sight of the motorcycle.

"You're not still following the kidnapper, are you?"

"I'm not going to do anything stupid." The intersection with the Washington beltway loomed ahead. "He's probably heading back to his office."

Sure enough, the motorcycle turned onto the beltway heading north. Kim followed. "He's slowed down; I don't think he knows I'm still following."

"You shouldn't be!"

"All I need is the rest of the license plate number, maybe a photo of the motorcycle sitting outside his building." The motorcycle was still too far ahead to read the plate. But the kidnapper seemed to be obeying the speed laws. "I'm not planning a citizen's arrest or anything."

"Kim, this is crazy. Get back here."

Kim gritted her teeth. Scott? Giving her orders? Who did he . . .

Be nice. Grandpa's gentle voice, always there in her head when she needed him.

But this time, Grandpa, I can't be nice. Not while you're in danger.

Best to end this conversation.

"I'll call you back later." She snapped the phone shut, cutting Scott off mid-sputter.

Construction on the beltway slowed traffic and allowed her to keep the kidnapper in sight. As soon as they left the highway, however, the dark, curving roads allowed the more maneuverable motorcycle to out-distance her. She rolled down a window, listening for the distinctive rumble. It sounded far away.

Didn't matter. She knew where Cunningham worked and, considering the unmade bed she'd seen, probably lived. As long as she arrived before he had a chance to hide the motorcycle, she'd get what she needed.

Beside her, the cell phone rang. She ignored it.

Ten minutes later, she turned onto Cunningham's street. The gray gloom that hovered over the area in daylight metamorphosed at night into sinister shadows, shapes and sounds. Vandals had destroyed all but one streetlight. Its thin, yellow glow revealed a deserted stretch of parked cars and blowing trash. Kim slammed the brakes as a rat scurried in front of her.

With a shiver, Kim cruised past the detective's building. She found the motorcycle wedged between two SUVs, its front tire aimed towards the street. Impossible to read the license plate.

At the next intersection, she turned around and headed back towards Cunningham's office. The door to an apartment building on her left opened. Two couples, arms draped around one another, staggered outside, laughing. Kim slowed. One of the men stopped in front of a four-door sedan. He shoved a key at the lock, missed, laughed and finally inserted it. The doors opened, the men and women piled in.

Kim waited until the weaving car was safely away before pulling into the vacant space.

From here she had a clear view of the detective's lighted office. Though the shade was pulled, she could see Cunningham's distinctive silhouette moving around the office. He opened what appeared to be the center drawer of a tall file cabinet and extracted a rectangular bottle. Crossing to his desk, he slumped into a chair.

Turning off the car, she considered her next move. To inspect the license plate, she'd need to leave the car. With Cunningham perched at his window, however, she'd be exposed if he glanced out.

Maybe she should wait until he fell asleep?

A pair of headlights illuminated the row of cars opposite her. The drunks returning?

No, this car was larger, blacker. Another one of those bomb-shaped luxury cars. It screeched to a stop, double parking directly outside Cunningham's building and effectively blocking the motorcycle from her view. The driver's door opened, but the dim light prevented Kim from seeing the man's features.

He jogged into Cunningham's building.

Reaching for her cell phone, she glanced at the time. Close to two a.m. Who visited an office at that hour?

Movement drew her eye back to Cunningham's window. A male silhouette approached the detective's desk. The driver of the car?

Whoever he was, he clearly wasn't happy. He waved his hands around, pacing back and forth. Returning to the desk, he leaned forward and smacked both hands down on the table top.

Cunningham remained seated. From Kim's vantage point, however, she could see the detective's hand snake down behind the desk. When his hand reappeared, it held something.

The standing man stiffened. Slowly, he raised his hands above his head.

A gun.

The detective must be holding another gun. Kim swallowed, but her mouth was suddenly too dry. Her hand tightened on her phone.

Cunningham stood. She could see the outline of the gun now, clutched in the detective's hand as he gestured.

Call the police.

Kim opened her phone, but couldn't tear her eyes from the scene in the window. The visitor launched himself at the detective, gripped the gun arm with both hands. She could see now he was taller than Cunningham.

Rat Man. It had to be Rat Man.

The two men grappled, wrestling for control of the gun. Cunningham was smaller, but strong. For a moment, the combatants looked evenly matched.

The larger man suddenly jerked backwards, pulling the detective across his desk. The two men tumbled to the floor, out of sight. A shot rang out.

Beside her, Rory whimpered and nudged her hand. Kim gripped his fur. Get out of here! But she couldn't move. She stared at the window. A man stood. For a moment, he gazed down at the floor. Then he turned and ran through the office door.

No time to drive away. Kim flung her arms around Rory and pulled him flat on the seat. She held her breath, praying the surviving man would leave without searching the street for witnesses. A car door opened and slammed shut. An engine growled. Headlights illuminated her car's window. Kim closed her eyes.

The car didn't stop. Its engine noise grew faint, fainter. In the distance, sirens wailed. Beside her, the cell phone rang.

CHAPTER 31

The grandfather clock chimed eight times as Kim unlocked the doors to Grandpa's living room balcony. With Rory at her side, she padded barefoot across wood still damp with morning dew. A warm breeze, fragrant with wet sand and brine, blew a lock of hair across her face. Frowning, Kim tucked the unruly curl behind her ear, leaned against the deck railing and gazed out at the glistening water.

Normally, the lapping of the waves soothed her. Despite a long, hot shower, however, her muscles still throbbed from last night's struggle with the kidnapper. Her mind was in even worse shape, a whirling swirl of anger, confusion and fear.

Decker Cunningham -- Dora's kidnapper -- was dead. The man who killed Decker, however, remained free. And he'd taken Cunningham's gun.

That much, at least, Lieutenant Brockley had been willing to share last night. But not until he'd berated her for following the kidnapper. Kim had been too exhausted to argue. She'd clung to Rory, eyes lowered, as the lieutenant pointed out all of the nasty things that could have happened if Cunningham's killer had spotted her.

Misinterpreting her silence as contriteness, Brockley also revealed he'd found evidence in Cunningham's files connecting the detective to Rat Man, a.k.a. Frankie Roberts, and Roberts' dead partner. The police put out an all-points bulletin for Roberts' arrest.

But while Brockley theorized the shooting indicated a falling out among thieves, Kim wasn't convinced. There were just too many unanswered questions. How had a crooked private investigator and two Baltimore thugs learned about Grandpa's blue diamond? Why had the kidnapper gotten angry when he saw the map to Jim's diamond find? What the heck was he talking about when he demanded a "formula"?

Lieutenant Brockley, of course, had no answers to her questions. Instead, he'd ordered her -- ordered! -- to "stop playing Nancy Drew" and let the police do their job.

Remembering Brockley's patronizing tone, Kim bristled. Why was it whenever a man wanted to belittle a woman's inquisitiveness, he brought up Nancy Drew? She was tempted to point out that at least Nancy always captured her suspect.

Nancy wouldn't quit, either. Not while Rat Man remained free to strike again. And what if Kim was right, that there was a fourth person involved? When Grandpa came home from the hospital, there'd be no way for her to protect him 24/7.

No, this Nancy Drew would not stop until she'd answered all her questions.

Problem was, she had no idea what to do next.

"Ready for tea?"

Kim jumped, then turned. Aunt Ginny stood by the balcony door gripping two steaming mugs. A belly pack dangled from her wrist.

"Thought you were still be in bed." Kim gratefully accepted the mug her aunt held out.

"I suspect Doris is the only one who slept last night." Ginny set the pack on the table before settling into a deck chair with her own mug. She motioned to Kim to join her. "She said getting kidnapped is exhausting."

Kim sat across from Ginny. "How's she doing?"

Last night, Kim hadn't had a chance to talk to Doris. Brockley and his cohorts had interrogated Kim for four hours. When she finally arrived home, she'd found Aunt Ginny dozing at the kitchen table. She'd wakened Ginny, learned that Doris was in the hospital and Scott had taken the others in a nearby motel, then sent her tired aunt to bed.

"Cranky." Aunt Ginny blew on her tea. "No serious injuries; they just kept her overnight for safety. But they won't release her until the doctors do their rounds. Which means at least another hour, plus paperwork."

"She knows to call for a ride, right?"

Aunt Ginny's eyes widened. "Didn't you know? Your young man wouldn't let me stay at the hospital last night. Said he'd get a motel room so he could be available to drive Doris back here."

"He's not my young man." Kim dragged fingers through her hair. And after last night, he'd probably never be.

"You two have a fight?"

"I don't want to talk about it." While waiting for her police interview, she'd finally answered her cell phone. Scott yelled, she yelled back.

"He tried to tell you what to do, didn't he?" Aunt Ginny's eyes were knowing.

Scott's exact words had been Stop acting like you have a death wish. As if she was some bimbo. Amber the drama queen or, God forbid, Tiffany.

Aunt Ginny laid her hand over Kim's clenched fist. "Try to remember Scott's under a lot of pressure, too. He just lost the man who raised him."

Kim groaned and flopped back in her chair. She had forgotten. Not Jim's death -- Grandpa would be devastated when he heard -- but that the scientist and Scott had a father/son relationship.

Scott acted so stoic that she hadn't stopped to consider his pain. Ironic, given that's exactly the way her family treated her. Kim was the strong one, therefore Kim didn't feel anything.

"I hate it when I act like a jerk."

Ginny patted her hand. "He'll forgive you." She nodded towards the belly pack. "And when you see him, you can thank him for retrieving your diamond. Doris saw you toss it into the bushes."

"This is my bag?" Kim opened the belly pack and pulled out the jeweler's envelope. The blue zircon she'd substituted for the diamond was inside, unharmed.

She returned the stone to the envelope and tucked it into a jeans pocket. "So did you get a chance to talk to Doris before the police arrived?"

Aunt Ginny nodded. "The kidnapper grabbed her in Max's driveway. Snuck up with a gun." She frowned. "I should have followed her outside when she left, made sure she got into the car and locked the doors. But I was so tired and it wasn't even dark out . . ."

"Don't blame yourself. If he was determined to grab her, he could have forced her off the road or followed her home."

Aunt Ginny sipped her tea, looking unconvinced. After a moment, she continued. "She said he dragged her to a car in the alley, threw a sack over her head, tied her hands and feet and shoved her into the backseat. And no one saw them."

"The alley is pretty quiet during the day. Most people work." Kim shivered, imagining the claustrophobia of having a bag over her head.

"They drove somewhere and parked," Aunt Ginny said. "Doris has no idea where they were. Couldn't hear much through the bag.

"She said the worst, though, was riding the motorcycle."

Kim felt her mouth fall open. "He drove her to the park on a motorcycle? Why didn't she signal someone for help? Or jump off when they came to a stop sign?"

"Too scared. Before shoving the helmet onto her head, he blindfolded and gagged her. Told her if she tried to run or get help or tip the bike, he'd run over her. She was so disoriented, it was all she could do to hang on. She's going to have nightmares for a while."

Kim's hands tightened on her mug. That someone would terrorize an elderly woman . . . If Rat Man hadn't killed Cunningham, she'd be tempted to do it herself.

"Did Doris know what time they arrived at the park or how long they were there before I arrived?" A time frame might help her determine if Cunningham had a nearby accomplice.

Aunt Ginny shook her head. "The only reason she even knew it was dark was because the temperature dropped . . . Is that Emily Johnstone?"

Kim turned towards the boardwalk. Emily Johnstone waved and trotted towards them.

"I know I'm awfully early," Mrs. Johnstone said, stopping at the base of the store stairs. "But I'm taking my grandson to the sandcastle competition and then there's the parade and the fireworks and, well, you are opening today, right?"

Kim stifled a groan. She'd forgotten that Grandpa always opened the store for a few hours on July 4. Though he seldom sold more than a few beach charms, he claimed the holiday opening generated the goodwill required to keep a small shop in business.

After last night, however, the last thing Kim wanted to do today was babysit a bunch of "only-looking" tourists.

But Mrs. Johnstone wasn't a tourist; she was Grandpa's best customer. So good she'd even picked a fight with Grandpa's nemesis, Alex White. Jason's father.

Hmmm . . . Wonder if Mrs. Johnstone would be willing to gossip.

"I'll be right down."

CHAPTER 32

Mrs. Johnstone swept in on a wave of humid warmth and announced she wanted to buy earrings to match the emerald bracelet her husband had given her for Christmas. Whipping a box from her purse, she handed it to Kim.

"Jonathan bought it here, so Max must have something that will match."

Kim opened the box and suppressed a whistle. The tennis bracelet sported brilliant-cut diamonds and emeralds, each easily a carat in weight. The emeralds' color match was darn-near flawless and the clarity amazing for emeralds this size. How could anyone feel comfortable wearing such a rare, expensive piece of jewelry?

"Uh, Grandpa has some lovely earrings in stock, but the stones aren't this large." Closing the box, she handed it back. "I think I can find a close color match." Grandpa was very particular about color. "But if you want stones the same size, we'll have to wait until Grandpa's out of the hospital."

Mrs. Johnstone waved a hand in dismissal. "Size doesn't matter. It'd be better anyway if the earrings didn't compete with the bracelet."

Leaving Aunt Ginny to entertain Mrs. Johnstone, Kim crossed to Grandpa's office, kneeled in front of the safe and began the tedious process of dialing the long combination.

A thrill coursed through her. If she sold Mrs. Johnstone emerald earrings, she'd make enough money to justify closing the store today. As for that goodwill stuff Grandpa always harped on . . . well, she'd just post a sign saying the store was closed due to illness. Surely no one would complain.

The safe clicked open.

Reaching into her pocket, she pulled out the envelope she'd taken to the rendezvous with the kidnapper. The sight of Grandpa's handwriting made her stomach knot, but she pushed the emotion aside.

Grandpa had entrusted her to manage his beloved store and she needed to focus on this potential sale. First, however, she switched the blue zircon and diamond stones back into their respective, correct envelopes. That done, she pulled out the tray of emerald earrings.

While Kim adored blue-tinged emeralds, the most valuable color was an intense, glowing green like the emeralds in Mrs. Johnstone's bracelet. It was also the rarest color.

She picked through the earrings. Too blue, too yellow, maybe, not-a-chance, pretty good . . . She sighed. She'd found only three possibilities, none an exact match. She may not make that big sale after all.

Carefully arranging the earrings on a velvet tray, she closed and relocked the safe and returned to the store.

She found the two women leaning against the display cabinet.

"Emily was starting to tell me why she's so angry at Alex White," Aunt Ginny said.

"Oh?" Too bad Grandpa wasn't here; he'd enjoy learning more about the Whites.

Kim found two seats for the ladies, then stepped behind the counter.

Mrs. Johnstone settled onto the tall footstool. "I was telling Ginny I met Alex in college. I was a freshman, he was a senior. A football star. I met him at a frat party." Mrs. Johnstone looked away. "You probably know what happened next."

"Er . . ." He asked her out? He rejected her? He . . .

Mrs. Johnstone met Kim's eyes, read the confusion on Kim's face. "The party was crowded.

He offered to get me a drink. I woke up the next morning, naked, and . . ." Her face flushed. "There was blood on the sheets."

Kim gulped. "He used a date rape drug?" What the heck was that called? Something that began with an R . . .

Mrs. Johnstone's smile was bitter. "Rohypnol? No, that wasn't readily available back in my day. Alex was more inventive. He simply spiked my drink with a couple of his mother's Valium. Unfortunately, the next morning I remembered every awful minute. You see, I was still a virgin."

Kim shuddered, but remained silent.

"Apparently, Alex White hankered for virgins. I heard later he'd become quite expert in seducing them." She snorted. "Didn't even try to woo me. I guess he'd just discovered the usefulness of tranquilizers mixed with alcohol."

"Wha . . " Kim swallowed. "What did you do?"

Mrs. Johnstone shrugged. "Not much I could do. Alex was the son of a school patron. I was a poor scholarship student. Who would believe me?"

"But if he had a reputation . . ."

Mrs. Johnstone shook her head. "People didn't discuss these things back then. I'd have looked a fool. Besides, I was one of the lucky ones. I didn't get pregnant."

Kim shuffled her feet. She didn't think of herself as a prude, but this conversation was almost as bad as when Mom handed her a packet of condoms "for your purse."

Sensing Kim's discomfort, Aunt Ginny changed the subject. "Is this why you decided to picket Alex White's store yesterday?"

"Of course not. I got over Alex decades ago." Mrs. Johnstone's eyes narrowed. "But he's still a sneak and a cheat. He scammed my niece. Then, when I went to his store to challenge him, he didn't recognize me -- even after I told him my maiden name!"

She threw back her shoulders and raised her chin. "So, yes, I've been stalking him, pushing him towards the nervous breakdown he deserves." The grin that spread across Mrs. Johnstone's face made Kim step back. "You should have seen his face last night when I showed him this article."

Plopping her purse onto the case, she fished around, pulled out several folded pages and handed them to Kim. "I told him not to be so high and mighty because some day these diamonds would put him out of business. His face turned as white as his name."

Kim unfolded the pages. "The New Diamond Age" proclaimed the headline. The article then went on to describe a Belgian gem trader as he estimated the value of a yellow diamond. It was worth, the trader said, several million.

At which point the owner -- a reporter -- produced several more diamonds from his pocket. All were identical to the first.

Kim glanced back at the headline. Ah, yes, the infamous Wired article.

She'd read it when working on her dissertation. The well-written story described the process of creating gem-quality diamonds in laboratories. Like the diamond Tiffany had made from her husband's ashes, these stones were chemically identical to diamonds mined from the earth.

And most jewelers -- including this well-respected man in Antwerp -- couldn't tell the difference.

The reporter predicted the demise of De Beers and the diamond industry, speculating that the price of diamonds would crash when women realized they could purchase a gorgeous lab-made stone for less than half the price of a mined diamond.

Grandpa had been one of the few jewelers who reveled in the story. Unlike many of his colleagues, Grandpa kept his diamond prices low to allow his customers to afford them. Which meant his business wasn't totally dependent on diamond sales.

However . . .

"You know, since this article was written, De Beers created several testers that separate lab-made diamonds from mined diamonds." She set the story aside. "Plus polls show women would rather own a mined diamond than a synthetic no matter the price difference.

"I'm kind of surprised Alex White was bothered by this story." Surely he'd seen the article when it was first released and had followed the subsequent debate.

Mrs. Johnstone shrugged and tucked the article back in her purse. "He's probably afraid I'm going to accuse him of selling synthetics as real." Her eyes suddenly widened. "You don't suppose he's doing that?"

"Uh . . . " Oh, she didn't want to get into this. She straightened her shoulders. "No, no I don't think the Whites or any other reputable jeweler would substitute a synthetic for a real diamond. Now, what do you think of these earrings?

To her relief, Mrs. Johnstone immediately focused on the glittery tray Kim held out.

As Mrs. Johnstone and Aunt Ginny debated the merits of one pair over another Kim's mind wandered. Grandpa had often grumbled about the Whites' sales tactics. But would they actually dare to sell synthetic diamonds as real?

Of course, a man who drugged an innocent woman's drink clearly had no morals.

She sucked in breath as another thought occurred to her: Did Grandpa know about Alex White's sexual exploits? That might explain why Grandpa had opposed her dating Alex White's son. Like father like son?

She stiffened. What would have happened if Jason hadn't stood her up for the prom? Would Jason have slipped something into her drink?

No, that was absurd and totally unfair. Alex White's behavior was not an inheritable trait. She didn't like it when friends of Amber the drama queen or Tiffany the air head expected Kim to be just another light weight. She had no reason to liken Jason to his father.

Mrs. Johnstone held up one of the earrings and flashed Kim a smile. Did that mean she'd made a decision?

Before Mrs. Johnstone could speak, however, the front door banged open and a familiar voice demanded "Why aren't the cases filled?"

CHAPTER 33

Kim stepped around the showcase to accept Tiffany's hug. "Didn't you read the sign, Tiff? We haven't opened yet."

Her cousin shrugged, then spotted Mrs. Johnstone. With a squeal, she embraced the older woman and offered air kisses. Kim rolled her eyes.

Years ago, Tiffany's marriage to husband number one had propelled her into Annapolis society and she'd wasted no time in adopting what she called "high-class behaviors."

She never noticed that Mrs. Johnstone never air-kissed anyone.

"Is this the diamond you were having made from Desmond's ashes?" Mrs. Johnstone snagged Tiffany's right hand.

The yellow gem caught the overhead light and flashed beams across the room. Even Aunt Ginny gawked at Tiffany's ring. The emerald earrings lay on the showcase, ignored.

Kim opened her mouth to suggest they finish selecting earrings when the front bell again jangled. Doris entered, followed by Maureen and another woman who must be Wilma, the friend who'd accompanied the ladies last night.

"My hero!" Doris flew across the room and wrapped Kim in a tight bear hug. "Thank you, thank you, thank you."

For a moment, Kim couldn't breathe. Doris released her and turned to the others. "Kim saved my life last night!"

Mrs. Johnstone and Tiffany gasped, then begged for details.

Even Aunt Ginny and her friends -- who surely must have heard the story several times -- listened to Doris with open mouths. As Doris described Kim's struggle for the kidnapper's gun, she made Kim sound like a cross between Indiana Jones and Spiderman. Kim felt heat climbing up her cheeks.

"Don't look so embarrassed; you really are a hero," a man's voice whispered.

Kim jumped and turned. Scott smiled down at her.

"When did you get in here?"

"I was right behind Wilma, but you were too busy trying to escape Doris's clutches."

Kim smiled. "She does get enthusiastic, doesn't she?"

"Oh, this is nothing compared to last night. The doctor had a heck of a time taking her temperature because she wouldn't stop talking." He grinned. "Adrenaline is a wondrous high."

His smile faded. "It can also make you act like a jerk. I'm sorry about last night. I shouldn't have shouted."

Kim shook her head. "No, I'm sorry. You were just trying to protect me. I shouldn't have hung up on you."

"'s okay. Max warned me not to tell you what to do."

"What?" Kim leaned towards Scott, close enough to smell whatever hotel soap he'd used. "What did Grandpa say?"

"Just that I shouldn't ever try to tell you what to do."

"That's right," Aunt Ginny broke in. "No one's ever forced Kim to do anything."

Kim turned to see six Cheshire-cat faces beaming at her. With a shock, she realized Doris had chosen this moment to stop chattering.

As if reading Kim's discomfort, Maureen stepped forward and linked her arm through Scott's.

"And did you hear what this young man did last night?" Maureen said. "He insisted that Wilma and I sleep at a motel while he spent the night at the hospital protecting Max."

Kim stared at Scott. He shrugged. "I knew I wouldn't sleep so I figured might as well let the ladies get a good night's rest."

"So we're all rested to watch tonight's fireworks," Doris said. "Ginny reserved front-row seats."

"Reserved . . ." Oh. She'd forgotten Osprey Beach catered to seniors by sectioning off part of the pier for them to sit during the fireworks. She'd assumed the seats were available on a first-come, first-serve basis. Now that she considered it, however, it actually made sense to allow reservations.

Still . . . "You know you can all watch the fireworks from Grandpa's balcony."

Doris's eyes slid away. Aunt Ginny stared at the ceiling. Maureen and Wilma shuffled their feet. Mrs. Johnstone and Tiffany looked as confused as Kim felt.

"What's wrong with watching from Grandpa's balcony?"

Scott leaned so close she could feel his breath on her neck. "I think the ladies want to reserve the balcony for just you and me."

"Oh, for heaven's sake, there are two balconies, we could . . . " Oops. Access to the upper balcony was through the master bedroom.

Scott flashed his crooked grin. Kim felt her face flush.

"So, how 'bout them Redskins?"

Scott chuckled, a throaty laugh that made Kim's toes curl. Maybe watching the fireworks from the bedroom balcony wasn't such a bad idea after all.

"The plan," Doris said, "is for all of us to get some rest today, then meet here for Chinese takeout."

"And after dinner," Scott said, "I'll drive the ladies to the fireworks and come back here to watch them with you. That sound reasonable?"

"Uh, I'm kinda surprised you all want to do anything today. After last night and all."

For the first time, Maureen spoke up. "We figured it'd be a good idea to do something normal today."

"Sort of like climbing back on the horse that threw you," Doris added.

"Well, if you're sure you'd like to get together tonight, I'm game."

"That's our cue to leave," Maureen said. "C'mon, ladies. Doris, leave your car here and come with us. You shouldn't drive until you've slept in your own bed."

As the ladies headed for the door, Scott said, "I'd better get going, too. Someone from the university is meeting me at Uncle Jim's to pick up Hank."

"Jim's CVD machine?"

"Yeah. Apparently, it's an old unit they let Uncle Jim borrow."

"I'm surprised anyone at the university is working on a holiday."

Scott shrugged. "Professors keep odd hours. This guy says he's flying to Europe tomorrow and wants to settle things before he leaves."

With a grin, he planted a chaste kiss on her cheek, then followed the others to the door. Kim locked it behind them. Now, to sell those earrings.

Tiffany, however, had other ideas. "I need to talk to you."

"Can't it wait until I'm finished with Mrs. Johnstone?"

"No, I've got to get back before Amber realizes I'm missing."

Huh?

"Go ahead, dear." Mrs. Johnstone waved the two younger women away. "I'm still trying to choose between the studs and the dangles."

Tiffany's eyes brightened as she spotted the emerald earrings. Before Tiff could confuse the issue by adding her opinion, Kim snagged her cousin's arm and dragged her into Grandpa's office.

"So." Kim crossed her arms. "What's going on?"

Tiffany deflated into Grandpa's desk chair. "It's Amber. She's seeing Darin again."

Kim's arms dropped. "After he hit her?"

Tiffany's blond curls bobbed up and down. "He called, all apologetic, saying he never meant to hurt her . . ."

"Yeah, right." She had no tolerance for men like that.

"Said he was just trying to protect her from some very bad men. And that . . ."

"Wait a minute." Kim's heart raced. "What bad men?" Was Amber's slimy boyfriend behind all of the attacks?

"He wouldn't say because he's . . ." Tiffany drew air quotes . . ."'protecting Amber.' But he did admit telling someone that Grandpa carried diamonds between here and New York. He just refused to say who."

Kim's teeth clenched. "Well, maybe he'll be more open with the police." She reached for the desk phone.

"No!" Tiffany slapped a hand over Kim's, preventing her from lifting the receiver. "Don't you see? If the police haul Darin in for questioning, he'll blame Amber and hit her again."

"Oh, lord . . ." Kim ran fingers through her hair. How could the police stop the attacks if they didn't have all available information, didn't know Amber's boyfriend had blabbed about Grandpa's New York trips to one of his sleazy friends? There had to be a way . . . "Do you think Darin would talk to me without getting mad at Amber?"

In reply, Tiffany reached into her purse, pulled out a piece of paper and slapped it into Kim's hand. "That's his cell number."

Kim stared at the paper. "Tiff, if all you wanted was for me to call Darin, why didn't you just pick up the phone and ask?"

Her cousin shrugged. "You never say 'no' in person. And there's one more thing: You need to talk sense into Amber. You know, use your psychology stuff, make her throw Darin out."

"She let him move in?"

"He lost his job, so . . ."

Kim groaned. "Tiff, I'm not a clinical psychologist. I've never worked with battered women . . ."

"Amber is not a battered woman." Tiffany leaped to her feet. Her face flushed, her chin jutted out, her hands clenched into fists. "You take that back. Right now."

Stepping away from her enraged cousin, Kim held up a placatory hand. "Okay, okay, so she isn't battered." Rather than fight, she dodged the issue. "I'm just not sure she'll listen to me."

Tiffany's hands relaxed. "You'll think of a way to make her listen. You always do." She swung her handbag onto her shoulder. "Look, I'd better get going. Richard and I promised to take Amber to the Annapolis celebration. Darin refused to go."

Tiffany wasted several minutes saying goodbye to Mrs. Johnstone and Aunt Ginny, but at least she seemed to have forgotten the emerald earrings. Kim locked the door behind her cousin and turned to Mrs. Johnstone.

"So. Did you decide on your earrings?" Please, please, please say you'll buy earrings. Now that she knew Darin had told someone that Grandpa carried diamonds in his briefcase, she wanted to call the slime ball right away. If she could get a name and pass it on to Brockley, maybe this whole nightmare would finally end.

"Ginny thinks the studs are the most elegant." Mrs. Johnstone held up a pair of earrings. The central emerald was completely surrounded by diamonds.

"Ginny's right." Kim smiled. "And the color is the best match to your bracelet."

As she handed over a credit card, Mrs. Johnstone's smile illuminated her face. Amazing that a woman who owned thousands of dollars worth of jewelry could still feel girlish excitement when buying yet another pair of new earrings.

The best part, however, was being able to close the store today without feeling guilty.

"So what did fluff for brains want?" Aunt Ginny said as she followed Kim upstairs and into the kitchen.

"Amber's in trouble again." No way was she getting into the details right now. She'd worry about Amber after Grandpa was safe. Now she needed to decide how best to approach Darin. Call or confront him in person?

Remembering Amber's black eye, she decided to call. Why give the thug a chance to swing at her?

"I must say, Tiffany has excellent taste in diamonds." Aunt Ginny opened the refrigerator, peered inside and frowned. "Too bad the yellow one is fake. When was the last time you went to the grocery store?"

"Wait a minute. Why do you think Tiff's yellow diamond is fake?"

"She said it was made from Desmond's ashes." Ginny closed the refrigerator and crossed to the bread keeper.

"It might be lab made, but it's still a real diamond."

Ginny turned. "How can that be?"

"Chemical composition is identical. The only difference is that Tiffany's yellow diamond was made in the lab while her engagement ring was created in the earth."

Aunt Ginny popped a piece of bread into the toaster. "So how can Max tell the difference? Want some toast?"

"Er, no. And if Grandpa suspects a diamond is synthetic, he can take it to New York for testing. Like he did with the blue diamond . . ."

No, it couldn't be.

Could it?

"I'll be right back."

Kim dashed downstairs and into Grandpa's office. She squatted in front of the safe, her fingers trembling so violently she could barely dial the combination. Finally . . . finally . . . the safe opened. She reached inside and pulled out the envelope Grandpa had given her to hide.

And there it was, written in Grandpa's own hand: Will it pass DiamondView.

Will it pass. Not does it pass.

How could she miss this? Grandpa's choice of words had bothered her from the moment she saw them. Does it pass implies lack of knowledge, an actual question of authenticity. Will it pass, however, implies knowledge. As if Grandpa already knew something and was trying to find out how the diamond would fare when put to the most stringent of the diamond testers.

Kim's mind whirred. Grandpa's words: A friend poked at a hornet's nest and I'm trying to help. Jim's CVD machine. His missing lab notes. The kidnapper's demand for a "formula". Grandpa's plea that she hide the diamond.

Of course he wanted her to hide it. He didn't want a lab-made diamond getting mixed up with diamonds mined from the earth.

Jim had used that cute little CVD machine to create a breathtaking blue diamond. He'd given it to Grandpa to see if it would pass DiamondView.

Her eyes dropped to the other word Grandpa had written: Yes.

Yes, the diamond had passed DiamondView. Yes, such a simple word, three innocuous letters that would change the gemstone world.

Yes.

Jim Hampton -- Grandpa's friend and Scott's uncle -- had done the impossible. He'd created a lab diamond that couldn't be detected by any current tests.

CHAPTER 34

Kim opened the jewelry envelope, tipped out the diamond and carefully unwrapped it. Her breath caught. Even knowing the diamond had been created in a laboratory did nothing to diminish the rush of desire. No gray sullied the intense, vivid blue. No inclusion marred the sparkle. At four carats in weight, the blue diamond encompassed many a woman's secret desire.

The scientist who'd sought to fashion a solid-diamond hip joint had instead created the perfect diamond.

The perfect diamond. And the perfect deception.

What was Grandpa's friend planning to do with the diamond and the notes detailing how he made it? Publish his results in a professional journal? Sell the process to the highest bidder? Or sell the diamond as the real deal?

Kim sat back on her heels, her mind reeling. She'd only met Jim once, but he'd seemed honest. And Grandpa would never help his friend sell the diamond as mined. Decker Cunningham and his hired thugs, however, wouldn't hesitate to sell the diamond for millions and then turn around and sell Jim's notes to someone in the diamond industry.

Someone like De Beers?

No, no, no. Not De Beers. Please don't let De Beers be involved.

Okay, deep breath. The De Beers company's century-long dominance of the diamond industry ended years ago. And even when they'd controlled the market, they'd used money, not force, to rein in anyone who attempted to break from the diamond syndicate.

Or so they said.

Sure, there were rumors of strong-arm tactics. But that was early in the 20th Century when gangsters ruled Chicago. And as for the Arkansas diamond mine, the rumors that De Beers hired vandals to force the owners out of business had never been proven.

Still . . . what would the De Beers folks do to stop undetectable lab-made diamonds from flooding the market?

Heck, what would anyone dependent on the diamond industry do to stop it? Was this the hornet's nest Grandpa mentioned? If so, how did Jim's cabin, the one he was going to buy in Montana, fit in? Was Jim planning to recreate the Great Diamond Hoax? Maybe as a joke and the wrong person learned about it, took it seriously and . . . And what about Darin? How did Amber's rotten boyfriend fit into all this? Was it possible two separate sets of thieves were involved?

Mmfff. The snort in her ear was accompanied by a friendly push. Kim toppled onto her butt.

"Rorrrry!"

In response, Rorschach slurped her glasses. Kim peered through smeared lenses at Rory's pointy nose, floppy ears and silly grin and started to giggle. She fended off more face washing and pushed to her feet.

"Okay, okay, you win." She bent to place a kiss on Rory's muzzle. "C'mon big guy, we have a lot to do today."

She used the hem of her t-shirt to clean her glasses, then returned the diamond to the safe. Her mind continued to whir as she followed Rory upstairs.

Whatever was going on, the missing lab book was the key. Scott had identified Rat Man and his partner as the men who stole Jim's safe and laptop; that they kept coming back indicated they didn't have the lab book. Scott hadn't found it in Jim's house and she certainly hadn't seen anything like it at Grandpa's.

But there was one other person who might know where Jim hid his laboratory notes.

"So what was all the excitement about?" Aunt Ginny demanded as Kim followed Rory into the kitchen.

"I'll tell you in a minute." Kim reached for the purse she'd left draped across the back of a chair. Pulling out her cell phone, she punched in Scott's number.

"Do you have an address for Jim's secretary?" she said when he answered.

"Just a minute while I find a place to pull over. . . Okay, I've got it. Got a pencil?"

Kim grabbed a notebook and pen from her purse. "Go ahead."

Scott read off Carole's phone number and address, then asked why she needed them.

"Let me put this on speaker phone so Aunt Ginny can hear." Kim set the phone on the table and began laying out her theory that the blue diamond was actually manmade.

"When we talked to Jim's secretary at the Smithsonian, it was clear she was hiding something," Kim concluded. "I think she knew about Jim's diamond-making attempts. She might also know where he hid his notebook."

Scott was silent for so long, Kim thought they might have been disconnected. "Scott?"

"Yeah, yeah, I'm here." He let out a rush of air. "Wow, I didn't see that coming."

"Well, from a psychological perspective, Jim creating a non-detectable synthetic diamond makes sense." Kim kept her voice gentle. "He blamed the diamond industry for his father's death. So he retaliated by creating the perfect synthetic. When word gets out, diamond prices will plummet. People won't want to spend thousands of dollars on a gem that might or might not be manmade. Sounds like the perfect revenge to me."

"And you're thinking Jim's old girlfriend might know more than she's saying."

"That's what I'm going to find out."

"Okay. I should be done with the university guy in a couple of hours . . ."

"That won't work," Kim interrupted. "Carole's family probably has holiday plans."

"So wait till tomorrow."

And sit here all day doing nothing? No way. "If I leave now, I can probably catch her before she gets involved with the family."

"You shouldn't go alone," Scott said. "What if Carole is the one behind everything?"

"I . . . I hadn't considered that." Surely a woman who escorted her grandchildren to the Smithsonian couldn't be a thief. Or worse. Remembering the sweet face of Liz, the eldest granddaughter, Kim shivered.

"She won't be alone." Aunt Ginny crossed her arms, raised her chin and met Kim's eyes. "I'm going with you."

As Kim opened her mouth to protest, Ginny added "Or would you prefer I stay here alone and unprotected?"

Kim couldn't help grinning. "Good one. Clear, succinct and just the right touch of guilt tripping."

Rory slapped a paw on Kim's knee. Kim scratched his ear. "Alright, we'll make it a family trip."

"I take it you're all going?" Scott said. "Call me when you're through? So I don't worry?"

Kim agreed and hung up the phone.

Aunt Ginny stood. "Give me a few minutes and I'll be ready to leave."

While she waited for Ginny -- and before fear could paralyze her -- Kim pulled out the phone number Tiffany had given her. Her hand trembled. She needed to convince Amber's boyfriend to reveal the name of the "dangerous friend," the one who knew about Grandpa's jewelry-buying trips. And without triggering another round of anger at Amber.

Despite the black eye he'd given Amber, Darin seemed to view himself as her protector. Maybe Kim could use that to extract a name.

The phone rang two, three, four . . . a mechanized voice told her to leave a message. No way. She snapped her phone closed. The last thing she needed was Darin calling and catching her off guard. She'd try again later.

"I'm ready."

Kim turned towards her aunt and giggled. Ginny had donned khaki slacks, pink camp shirt with the collar turned up and a Humphrey Bogart straw fedora.

"What? You don't like my private investigating outfit?" Spreading her arms wide, Aunt Ginny turned around.

"No, no, you're perfect." Kim kissed her aunt's cheek and led the way to the car.

Forty minutes later, Kim, Ginny and Rory made their way up a concrete walkway to a small bungalow and rang the doorbell. Someone had painted the home a cheery yellow with forest-green shutters. Not a single cobweb or speck of dust marred the green door. The small front lawn had been mown within an inch of its life. Even the old Honda parked in the driveway had been recently polished and shined.

"Anal," Kim said. "Very anal."

Aunt Ginny shrugged. "Good qualities for an executive secretary."

"I guess." Kim found it hard to attribute anything good to Carole. Not after the way Carole revealed Jim's health problems, used them as a weapon to divert Scott's questions. Well, Kim wouldn't allow Carole to weasel out this time.

She was about press the doorbell again when it opened.

"You." Carole frowned and crossed her arms. "I don't know what you want but as you can see, I'm about to go out."

Kim studied the woman who might hold the key to recent events. Dressed in trim slacks and modest tank top, she radiated cool competence. Except for one thing: One eye was made up with eyeliner, shadow and mascara while the other eye was totally bare. The lopsided effect magnified the glare Carole aimed at Kim.

"This won't take long." Sensing Carole was about to slam the door in their faces, Kim eased the tension on Rory's leash, allowing him to push Carole aside so he could explore the living room. Kim followed close at his heels.

If anything, the home's interior was more pristine than the exterior. A floral sofa had been arranged beneath the front window. Kim could actually see her reflection in the walnut coffee table that separated the sofa from two easy chairs. In the far corner, a hutch displayed gold-rimmed china. The only softening touch came from a collection of grandchildren photos arranged on a nearby wall. Kim couldn't help smiling back at a gap-toothed photo of Liz, taken when the girl was five or six.

Kim settled onto the sofa with Rory laying in front of her. Aunt Ginny joined her, leaving the chairs for Carole.

"You have five minutes." Carole perched in one of the chairs, glared at Rory, then pointedly studied her watch.

Kim swallowed her angry retort. Carole had every right to be testy after Kim pushed her way in. Best to remain calm and reasonable.

"We're hoping you can help us locate Jim's most recent lab notebook."

Carole's eyes widened. "His lab book's missing?"

"Scott found all but the most recent one. Do you know where he kept it?"

Carole reached up to clutch the pendant she'd worn to the Smithsonian. "Wasn't it in his workshop?"

"No. And it wasn't with the other lab books."

Carole jerked the necklace back and forth. "You . . . you don't suppose it was stolen?"

"We know it wasn't."

The necklace stilled. "How could you possibly know that?"

Kim leaned forward, her eyes boring into Carole's. "Because my aunt was kidnapped and ransomed for that damn notebook." No sense getting into the mix-up with Doris.

All of the color drained from Carole's face. Her eyes darted to Aunt Ginny's. She opened her mouth, but no words came forth.

Kim's shoulders relaxed. This poor woman wasn't involved with Rat Man. It would be very difficult to fake that pasty whiteness.

"Are you all right?" Kim reached for Carole's free hand. It was icy. "Can I get you a glass of water?"

Carole shook her head. "No, no I'll be alright. Who . . . Do you know who . . ."

"The kidnapper is dead and an accomplice is on the run." Kim tightened her grip on Carole's hand. "But we need to find out who else is involved. Someone told those men about Jim's experiments."

Carole's eyes widened. "You think it was me? I would never . . . I loved Jim."

Kim believed her. Whatever triggered the attacks, it wasn't Carole confiding in the wrong person.

"Why don't we start at the beginning?" Kim kept her voice gentle. "When did Jim decide to make diamonds instead of hip joints?"

Carole sank back into her chair. "You know about that, too? I thought maybe, with Jim's death, all of that would end. But it's not going to, is it?"

Kim shook her head.

"I think I would like that glass of water."

"I'll get it." Aunt Ginny stood and headed towards the rear of the house.

Kim met Carole's eyes. "The diamond?"

Carole nodded. "He started trying to make diamonds about a year ago, maybe earlier. When he was first diagnosed with prostate cancer. The doctor said it was a slow moving cancer, but Jim . . . When you get to our age, any illness reminds you of your mortality. The cancer made Jim realize he wouldn't live long enough to complete his research . . . Thank you." She accepted the glass Aunt Ginny offered, took a long sip, then continued.

"For a while it looked like he was okay. He started eating healthier, joined a gym, said he'd by golly kick the cancer." Another gulp of water. "The problem was, Jim defined himself as a scientist and what's a scientist without his research? He enjoyed fishing, enjoyed traveling, but it wasn't enough." Carole shook her head. "So I suggested he make me a diamond." A wry smile. "It seemed like a romantic idea and it gave Jim something to focus on. He seemed happy."

"The diamond you're wearing . . .?"

"Was his first success."

"May I?" To Kim's surprise, Carole removed the necklace and passed it over. Kim angled the pendant towards the light streaming through the window. Like the diamond Grandpa had given her, this stone's color was a vivid blue without a hint of gray.

"How'd he create such a lovely blue?"

"Don't know." Carole accepted the necklace and gaze down at it. "The first diamond he made had a trace of blue in it. Jim said there must have been some impurity in the gas he used. That diamond also had a lot of feather-like flaws in it. But even with the flaws, I got so excited when I saw the blue tinge that Jim set out to specifically make blue diamonds."

Kim nodded. "Probably used boron. Does your diamond have inclusions?" The stone was eye clean, but without magnification she couldn't be sure about internal flaws.

"No, it's perfect." Carole beamed at the pendant, then frowned. "Well, almost perfect. It didn't pass some fancy test your grandfather did on it."

Every muscle in Kim's body tensed. "DiamondView? That test?"

"Sounds familiar." Unaware of Kim's agitation, Carole calmly hooked the pendant around her neck. "Jim was disappointed, thought he'd figured out a way to outfox the tests."

Kim's heart beat faster. She was right! Jim had made the blue diamond, he was the friend Grandpa tried to help. "Did Jim say why it was so important the diamond pass the tests?"

Carole waved the question away. "You know Jim. He never got over his father's death; blamed the diamond industry."

"I knew that, but what's that got to do with his diamonds passing DiamondView?"

Carole sighed. "Oh, he had all kinds of grandiose plans. For a while he joked about using the diamonds to recreate that old diamond hoax, you know, salt some land, sell it to someone like De Beers. . ."

"Go to jail."

Carole nodded. "Exactly what I told him. But he claimed he wouldn't get caught because he'd choose land where there already are diamonds, even though they aren't blue ones."

"Wyoming," Kim said. Where Jim intended to buy a cabin.

"Or Colorado. But, even so . . . You don't mess around with some of these people. I had nightmares of finding him at the bottom of a mine shaft or something. That's when I sent him that movie quote . . ."

"'I won't watch you die,'" Kim said.

"A bit melodramatic, huh? Except, he did die, didn't he?" Carole's blue eyes watered. She rubbed her eyes. "When he found out about my nightmares, though, he stopped talking about recreating the diamond hoax.

"But he couldn't stop obsessing about revenge. It was like the proximity of death released something ugly in him. He grew consumed with the idea of making a perfect diamond, something unique. But the diamonds weren't perfect. When he saw the flaws, he'd get this look in his eyes . . ." Carole shivered. When she spoke, her voice came out as a whisper. "And then he'd take a hammer and smash the diamond. Just smash and smash and smash until nothing was left but dust."

Kim shivered. Talk about your Jekyll and Hyde! Had Grandpa seen the Hyde side of his friend?

"Jim must have been thrilled when he created your diamond." Kim nodded at Carole's pendant.

Carole smiled and touched the necklace. "He was so proud." She sighed. "He should have just stopped there. But, no, he had to give the diamond to your grandfather, tell him to take it to New York for testing. I mean, who cares if some stupid test reveals the stone's manmade?" Her hand closed over the pendant. "When the diamond didn't pass, I was so afraid Jim would smash this one, too."

"Why didn't he?"

"I wouldn't let him. That's when we had our big blow-up. I . . . I just couldn't take what he'd become."

"When did you last talk to Jim?"

"Two, three months ago."

"Did he tell you he'd succeeded?"

Carole's eyes widened and for a moment she couldn't speak. "He did? He didn't say. He never called . . ." Tears started falling. "We fought and I walked out and he never called. I thought he'd call . . ."

Kim pulled a packet of tissues from her purse and passed it to Carole, thinking of course Jim never called. He was a scientist! The scientists Kim had known were so literal Kim never knew how they'd react to a simple "Good morning." If Carole told Jim she never wanted to see him again, it'd never occur to him to go against her wishes and call.

Kim waited for the worst of the tears to stop before posing the critical question. "If Jim was going to hide his lab book, where would he put it?"

Carole gulped water before replying. "I suppose he'd give it to his nephew or your grandfather or . . . or me."

"Scott doesn't have it and I couldn't find anything like it at Grandpa's. So you're the logical person."

Carole shook her head. "The only thing I have is my copy of what I typed in Jim's computer."

"Jim's computer?" Kim's breath quickened. She leaned forward. "Did you transcribe Jim's notes?"

But Kim knew the answer even before Carole nodded. "Jim said he needed type-written notes for peer-review or something." Carole snorted. "Since Jim hated computers, guess who got to transcribe his illegible handwriting into the computer? And before you ask, yes, I have copies. But the most recent is three-months old."

"Can you make me a couple of copies of what you do have?" Kim stood. "Maybe I can find a scientist to look at it."

She followed Carole into a small bedroom used as an office. As they waited for Carole's computer to copy the transcription onto the disks, Kim had another thought.

"Carole, could you stay with your daughter for a few days?"

"I suppose." Carole ejected the disk and handed it to Kim. "But why would I do that?"

"Whoever is searching for Jim's notes might think he gave them to you." Kim's eyes met Carole's. "You might be in danger."

CHAPTER 35

"Do you really think Carole's in danger?" Aunt Ginny stared out the van window at Carole's departing car.

"I wouldn't have insisted she pack her suitcase if I didn't." Kim locked her own car doors, but didn't turn the ignition key. Carole was safe now, on the way to her daughter's house.

But with Rat Man still prowling the streets, everyone Kim loved remained in danger.

She drummed her fingers on the steering wheel. With the right buyer, Jim's diamond-making process would be worth millions. Plenty of incentive for murder. Unless . . .

Unless she could find Jim's lab notes and publicize them. Put them on the internet, take out an ad in the Washington Post. Once the process was available for free, Jim's notes would be worthless.

Kim winced. Scott might object to that. After all, he was Jim's heir. But if the police never caught Rat Man, publicizing Jim's notes would be the only way to keep everyone safe. Surely Scott would agree.

Problem was, she didn't have Jim's complete notes. Just his process for creating inclusion-free blue diamonds. Interesting, but not in the same league as a method for foiling the current tests.

But would Rat Man know that?

"What would happen," she said aloud, "if we publicized these notes." She tapped a finger on a CD. "And pretended they're Jim's process for creating undetectable synthetic blue diamonds?"

Before Aunt Ginny could reply, Kim shook her head. "No, that won't work. Rat Man and his partner stole Jim's computer. They already have these notes."

Familiar with Kim's tendency to think out loud, Aunt Ginny merely nodded.

"What we need are fake notes," Kim said, "realistic enough to fool Rat Man, keep him distracted until the police catch up to him."

"Can't you do it?" Aunt Ginny said. "You've got the geological knowledge."

"Geology won't help. We need someone who understands the CVD process . . . Oh!"

Kim reached for her cell phone and punched the redial button. Scott answered on the first ring.

"You okay?"

Recognizing the concern in his voice, Kim winced. She should have called him sooner. "We're fine. Carole wasn't involved. I'll tell you more later. In the meantime, the man who's picking up the CVD equipment, he's Jim colleague, right? A scientist?"

"Yeah . . ."

"So he knows how to operate Hank."

Scott snorted. "Of course."

"How soon is he arriving?" Kim transferred the phone to her left hand and, with her right, turned the ignition key.

"Should be here any minute. What's going on?"

"I'll tell you when I get there. Just don't let him leave; I need to talk with him."

"Better hurry, then. He's catching a plane to London sometime today."

Jim's colleague was at first disbelieving, then horrified when Kim told him the college's precious CVD machine had been used to manufacture gem-quality diamonds. Once she'd shown him her bruises, however, he agreed to Kim's scheme. Accepting a copy of the disk Carole had given her, he promised to create notes that would fool Rat Man. He'd email Kim the results.

Unfortunately, the scientist wouldn't have time to even look at Jim's diamond-making notes until his flight to London was airborne.

Disappointed, Kim drove home and spent the rest of the afternoon and early evening cleaning Grandpa's house. With everyone planning to arrive at seven-thirty for a combination July 4/Doris-is-free celebration, she figured the busy work would occupy her mind.

Wrong. Sweeping and scrubbing and straightening simply freed her brain to obsess. On Grandpa. On Scott. On the blue diamonds.

Carole had described Jim's diamond-making efforts as a romantic gesture, an expression of his love. Kim sighed. Why didn't otherwise intelligent women understand that love was disclosed through actions, not things? Actions like cleaning scraped knees without hurting you. Offering a shoulder to cry on. Cheering when you succeeded.

Besides, "love and romance" might explain why Jim struggled to create a flawless blue diamond. But not why, after succeeding, Jim pressed on.

Why was Jim so intent on creating a diamond that passed all tests? What did he plan to do once he succeeded? And where were the notes for his diamond-making process?

The questions whirred through her mind, keeping beat with the push of the vacuum, the swipe of the dust cloth.

Doris, Maureen and Wilma arrived at seven thirty sharp. Kim hustled the ladies into the living room, then spent the next fifteen minutes setting out appetizers and glasses of iced tea.

Scott arrived last, his arms laden with Chinese take-out. Kim swung the door open, doing a shuffle step as Al dashed between her legs to greet Rory. Reaching for one of the heavy bags Scott held, she inhaled the aroma of soy sauce, spring rolls and ginger.

"I hope no one wanted Moo Goo Gai Pan." Scott set his bag on the table and pulled out an open, gooey carton. "Al thought it was delicious."

"Looks like there's still plenty of food for everyone," Aunt Ginny said from the hallway door. "Well, aren't you cute?"

Kim couldn't help grinning as Ginny scooped Al into her arms and cradled him on his back like a baby. His normally flat belly was extended twice its size.

"How much did he eat?" Kim tickled Al's round belly.

"The entire quart." Scott pulled more takeout cartons from the sacks.

"Uh, how'd he reach the food? Wasn't he wearing his seatbelt?"

Scott tossed her a sheepish look. Kim bit back the lecture on dogs and responsibility. There'd be plenty of time to whip Scott into dog-owner shape if their growing friendship extended beyond the current crisis.

She crossed to the cabinets and began removing plates and silverware. But her stubborn mind wandered back to the question that had been nagging her all afternoon. What had Jim intended to do with the blue diamond? And why did she feel as if she should already know the answer?

Sighing, she added a roll of paper towels -- makeshift napkins -- to the table. Sometimes if she focused on food and conversation, her subconscious would reveal what was bothering her. "Shall we fill the plates in here and then eat out on the balcony?"

But after devouring two helpings of beef with broccoli, four spring rolls and a serving of sweet and sour chicken, she was no closer to identifying that nagging thought.

She'd like to blame her distraction on Aunt Ginny's noisy friends. Doris -- seemingly recovered from her kidnapping ordeal -- talked incessantly, her chatter accompanied by an occasional tinkling laugh. Aunt Ginny and the others tolerated Doris's babbling by simply interrupting whenever they wanted to speak. Trying to follow the discussion made Kim's head spin.

In all honesty, however, it was the nearness of Scott that kept turning her thoughts to goo. She'd arranged six chairs around a table that normally accommodated only four. Every time she shifted in her chair, her leg brushed Scott's and she caught a whiff of Irish Spring soap.

A curly black head appeared between Aunt Ginny and Doris. Kim leaned forward as Rory laid his chin on the table.

"Rory, no."

Rory rolled his eyes Kim's way, but his chin didn't move. "Rorschach . . ."

With a heaving sigh, Rory lifted his head and disappeared from sight.

"You named your dog after an inkblot?" Maureen cocked one eyebrow.

"No, after the man who invented the ink blot test. I thought it was appropriate. You know, ink blot, black dog, psychology professor . . ."

"I think it was a Freudian slip," Aunt Ginny interrupted. "She didn't want to be the only one with an embarrassing name."

"Kim?" Doris frowned. "What's wrong with that?"

"Kim says she was named after a hole in the ground."

Before Kim could stop her, Aunt Ginny recounted ten-year-old Kim's reaction when she discovered she'd been named after the African diamond mine.

"Don't feel bad, dear." Wilma smiled at Kim. "I was named after a great aunt. But growing up, all of my friends thought I'd been named for Wilma Flintstone. You know, the cartoon character?"

Kim grinned and gave a theatric shudder. "You're right; that's worse than Kimberley. At least children don't think about diamond mines when they hear the name."

"Kinda interesting the way names influence people." Scott bent over to lift Al onto his lap. "Apparently, my Aunt Cary was not only a tomboy, but she settled a lot of arguments with her fists. Claimed it was the only way to defend herself since she was named after a man."

"Cary Grant?" Aunt Ginny said.

Scott nodded and launched into the story of his grandmother's obsession with Hollywood and how she'd named her children after movie stars.

"I was real lucky Mom didn't continue the madness," he concluded. "But I've got cousins named after Grace Kelly and Frank Sinatra. Oh, and there's a golden retriever named Bogie."

"So what about this little guy?" Aunt Ginny nodded at Al. "Was he named after Alan Alda?"

Scott snorted. "I wish. His full name is Almas. Which is another name for Bigfoot, Yetti or Mongolian wild man."

Aunt Ginny opened her mouth, but her words were drowned out by the sudden bangity-bang-bang of firecrackers. Rory whimpered and pushed his head under Kim's arm. Al yawned and rolled over.

Doris leaped to her feet. "Oh my goodness, are they starting?"

"Relax," Kim said. "We've got at least another hour before it's dark enough for the big fireworks."

"We should leave, anyway." Aunt Ginny stood and began gathering plates. "Even though we have reserved seats, they'll give them away if we don't arrive fifteen minutes early."

"Sure you don't want to watch from here?" Kim stacked empty take-out cartons. "The view is wonderful."

"No," Aunt Ginny said. "From the pier we can watch the children as well as the fireworks."

"Okay, then you'd better get started," Kim said. "Traffic will be a nightmare. I'll take care of cleanup."

Scott and the ladies, however, insisted on helping Kim carry everything into the kitchen. While Aunt Ginny dashed upstairs to collect her purse, Kim started loading the dishwasher. She turned to grab a new stack of dishes and bumped into Scott. Before she could step away, he leaned in and murmured in her ear "Looking forward to the fireworks tonight."

The double entendre made Kim's breath catch and her toes curl. She could smell the soy sauce on his breath and wondered if he'd taste like a Chinese meal. As if he could read her mind, Scott flashed his Indiana Jones smile and traced a finger down her cheek.

Kim shivered and stepped back, suddenly grateful that Scott had insisted on driving Aunt Ginny and her friends to the fireworks display so the women wouldn't need to search for a parking space. That would give her at least thirty minutes to decide how romantic she wanted to be tonight.

She escorted everyone to the kitchen door and, remembering the way Doris had been kidnapped right in Grandpa's back yard, watched from the top of the stairs until everyone had crawled into Scott's car.

Leaning against the railing, she inhaled the aroma of grilling hamburgers, hotdogs and . . . She wrinkled her nose. Marijuana. Yuk. The smells seemed to drift from the house across the alley, where old Beatles music blared. A firecracker made her jump. Rory streaked back into the house.

Kim hurried after him.

"It's okay, sweetie . . . Almas, no!" Slamming the door behind her, she raced to the kitchen table and snatched the little dachshund from the carton of leftover rice. "How did you . . ." Her eyes fell onto the kitchen chairs. One had been left slightly pushed away from the table. A determined dog could hop on the chair and then onto the table. Even a dog with short legs.

Still holding Al, she lifted the carton. Empty.

"What did you do?" She shook the carton at Al.

The gesture would have made Rory drop his ears and beg forgiveness. Al, however, gazed back at her, white grains dripping from his ears and muzzle. The tan markings on his eyebrows and muzzle created a black mask around his eyes. His bold, unashamed eyes.

Kim snorted. "Should have named you Bandit."

She studied him, now worried about all of the food he'd stuffed in. Though his belly was even more distended, he didn't act distressed. Instead, his eyes rolled back, his lids closed and he gave a contented burp.

Kim shook her head, suppressing a smile. The little dog was so darn cute he'd probably ruled Jim Hampton's house.

"All right, Bandit. Let's find a safe place for you to sleep it off." She started down the hallway. If she set up Rory's travel crate, Al could stretch out and sleep through the fireworks. And she wouldn't have to worry about him getting into something else.

She froze, one foot still in the air. Why hadn't Jim named the dog Bandit? Or Zorro? Something befitting the dog's personality and appearance. Almas was an odd choice for someone whose family members selected Hollywood names.

"Are you really a Mongolian wild man?" She grinned at the little dog as she stepped into the living room. Heck, maybe he was. She had no idea what a Mongolian wild man might be.

However, she could easily find out. Her laptop sat on the coffee table, exactly where she'd left it. She settled on the sofa, Al at her side, Rory draped across her feet. Reaching for the computer, she called up Google and typed in Mongolian wild man.

A series of photos popped up, along with a collection of links to Bigfoot-like creatures, brown versions of the mythical Abominable Snowman.

"No way." She looked from the computer to the sweet little dog now sound asleep. Back to the computer. This time she typed in "Almas meaning." A new list of links appeared.

Girl's name, girl's name, girl's . . . where was the boy version? Was she spelling it wrong? She deleted the search and started to type again when her eyes fell onto the first link.

She blinked and read it again.

"The meaning of the name Almas is Diamond."

CHAPTER 36

Diamond. Almas meant Diamond.

Kim stared down at the sleeping dachshund. Didn't Scott say his uncle's last words were "Al"? Scott assumed -- heck, they both assumed -- Jim was trying to tell his nephew to please care for the little dog.

But what if Jim was trying to tell Scott something else? What if he mentioned Al because the dog's name was important?

"If Almas means diamond," she said aloud, "then . . ." She gazed down at Al. "What did you do, eat one of Jim's creations?"

She stroked his fur. "No, Jim wouldn't find that amusing." Besides, if Al swallowed a diamond, it'd pass through his system and come out the other end, hopefully without cutting his insides. Not something Jim would worry about when critically injured.

So. Let's assume Jim was trying to tell Scott that Al was a crucial piece of the puzzle. How would Jim use the little dog?

Her mind instantly jumped to the missing lab book. The one that presumably explained how Jim made blue diamonds that passed all current tests.

"If this was a movie," she told Rory, "the mad scientist would copy his notes onto microfilm, stick it in a little container and inject it under Al's skin."

Rory slapped a paw on her knee. Al continued to snooze.

Of course, if Jim really wanted to hide something under Al's skin, he could use one of those microchips that enabled dog catchers to reunite strays and their owners.

She'd had one inserted in Rory to protect him in the unlikely event they became separated. If he was hauled in by a dog catcher, a quick check with a hand-held scanner would reveal Rory's personalized identification number. A call to the national data-base would then allow them to obtain Kim's contact information.

Which reminded her; she needed to call the data center to give them her new address.

She made a note on her growing to-do list, then frowned. No, a microchip wouldn't help Jim. To inject the chip, he'd need a vet's help. No reputable vet would get involved.

Beside her, Al started to snore. Kim grinned. Looked like the little thief was down for the night. She should probably tuck him into Rory's travel crate so she didn't have to worry about him waking up and going exploring while she wasn't looking.

First, though, she needed to remove Al's collar. She'd heard too many stories about unattended dogs snagging their collars and choking. Which is one reason she never used a flea collar on Rory.

Reaching over, she gently slipped Al's new collar over his head. He opened one eye, sighed and rolled into a tighter ball.

But Kim wasn't paying attention. She was staring at the collar in her hand, thinking about another collar. The original collar. The stupid leather, rhinestone-covered buckle collar that was totally inappropriate for this little dog.

Maybe that was the point. Maybe the collar Jim stuck on his dog served a totally different purpose from keeping Al attached to his leash. Like hiding a message.

She'd left the collar on her bedroom dresser.

Scooping Al into her arms, she headed for the stairs. In the bedroom, she laid Al on the bed, then erected Rory's travel crate and arranged soft towels on the bottom. Lifting the still-sleeping dachshund, she tucked him inside the crate and secured the door.

Satisfied that Al would be safe while she was otherwise occupied, she crossed to the dresser.

Even in the dim bedroom light, the silly rhinestones sparkled. As she lifted the collar she smiled, remembering Scott's chivalrous mien as he'd buckled the soft leather over her wrist. Pushing the thought aside, she studied the collar. The most logical place to hide a message would be on the underside.

She flipped the collar over, expecting to see words or numbers burned into the leather. Nothing. Turning the collar, she studied the edges. Nothing written there, either.

Maybe the buckle? She ran her fingers across the smooth metal, searching for a rough patch that might indicate engraved words. Her finger brushed against something scratchy.

Her heart quickened as she leaned forward and peered at the spot. Yes! There were letters here. But they were too tiny to read.

She needed one of Grandpa's loupes.

With a sigh, she double-checked the lock on Al's crate then carried the collar down to Grandpa's office. She flipped on the work light, snagged a loupe and peered at the buckle. The words swam into view -- the manufacturer's logo.

She blew out a puff of frustration. Darn it, she'd been so certain.

She turned the collar in her hands. Was there a place to hide that microfilm she'd joked about?

The collar's rhinestones caught the light and glittered. She smiled, remembering the rhinestone-covered barrette Grandpa had given her . . . was it twenty years ago? It'd been butterfly-shaped, its wings encrusted with multi-colored rhinestones. She'd told Grandpa the stones sparkled just as much as Aunt Emerald's stupid diamonds . . .

Kim's breath caught. No. It couldn't be that simple. Could it?

Her fingers trembled as she studied the stones. Were they all rhinestones? Or had Jim substituted one of his synthetics?

She remembered Tiffany's lab-made diamond and the message she'd had laser inscribed on its girdle. So simple. Take a lab-made diamond, inscribe something on the girdle and substitute the stone for one of the rhinestones. Who'd think to look on a dog's collar?

She held the collar towards the light. Three rows of prong-set red, blue and yellow rhinestones wrapped totally around the collar.

Normally her first step would be to breathe on the stones. Moisture from her breath would condense on the glass rhinestones, causing them to fog. Diamonds, however, conducted heat so any moisture would quickly evaporate.

The size and density of the stones in the collar, however, would make it impossible to breathe on individual stones. Grandpa's sharp eyes could probably pick out any differences in the stones. Kim, however, was out of practice.

Best go to step two: Examine the stones through a loupe, looking for rounded-edges on the facets and/or bubbles in the body of the stones. Since all of Jim's creations had been blue, she'd focus on those colored stones first.

Bringing the loupe to her eye, she peered at the first blue stone. Scratches marred the table. Diamonds wouldn't scratch; she didn't need to look further into this stone. On to the next.

Most of the stones were scratched. Al had been hard on his collar. A handful of blue stones, however, had escaped Al's rough treatment. She peered closer. The first one's facets were clearly worn. Second one had small bubbles, a sure indication of glass. The third one . . . She leaned into the stone.

The third one was flawless. No scratches, no wear on the facets, no internal bubble-like inclusions.

Placing a thumb over the stone to mark her place, she reached for Grandpa's finest needle-nosed pliers. She gently bent each of the prongs that held the blue stone in place, tipped the collar upside down and caught the loose stone. Her hands trembled as she used tweezers to grip the top and bottom of the stone. Finally, she raised the loupe and brought the stone's girdle into view.

Nothing. She rotated the stone a quarter turn. Still nothing. Another quarter turn rotation.

There was something written there.

CHAPTER 37

She'd hoped the inscription on Jim's synthetic diamond would contain a clear message, an indication of what he'd done to make the diamonds pass current tests.

Instead, someone had inscribed a series of numbers and letters: R34L07R22.

What the heck was that supposed to mean?

Okay, Jim was a scientist. Maybe the letters were symbols for an element from the periodic table. She frowned, trying to remember what she'd learned in school. C stood for carbon, O for oxygen, H for hydrogen. But R and L? She couldn't think of an element represented by those single letters.

So. Not scientific symbols. Or at least not ones she'd recognize. But something about the inscription looked familiar. It looked like . . . like the numbers she'd found in the book Scott had given her, the one where Jim had written the combination for his office safe.

Her shoulders slumped. Scott already searched that safe. That's where he'd found the small blue diamond that'd he'd tried to return to Grandpa. But Scott said there'd been nothing else in the safe.

Of course, maybe these weren't the same letters and numbers. She'd left the book upstairs on the nightstand.

Buckling the collar onto her left wrist, she turned out the task light and, with Rory clinging like Velcro, headed for the elevator. The occasional pop of firecrackers had turned her normally confident poodle to mush.

She laid a comforting hand on his head and punched the button for the top floor.

Minutes later, she perched on the edge of the bed and opened the book to the title page. A man's hand had written: R22L00R16.

Same letters. Even the same pattern of letters: R, L, R. But different numbers. Which probably meant the diamond's laser inscription was indeed a combination. But a combination to what?

She pulled her cell phone from her pocket and dialed Scott.

"This traffic is worse than any Washington rush hour," Scott said by way of greeting.

"Are you on the way back?"

"Haven't even arrived yet. If traffic doesn't start moving faster, the ladies may have to walk."

Kim winced. Aunt Ginny wasn't known for her grace and with children pushing through the crowds, she might fall.

"Maybe you can convince them to come back here and watch the fireworks from the balcony."

"Tried that. They're determined to sit on the dock . . . Hang on a minute, the light just turned green."

Through the phone, Kim could hear cars, firecrackers and Aunt Ginny's laughter. She bit her lip. To think that Ginny had been targeted by the kidnapper . . . The police were looking for Rat Man. Lieutenant Brockley said the thug would be too busy dodging cops to worry about Kim. She wasn't convinced. Rat Man must know Jim's diamond-making process was worth millions. Until she found Jim's lab book, everyone would remain in danger.

"I'm back," Scott said. "Looks like we're going to make it after all. What's up?"

"Did Jim have another safe besides the one in his office?"

"Just the safe in his lab, the one that was stolen. Why?"

Kim flopped onto the bed beside Rory. She'd forgotten about that safe, darn it. "One of the stones on Al's collar is a synthetic blue diamond. Jim had some numbers and letters laser inscribed on it. Looks like the combination to a safe."

For a few moments, Scott was silent.

"Doesn't make sense," he finally said. "Jim kept those combinations nearby so he could quickly reach them when he wanted to get into a safe. The inscription on the diamond . . . he'd need to catch Al, remove the collar, then use a magnifying glass to read the inscription, right?"

"Worse than that. I had to remove the diamond from its setting before I could study the girdle . . . er, the inscribed edge."

"There you go."

Kim frowned. Darn it, she was so sure the inscription was a lock combination. Could it possibly be some scientific shorthand?

"I'd better let you concentrate on your driving," she said. "See you later."

Tossing the phone on the bed beside her, Kim stared at the numbers and letters she'd written. If not a combination, then what the heck was this?

The sudden ringing of her cell phone made Rory jump. Poor dog was skittish tonight. Maybe chewing a rawhide would help. She'd left it on top of the grandfather clock.

Swinging her legs off the bed, she snagged the phone and glanced at caller I.D. Lieutenant Brockley.

"Just got a call from the Baltimore police," he said. "They picked up Frankie. Idiot was pumping iron at the gym."

"Did he say who hired him?" As she talked, she trotted downstairs to retrieve Rory's rawhide.

"Clammed up and demanded a lawyer. I'm on the way there. Given the struggle you witnessed through Cunningham's window, we might make Frankie talk by reducing the charges from murder to manslaughter."

Kim gritted her teeth. "What about the attacks on Grandpa?" And me.

"Let's take it one step at a time," Brockley said.

Kim bristled at the patronizing tone. "Would you at least check for dog teeth marks on Ra . . . er, Frankie's right arm?" While the police assumed Rat Man had been Grandpa's attacker, Kim wanted to make darn good and sure before Grandpa was released from the hospital.

Lieutenant Brockley didn't seem to notice the anger in her voice. Or maybe he chose to ignore it. Instead, he agreed to examine Rat Man's arms and hung up.

Kim flipped the phone shut, grabbed Rory's rawhide -- darn thing weighed a ton -- and returned to the bedroom. Rory accepted the bone, his tail thumping. Kim breathed a sigh of relief. At least one of them was happy. She wouldn't rest easy until Rat Man revealed his employer.

She plunked onto the bed beside Rory and scratched behind his ear. "They caught Rat Man. Guy must be a real numbskull. He was at a public gym lifting weights . . ."

Her hand froze. A public gym.

She'd been to one. Years ago, in Oregon, a friend convinced her to try out a new local health club. Kim quickly grew bored. She just couldn't see the point in bicycling in place or walking to nowhere, let alone hefting weights over her head. Better to dig in the garden or walk the dog, look at the view.

But while she hadn't returned to the club, she did remember the rows of orange colored lockers, each one secured with metal locks supplied by the club's patrons. Some people used keys to open their locks. Others dialed a combination.

Didn't Scott say his uncle recently joined a health club?

She snagged her notebook and flipped through the pages, searching for the notes she'd taken after interviewing Scott about his uncle. Here it was, a list of Jim's recent behaviors that struck Scott as out of character.

At the top of the list was buy a dog. She glanced towards Rory's crate. Al slept on, his little chest rising and falling. Whether or not Jim needed a dog, he sure picked a nice one.

She scanned the rest of the list. Scott said his uncle had seemed jumpy and secretive. Then there was the phone call to Grandpa, the one warning that he was being followed. Finally, towards the bottom of her list, she found it: Jim had joined a health club.

And not just any health club. This one was a brisk walk from Grandpa's house.

No way was that a coincidence.

Snatching her phone, she again dialed Scott's number.

"Are you on the way back?" she asked when he answered.

"Yep. Just dropped off the ladies. Traffic is heavy, but I should be there in ten, fifteen minutes."

"Don't come here. Meet me at the new health club. It's on your way. When you get to Fifth Avenue, turn left, away from the Bay. It's about a block down Fifth."

"If you're looking for exercise," Scott said, "I can think of more interesting activities than walking on a treadmill."

Kim ignored the heat climbing her cheeks. "I think Jim hid his lab book in one of the club's lockers. I'll meet you there."

She hung up the phone before he could protest or she could change her mind. While the thought of snuggling with Scott gave her goose bumps, she knew she wouldn't rest until she'd located the missing lab book.

Besides, this shouldn't take long. The new health club was maybe a five-minute walk from Grandpa's. Given the holiday, the club should be empty. They could zip inside, find Jim's locker, retrieve the lab book and return to Grandpa's in time for the fireworks.

Fireworks.

She cast a guilty look at Rory. No way could he tolerate fireworks alone. But . . . surely no one would be exercising tonight. At least not during the fireworks display. She should be able to sneak Rory into the building.

"Go for a walk?"

Rory jumped off the bed, the rawhide still clenched between his teeth. Kim sighed, removed the bone from his mouth and tucked it into her purse. He could chew it while she searched for the correct locker.

She slipped her new clicker over her wrist -- might as well do some training as they walked -- and with Rory at her side, headed out into the deserted alley.

CHAPTER 38

Though she could still hear voices coming from the backyards that bordered the alley, hers were the only footsteps crunching the gravel. She cursed herself for not bringing a flashlight. House lights from Grandpa's neighbors did little to illuminate the alley.

She pulled Rory close, her eyes darting from shadow to shadow. The police have Rat Man in custody, she scolded herself. So why was she so darn jumpy?

Whatever the reason, she breathed easier when they reached Second Avenue and turned west towards the honking horns and bumper-to-bumper traffic of Main Street. She couldn't remember this many cars during the fireworks of her childhood.

No wonder Grandpa preferred to watch from his balcony.

Crowds, however, offered safety. The Three Beaches maintained the small-town, help-your-neighbor attitude; no way could anyone attack her without someone stepping in to help.

Unless, of course, the attacker had a gun.

She pushed that thought aside. The police had Rat Man in custody; he couldn't hurt her.

Rory suddenly slammed to a stop. Feet planted, tail straight up, he stared across the street.

"Rory, heel."

The big poodle ignored her. Kim stiffened. What had he seen? She tried to follow his line of sight, her eyes scanning the crowded sidewalk on the other side of the street.

Most people were headed towards the boardwalk and a view of the upcoming fireworks, their arms laden with beach chairs, blankets and small coolers. Parents and grandparents clung to the hands of small children while older children raced ahead. Directly across the street, a man and woman struggled to control a toddler, two elementary schoolers and a small white dog. The fluffy creature tugged on its leash, tail wagging, emitting excited yips.

"Rory, leave it. Heel."

With a sigh, Rory moved to her side. She clicked the behavior, then pulled a treat from her pocket.

The treat disappeared in one crunch, but Rory now clung to her leg, gazing up at her.

Kim set a brisk pace. Turning left, they headed towards Fifth Avenue. When they reached Fifth, the congestion worked in their favor, allowing them to safely cross Main Street.

Unlike the other streets, however, Fifth was dark and empty. No streetlights brightened the narrow sidewalk, no houses beamed a welcoming glow. The only illumination came from the windows of the health club up ahead. Kim walked faster, then broke into a trot.

She arrived at the fitness center door slightly out of breath. Gripping the handle, she paused to look around. The lighted parking lot held two small, light-colored cars. Commuter cars. Nothing like the black behemoth that drove away from Decker Cunningham's office -- was that just last night? No wonder she was so jumpy.

The stainless door handle retained the afternoon's heat. When she pulled on it, however, the door didn't move. Frowning, she pushed. Nothing.

She stepped back. The sign over the door read "Open."

So why the heck . . . Oh. To the left of the door, a slotted metal gadget waited for someone to insert a key card. She resisted the urge to kick the door. Great. Just great. The club was open twenty-four hours, but you needed a key to gain entrance. And the key was probably somewhere in Jim's house.

She leaned against the cool brick facade and considered her options. She could pound on the door and hope that someone inside would not only hear her, but would investigate the racket. She could hang around for someone to enter or exit. Or she could wait for Scott, return to Grandpa's and enjoy the fireworks.

Blowing air through pursed lips, she crossed her arms. There was no guarantee that Jim had hidden the notebook here. But to be so close . . .

Headlights illuminated the health club door, temporarily blinding her. She dropped her arms. Thank goodness. Someone to open the door. She stepped forward, then froze. Her breath caught. The car was a black Mercedes.

Had the driver seen her?

Kim stepped away from the lighted door and eased into the shadows. The nearest house was in the next block, an uphill jog. Would someone be home?

The car door opened and a woman emerged.

Rory whimpered and wagged his tail. Kim released the breath she'd been holding.

The woman looked vaguely familiar, perhaps someone from the boardwalk. She was dressed in pink sweats and carried a matching canvas tote bag. As she approached the door, she spotted them and froze. Hugging the canvas tote to her chest, her eyes darted from Kim to Rory and back to Kim.

Kim suddenly realized the shadows hid her own face. She stepped into the light.

"I'm sorry to startle you." She turned palms toward the woman. Look at me, I'm harmless. "I'm glad you're here. Forgot my key."

The woman's eyes dropped to Rory. Wagging furiously, the big poodle trotted towards the woman, leaned against her leg and gazed up.

So much for hiding him.

"He's afraid of fireworks," Kim said.

As if on cue, a series of cracks lit the night. Rory streaked back to Kim and tucked his head between her legs.

The woman's shoulders eased and she actually smiled.

"My collie's terrified, too," she said, shifting her tote to her side. "The big baby's in bed with my husband, hiding under the covers." She inserted a key card into the slot and pulled the door wide. "Just don't let him hog the treadmill."

Kim flashed a genuine smile as her Good Samaritan held the door for Kim and Rory to enter, then headed down a hallway to the left. Kim watched her disappear through a glass door into a brightly lit room of treadmills, stationary bicycles and other instruments of torture.

Which must mean the lockers were towards her right. Should she wait here to let Scott in or go exploring on her own?

Pulling out her cell, she dialed Scott's number.

"I'm still sitting in traffic," he said. "Probably be faster to walk, but there's no place to park the car. Looks like the side streets are also jammed."

"You might make better time if you get off of Main and take a parallel road," Kim said. "Call me when you get here so I can let you in."

Kim hung up, then followed the signs towards the locker rooms. Might as well take a peek while she waited. With any luck, there wouldn't be any men in the locker room, she could dash in, find Jim's locker, retrieve the lab book and be outside waiting for Scott when he finally arrived.

The squeak of her sneakers and click of Rory's toenails made an eerie combination. She was grateful when she reached the men's locker room door.

Lifting a trembling hand, she knocked.

"Hello? Anyone in there?" No one answered. She pressed her ear to the door, straining to hear movement or the sound of showers. Nothing. She knocked again. Silence.

She opened the door a crack.

"Hello? Anyone here?"

Hearing nothing, she stepped inside. The odor of wet sneakers and disinfectant assailed her. Another hallway led past two rows of private, curtained showers. She loosened Rory's leash, allowing him to trot ahead. Surely, if anyone was still here, he'd remark on the appearance of the standard poodle.

But no voice stopped them from entering the room of orange colored lockers.

Kim started to congratulate herself for her good fortune, then stared in dismay. Almost every single locker had been secured with a combination lock.

Kim sagged against the nearest locker. This could take forever.

Rory whimpered and nudged her hand. She dug fingers into his soft fur and smiled down at him.

"It's okay, sweetie. We're just going to be here a little longer than I thought."

Setting her purse on a metal bench, she removed Rory's rawhide and set it in the middle of the floor. Rory grinned, plopped to the floor and began chewing. The gnawing sound reverberated off the room's metal and concrete, reminding Kim of giant rats. She shivered.

Okay, the sooner she found Jim's locker, the sooner she could get out of here.

Pulling the combination from her purse, she started at the end of a row and dialed the first lock. She tugged. The lock didn't open. She released it, the lock clinking against the metal locker, and moved on to the next lock. After a few unyielding locks, she fell into a rhythm: dial, tug, release, move on. The jangle of metal against metal joined the crunch of Rory's rawhide.

Kim had reached the end of the first wall when Rory emitted a soft growl. Spinning around, her breath caught as the door opened.

An elderly man, dressed in khaki shorts and t-shirt, entered. Spotting the standard poodle standing rigid in the middle of the room, the man froze. Before Kim could reach for Rory, however, his growls disappeared and his tail began wagging. He trotted to the man and leaned in for an ear scratch.

"I'm sorry," Kim said. "My, uh, uncle left his medicine in one of the lockers but didn't tell me which one." She waved the piece of paper she held. "I didn't think anyone would be here during the fireworks." She stepped forward and slipped a hand under Rory's collar. "We'll get out of here . . ."

"Don't leave on my account." The man smiled. "I forgot Jimmy's -- my grandson's -- baseball cap. He claims he must have it for the fireworks."

Kim smiled and herded Rory back across the room. She waited until the man had collected his grandson's hat, tossed her a wave and left before snapping Rory's leash back on.

"Why don't you lay beside me, sweetie?" She transferred the rawhide to the bare floor at her feet, waited until Rory settled, then placed her foot on the end of his leash. No sense scaring yet another patron; the next guy might not be so understanding.

She reached for the first lock in the next bank of lockers. Two spins to the right to number 34, spin left passing 34 to 7, right again to 22, pull. The lock made a snapping noise as it held tight, then rattled when she released it to move to the next lock.

Slowly, she re-established her rhythm. Right 34, left 7, right 22, pull, move on, right 34, left 7, right 22, pull, move on, Right 34, left 7, right 22, pull, move on . . .

She froze and stared at the open lock.

For a moment, she couldn't breathe. Hand trembling, she slipped the lock from the hasp and opened the door. The locker room light illuminated the contents: a student's composition pad. Just like the ones on Jim's shelves.

Kneeling, Kim reached for the book. Rory suddenly leaped to his feet, barking.

"I'll take that."

Startled, Kim dropped the book. She looked over shoulder. A masked figure clothed in black loomed by the locker-room door. He held a gun . . . pointed at Rory.

CHAPTER 39

"No!" Still on her knees, Kim scooted in front of Rory. Rory peered over her shoulder. She could hear a deep growl rumbling in his throat. "Please. Don't shoot my dog."

The gun moved from Rory to Kim and back to Rory. The hand holding the gun trembled.

From anger? Fear? Indecision?

Whatever the reason, this man was no gun expert. Not only was his hand trembling, but his shoulders were rounded and he kept shifting his weight from one leg to another. He clearly was uncomfortable with the gun.

Could she use that to her advantage?

"The lab book . . ." She swallowed, trying to force saliva into her dry mouth. "What you're looking for is in here." She tipped her head towards the open locker. "Take it." She stared into the gunman's icy blue eyes. "We're no threat to you. Please, just take the book and go."

The man's eyes shifted from hers to the locker. Kim studied him, assessing. Hard to tell from a kneeling position, but he didn't appear to be much taller than her. Too nervous to be Rat Man and too slight to be the knife-wielding thug who'd attacked Grandpa.

So who was he? Could this possibly be the mastermind behind all of the attacks?

As if reading her mind, the man's eyes shifted to her face. Kim bit her lip, projecting her most innocent expression.

"Move away from the locker. No, don't stand. I like you on your knees."

Kim gripped Rory's collar and shuffled to her right. Her knee touched something hard. She glanced down. Rory's bone. A weapon? Her eyes flicked back to the gunman's. He jerked the gun sideways, urging her to move. But his eyes showed irritation, not alarm.

He couldn't see the bone from where he stood.

But he'd see it as soon as he neared the locker. Unless . . . Keeping her eyes on his, she shuffled sideways, nudging the bone with her knee until it was hidden by the bench. If she could move far enough to put the bench between her and the gunman . . .

"That's far enough." The man took a step towards the locker.

She was still trapped behind the bench.

Okay, go to Plan B. From here, she could reach the bone with her left hand. Maybe when the man leaned towards the locker, she could catch him off balance, use the bone as a club.

As if reading her mind, the gunman stopped.

Kim dropped her eyes. Look contrite! She relaxed the muscles around her mouth. Through her lashes, she could see the man's feet. One pointed towards the locker and the notebook. The other turned slightly towards the locker room door, a clear sign of indecision.

For a moment, she allowed herself to hope he'd change his mind, decide to leave without harming her or Rory. But she forced herself to be realistic. This was the man who'd hired Rat Man and his partner to attack Grandpa, to steal from Jim, to terrorize her. Maybe Jim's death had been an accident. Even so, this man's greed triggered the series of events that resulted in Jim's death.

So why should he show mercy now?

Keeping her shoulders hunched to indicate submission, she made a list of possible weapons. Her nice, heavy purse lay right where she dropped it -- on the other side of the room by the first set of lockers. Too far away to be useful.

Closer to hand lay the rawhide bone, heavy enough to do some damage if she threw it or used it as a club. The training clicker still hung from her wrist, but what good would that do? If the killer started shooting, the bench wouldn't offer much protection. The darn thing was bolted to the floor. Of course, if she could take the gun out of the equation, she had Rory.

The sound of the Indiana Jones movie theme pierced the silence. Kim's eyes flew up. The gunman stiffened, his eyes flicking from Kim to her purse, where the phone continued to sing. Kim bit her lip. Scott. It must be Scott, calling to say he was outside and waiting for her to let him into the building.

What would he do when she didn't answer?

The ringing stopped. The man with the gun opened his mouth. The phone rang again.

"That's the police," Kim said. "They know I'm here. If I don't answer, they'll know something's wrong."

The man's eyes narrowed. Though he didn't say anything, she could tell he was thinking.

"Please, just take the notebook and leave before the police arrive."

"And how do I know they aren't out there waiting?"

Damn, she'd made it worse. She needed to redirect this line of thought before it escalated into a hostage situation.

"They haven't had time to get here," she said. "They've been questioning Frankie . . ."

"Who?"

Now the man just looked confused. Maybe he knew Rat Man by a different name.

"The man you hired to steal from Jim. The police are questioning him now . . ."

The gunman's snort interrupted her. "Decker Cunningham's not talking to anyone. He's dead."

The cold, flat voice chilled her. How did he know the slimy detective was dead? There wasn't time for it to reach the news . . .

A memory from last night flashed into her mind. The lighted window of Cunningham's office. Cunningham standing and aiming a gun. The two silhouettes struggling for the weapon. Two men, the same height, equally matched in strength and weight, their silhouettes so similar she didn't know which one was alive until Brockley told her.

She'd assumed -- they'd all assumed -- Cunningham had been killed by Rat Man. But though she'd never seen Rat Man with Cunningham, she knew Grandpa's attacker was taller than Cunningham, taller and broader through the shoulders.

Rat Man didn't kill Cunningham. This man with the gun did.

The door to the locker room opened. The killer glanced away. Kim reached for the rawhide as she drew her feet under her. The gun swung back, halting her in a crouch position. Rory broke into a fit of barking, pulling so hard he almost tugged her off her feet. Scott? Kim swiveled towards the door.

Not Scott. Jason.

Jason White -- all six feet, two inches of him -- stood illuminated by the fluorescent lights. Clad in tight jeans and t-shirt, his muscles rippling, his blond hair wind-blown, her high-school flame embodied the quintessential romantic hero.

But even heroes could be killed by a gun.

"Jason, look out!"

But Jason ignored her. Instead, he stared at the gunman.

"Dad?"

"Damn it, Jason, what are you doing here?" Keeping the gun aimed at Kim, the man yanked off the ski mask.

Alex White.

Kim's stomach clenched into a knot. Scattered memories drew together to form a pattern. The young Jim Hampton, blaming White Family Jewelers for his father's early death, then fighting with Alex White. Jim's subsequent fascination with the Great Diamond Hoax and his search for a potential Wyoming diamond field. Alex White's explosive reaction to Mrs. Johnstone's accusations of deceit, his terror when she showed him the article about synthetic diamonds.

It all made a twisted kind of sense. Jim Hampton spent the last years of his life developing a non-detectable synthetic diamond for one purpose: To seek revenge on the family he held responsible for all his childhood woes.

Grandpa must have called Jim from New York, told him the diamond passed all tests. And Jim did . . . what? Tried to sell the diamond-making method to his nemesis? No, more likely he'd taunted Alex White with his success, bragged about the impact an undetectable synthetic portended for the diamond industry. For Alex White's business, his livelihood.

Jason gawked at his father. "Where'd you get the gun, dad?"

Alex's shoulders slumped, but the gun retained its deadly aim. "I killed a man, son."

"It was self defense," Kim squeaked. She swallowed. "I saw it through the window. Decker Cunningham pulled a gun on you. When you defended yourself, the gun went off. I'll testify for you."

"Don't believe her, Dad, she's a damn liar." Jason crossed his arms.

Kim stared at Jason's bare arms, her mind scrambling to comprehend what she was seeing. There were bruises on Jason's right forearm. Bruises in the shape of a dog's teeth.

She forced herself to look away, up, up into the ruthless, empty eyes of the psychopath.

CHAPTER 40

"You tried to kill Grandpa." Kim's hands clenched as anger pushed aside the fear. "You stabbed him with a knife and left him for dead. And when he didn't die, you tried again in the hospital." Rory's growl echoed her fury. "What kind of a monster are you to attack a helpless old man?"

"You knifed Max?" Alex White's eyes widened. "I thought it was one of those thugs Decker hired."

"It was," Jason said. "Don't believe a word that bitch says."

"The proof is right there on your arm." Kim lifted her chin. "Those are the marks Rory made when he defended Grandpa. The police have your DNA. They took samples from the blood on Rory's teeth."

"But why?" Alex stared at his son. "Why attack Max? I told you Jim Hampton had the formula."

"Yeah, but Max had the blue diamond."

Alex frowned. "Why do we need the diamond if we have the formula?"

"We don't need the diamond," Jason said. "I do. You think I want to spend the rest of my life always under your goddamn thumb?"

Alex straightened. "Jason, watch your language."

"Damn the language!" Jason smacked his palm against a metal locker.

Rory barked and lunged forward. Kim held on with two hands, conscious of the gun held in a shaking hand.

"When I sell that diamond," Jason growled, "I'll have millions of my own money. And I won't need you or anyone else."

"Sell the diamond?" Alex White's eyes bugged out. "If that diamond gets into circulation, it could ruin the industry."

"Fuck the industry." Another bang on the lockers.

Rory barked and lunged.

Jason pointed at him. "Would you at least shoot that damn dog?"

"No!" Kim wrapped both arms around Rory, cradling him as she turned her back to Alex White. She tensed, waiting for the blast of the gun. Would she feel the bullet smashing through her? Smell the gunpowder?

Instead, she heard Jason's callous voice. "Don't shoot the bitch. She needs to retrieve the diamond for me."

And then what? Would he take the diamond and leave? Or remove her as a liability? Like he tried with Grandpa.

"You think I'm going to help you destroy everything I've worked for my whole life?" Alex said.

"It's always about you isn't it? You and your damn family."

Kim turned towards Jason. He'd planted himself just inside the locker-room door, legs spread, arms crossed, chin raised. The romance hero had metamorphosed into a recalcitrant teenager. When he spoke, his voice had a distinctive edge, an entitled superiority that used to grate on her nerves . . .

She recognized that tone of voice. And Grandpa must have recognized it as well.

"That 'damn family', as you so crassly put it, put you through college, gave you a job . . ."

"Yeah, yeah, yeah." Jason dismissed his father's words with a wave of his hand. "And completely smothered me. Did it ever occur to you that I might not want to be shackled to the family business?"

Alex sputtered a protest. The two men continued to argue, but Kim didn't hear the words. She cast a glance at Alex. He'd squared off against his son, the gun now hanging by his side.

This might be her only chance.

"Rory, wait," she whispered in the dog's ear.

Keeping a firm grip on Rory with one hand, she inched the other towards the rawhide. The training clicker hanging from her wrist made a scritching sound as it dragged across the tile, but neither man seemed to notice. They were too consumed with their argument.

If she could just reach the bone. Her index finger brushed against it. Almost there.

Rory whined, his gaze no longer on Jason. Kim followed Rory's line of sight. The door to the locker room crept open. From her angle, she could see Scott trying to peer inside.

Scott could surely hear the two men arguing, but he couldn't see their positions. Couldn't see Jason, standing with his back to the door, close enough to touch. Couldn't see Alex, facing his son, trying to reason with him. Couldn't see the gun.

She needed to draw Alex's attention away from the door.

She flipped the clicker into her hand and rapidly depressed the button.

Clickclickclickclickclick.

"What the . . ." Alex turned towards the sound.

Kim dropped the clicker and snatched the rawhide. Scott charged through the door. Kim released Rory, grasped the bone with two hands and hurled herself at Alex.

Alex raised the gun, but not fast enough. Kim's swing connected with the man's shoulder, spinning him around. The gun went off. Someone cried out.

Kim swung again, smashing the hand holding the gun. The gun flew from his numb fingers. Alex moaned, dropped to his knees and clutched the injured hand.

Rory yipped, a high-pitched combination of pain and indignation. Kim whirled around in time to see Jason aim another kick at Rory. Rory skipped out of the way.

Quickly assessing the situation, she decided Jason wasn't an immediate danger. Rory had backed him into a corner and now held him there with growls, barks and flashing teeth. Jason's eyes were slitted with rage. But his long-standing fear of dogs prevented him from doing more than attempt an occasional kick. Rory had learned his lesson and stayed well away. He didn't appear injured.

And Scott?

She heard a groan to her right. She turned in time to see Scott push into a sitting position. His right arm clutched his stomach. Blood oozed from his left arm.

Kim's breath caught. Rushing to Scott, she dropped to her knees and reached for the injured arm.

"No." Scott's voice came out in a hiss. "'s okay." He gasped for breath. "Bullet just grazed me."

Kim studied Scott's pale face. Was this macho hogwash?

As if reading her mind, Scott offered a half-smile. "I'm not being brave. The pain is from getting kicked in the kidneys after the bullet . . . Watch out!"

Kim whirled around, gripping the rawhide, just as Jason dove for the dropped pistol. Rory barked, but a bench prevented him from reaching the enraged man. Kim hurled herself across the room, swinging the rawhide underhand.

The blow contained fifteen years of pent-up anger at Jason's lies, schemes and deceptions, at her own gullibility, at the nearness of Grandpa's death. Rory's bone smacked between Jason's legs with a solid thunk.

Jason screamed, dropped the gun and clutched his gonads. He fell to his knees, tears in his eyes, cursing.

The locker-room door opened and two uniformed men ran inside.

"Police. Nobody move. Drop your weapon. Ma'am, put down your weapon. Ma'am?"

For a moment, Kim stared at the man who'd tried to kill Grandpa. Then, handing the bone to Rory, she twined her fingers in the poodle's curls and turned away.

The room began to fill with police and emergency technicians. Two EMTs bent over Scott, examining his arm. Kim stood out of their way, watching. Scott looked up and attempted a smile.

"Remind me to never make you angry." He tipped his head towards the group crowded around Jason. "You've got a good aim."

"I was aiming for his gut." She shrugged. "Must've been a Freudian slip."

CHAPTER 41

"Grandpa?" Kim hovered in the doorway of the ICU room, staring at the fragile looking figure in the hospital bed. The breathing tube had been removed, but Grandpa was still attached to a frightening number of monitors. And he laid so still.

Was Mom wrong? Was Grandpa still in a coma?

"Grandpa?" she said again.

Grandpa opened his eyes. "Hello there, Monkey."

Kim rushed to the bed. Throwing her arms around Grandpa's shoulders, she buried her face in his neck. "I thought I'd lost you." She blinked, fighting the hot tears that streamed down her cheeks.

She wasn't going to cry. She wasn't. But after everything that had happened tonight . . .

Grandpa tugged her ponytail. "I'm not going anywhere."

Kim stepped back and brushed the tears from her eyes. She reached out and gripped Grandpa's hand. She never wanted to let go.

"I see you've ruined another pair of jeans." Grandpa grinned.

Kim looked down at her dirty, ripped jeans. After the ambulance took Scott to the hospital, she'd driven home to check on Al. She'd just finished emailing Jim Hampton's colleague, telling him she no longer needed a fake diamond-making formula, when Mom called to say Grandpa was awake. She hadn't bothered changing clothes before rushing to the hospital.

"Your granddaughter fights dirty," Scott said. He'd remained outside while Kim greeted Grandpa. She gestured for him to enter.

"She give you the broken arm?" Grandpa pointed at the sling Scott wore. Though the bullet had only grazed Scott's upper arm, it'd left a groove that required stitches and a sling to keep the arm immobilized.

Scott grinned. "No, but thanks to Kim, Jason and Alex White will need to see doctors before they go to jail."

Grandpa's eyes widened. He gripped Kim's hand. "Did they hurt you?"

"I'm okay." No need to tell him about the cuts and bruises all over her body. With any luck, she'd be completely healed by the time the hospital released Grandpa. "Do you have enough strength to tell us what happened? We know some of it, but . . ."

Grandpa's eyes flick to Scott.

"It's okay," Scott said. "We've figured out Uncle Jim was trying to scam the Whites . . ."

Grandpa shook his head. "Not scam. Well, maybe Jim considered that, but that was just fantasy. . . The nurses said . . ." He swallowed. "Is it true that Jim's gone?"

Scott nodded. Grandpa's fingers dug into Kim's hand. She tried a reassuring squeeze.

"He didn't suffer, Grandpa," she said. "And he would have suffered a lot once the cancer got worse . . ."

"Cancer?" Grandpa looked from Kim to Scott. "Jim had cancer?"

"Uncle Jim's girlfriend told us that the cancer triggered this whole mess. He didn't tell you either?"

Grandpa shook his head. "Never said a word. I guess that explains why Jim suddenly announced he'd never complete his artificial joint research before he died. Nothing I said seemed to cheer him."

"No one wants a reminder of their mortality," Kim said quietly. She knew she'd be dreaming of guns for a long time.

"Could you pass me some water?" Grandpa pointed to a bed-side tray that had been pushed out of the way.

Kim retrieved the cup of water and held it while Grandpa sipped through the straw. Much as she hated to leave him, she needed to wrap this up so Grandpa could get some rest.

"Did you know what Jim was going to do with the blue diamond once it passed DiamondView?" She set the cup back on its tray.

Grandpa grimaced. "No. Not until I called from New York to tell him the diamond passed and he started babbling about telling Alex White that the undetectable diamond would destroy the industry. I had no idea what he was planning, but told him to wait until I returned before doing anything. But I could tell he wasn't listening.

"So there I was, still in New York, trying to figure out how to prevent Jim from doing something stupid." He smiled at Kim. "That's when I remembered I knew an expert in all of this psychology stuff." The smile turned into a grimace. "I thought there was time for you and me to talk, to figure out a way to reason with Jim. But he didn't wait."

"And when you came home, you confronted a robber?"

Grandpa nodded. "He must have followed me from the train station. Came up behind me as I unlocked the office door, pushed me inside, showed me the knife. He demanded my briefcase."

"And you recognized Jason's voice?"

Grandpa shook his head. "He was disguising his voice. Except when I smacked him in the shin with the briefcase. Then he cursed in his own voice. I knew I'd heard that voice before, but he came at me with the knife and then you and Rory showed up . . ." Grandpa stiffened. "Is Rory okay?"

"He's fine. Quite the hero dog. Uh, when did you figure out the attacker's voice was Jason's?" And why didn't you tell me instead of wasting your breath about the stupid blue diamond, she silently added.

"Just now, when Scott said Jason is going to jail."

Kim frowned. "I guess Jason thought you'd recognized his voice when he attacked you. That would explain why he came to the store with your briefcase. He wanted to see if you'd told me.

"But even if you had, so what? Jason would be arrested for robbery. The Whites have enough money to hire the best lawyer. Jason probably wouldn't spend any time behind bars. So why did he sneak into the hospital to try to murder you?"

"Probably because once Mr. Hershey identified him, Jason White would also face accessory to murder charges," Lieutenant Brockley said from the doorway.

Darn. She'd hoped it'd take the lieutenant longer to travel from Baltimore to Calvert. He must have been nearby when he told her to wait for him at the hospital. "Uh, Grandpa, this is the officer who's been investigating the, er, robbery." No need to tell Grandpa about the kidnapping and other attacks. At least not right now. "Are you saying Jason's an accessory to murder?"

"Jason White hired Frankie and his partner to rob Jim Hampton," Brockley said. "That makes him an accessory in Mr. Hampton's death."

"But ... but Rat Man attacked Jason."

"Frankie and Jason never met." Lieutenant Brockley crossed his arms. "Frankie claims all transactions with Jason occurred over the phone."

"So Jason sent those thugs after me?" Ooh, how she'd love to take another swipe at that guy with Rory's bone.

"No, by then Frankie and Alan were working for Decker Cunningham, who was working for Alex White." Brockley shook his head. "That's one screwed-up family. While the father was trying to retrieve Jim Hampton's notes, the son was hunting the blue diamond. The father, at least, thought they were working together."

"But as always Jason only thought of himself," Kim said. "But you said Frankie's partner was dead. Who ...?"

"Decker shot him when they tried to collect their fee. Frankie was standing closer to the door and was able to get away."

A nurse appeared behind Brockley. "It's time for all of you to leave and allow Mr. Hershey to rest."

Brockley whipped out his wallet and showed the nurse his police identification. "I need to question Mr. Hershey."

"You can do it in the morning." The nurse folded her arms and lifted her chin.

Brockley sighed. "Fine." He pointed a finger at Scott, then at Kim. "But you two can give me your statements now."

"Let's do it in the lounge," Scott said, heading for the door. "We can get coffee."

The two men disappeared through the door. The nurse raised an eyebrow at Kim.

"One minute?" Kim tried her puppy-dog expression. The nurse's shoulders relaxed.

"One minute only." She turned away.

"This isn't how I'd planned to celebrate your homecoming," Grandpa said.

"There'll be plenty of time to celebrate once you're out of the hospital." Kim leaned over and kissed his cheek. "Oh, I almost forgot." Swinging her purse onto the bed, she opened the zippered center compartment and pulled out Fluffy. "I thought Fluffy could keep you company until you come home." She tucked the stuffed poodle under the sheet.

When she looked up, Grandpa had tears in his eyes. "I've missed you, Monkey. You're going to stay home this time, right?"

"Only if you promise to tell me more stories." She grinned, blinking back her own tears. "Like how opals got their color from butterfly wings."

DEAR READER

Thank you for reading *The Blue Diamond*. If you enjoyed it, please tell a friend. Or tell many friends by writing a review on your favorite site. Sometimes it's hard to find a new author, so we must rely on each other for recommendations.

This book was such fun to write in part because it gave me a chance to explore the fascinating history and legends surrounding diamonds. Plus who could resist hanging around jewelry stores? To read more about the stories behind the story, please visit my web site and join *The Diamond Digest*, my occasional email to select readers.

I've never been the greatest speller, so all of my books are extensively reviewed by professional editors and proofreaders. If, however, you do find an error, please email me at Lynn@LynnFranklin.com so I can fix it.

Actually, you can email me even if you don't find problems. I love to hear from my readers. You are the reason that I write.

Read on for a fun preview of *The Pirate's Ruby*, the next Kimberley West mystery.

LYNN FRANKLIN

Excerpt from

The Pirate's Ruby

*A late-night call from a local busybody sends
Kimberley West racing to Osprey Beach's gloomy new
pirate museum. But when Kim, her grandfather and
standard poodle Rorschach arrive, the caller is nowhere
in sight.*

The entryway was lit by a single bulb.
Apparently, the oh-so-economical Dorothy Tyson
hadn't turned on the overhead lights. The safety
lights barely illuminated the area.

"Dorothy?" Grandpa peered into the shadows.

Kim stepped around the ticket counter and
started toward the pirate ship replica. Rory
slammed to a stop. Planting his feet, he sniffed the
air. The hair on his back bristled and his throat
rumbled.

Grabbing Grandpa's hand, Kim hissed,
"Something's wrong."

"Rory's just never been in a museum," Grandpa
said.

She started to point at Rory's raised hackles when
he suddenly charged forward, pulling the leash
from her hand.

Kim ran after him. "Rory, no!"

Rory barked and seemed to increase speed. She followed him around the pirate ship, but slipped as they rounded the corner into the dark hallway of pirate photos.

Somewhere ahead, a door alarm clanged.

"Rory!"

She skidded around the last narrow turn in time to see Rory disappear through the far doorway into the gem exhibit.

She raced after him. Through the door, careening left, her mind barely registering something wrong with the exhibit on the right, no time, gotta catch Rory, through the entry into the final exhibit.

There, just ahead. The big poodle stood at the back door, barking and scratching. She snagged his leash, her heart racing, her mind trying to make sense of what just happened.

Someone had been in the museum, had run from Rory.

Dorothy?

No. His hackles wouldn't have risen if Dorothy was the only one in the museum.

So who just ran through the door?

She turned to look for Grandpa. But the large room was empty. Hadn't he been right behind her?

"Grandpa?"

"In here." His voice sounded strange, like his throat muscles were too tight. . .

Kim and Rory retraced their steps to the entrance of the gemstone exhibits. Rory braked to a halt and refused to enter the room.

Kim told him to lay down, then gave him the stay command. Turning, she entered the gem exhibit. Something crunched under foot. Glass.

More than half of the display cases had been broken. Glass and scattered artifacts littered the floor. The case that once held the pirate's ruby amulet was empty. Bare spots dotted the display of pirate weapons.

Grandpa knelt in front of the empty jewelry display, his back to her. She could see a woman's stocking-covered foot; her shoe lay a few inches away.

"Grandpa?"

He slowly rose, revealing the woman's face. Dorothy Tyson.

"Is she...?"

Grandpa nodded. "She's dead."

Buy the print version of The Pirate's Ruby at Amazon.
Buy the eBook version of The Pirate's Ruby at Amazon or Kobo.

ALSO BY LYNN FRANKLIN

Kimberley West Books

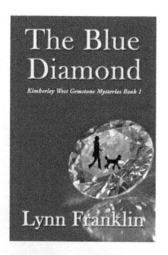

LynnFranklin.com

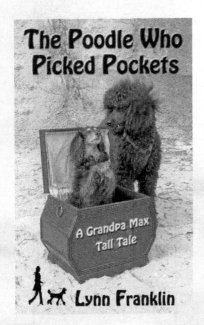
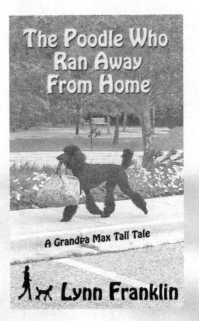

FACT OR FICTION?

While *The Blue Diamond* is a work of fiction, it is full of fact. As the author is an Accredited Jewelry Professional, most details about gemstones are meticulously accurate. As for the lore -- oh that wonderful lore -- the reality is too good to make up. A pair of conmen really did convince a group of businessmen, a U.S. geologist and Charles Tiffany that they'd discovered diamonds in Wyoming. Ironically, decades later diamonds were in fact discovered on the Colorado/Wyoming border, not far from the spot where the "prospectors" staged their con.

The Crater of Diamonds is a very real, and very beautiful, state park in Arkansas where visitors can dig for diamonds with their own hands. As mentioned in the book, the mine was once a commercial operation forced to close after vandals destroyed equipment and workings and ultimately pushed the owners out of business. Fingers were pointed at the De Beers Company -- fingers were always pointed at De Beers -- but no proof was ever found. You can learn more by visiting the park's website, and there is more -- much more -- to come later in the jeweler's granddaughter mystery series when Kim finally drags Grandpa on that promised trip.

Diamonds, in addition to serving as sparkling threads in mystery writers' plotlines, are extremely useful. In part what makes them valuable is their hardness, which exceeds that of any other gemstone. More interesting, though, is their glittering ability to lower the IQ of certain women. And as cousin Tiffany discovered, the advent of manmade diamonds has given women something to do with tiresome husbands. Aside from water, most of the body is made up of carbon, which is concentrated in the crematorium. The resulting cremains are only one brief step from what can be further heated and concentrated to become, as the marketers say, "memorial diamonds."

Osprey Beach is a fictional town, but North and Chesapeake Beaches are both real and lovely. Located on Maryland's western shore, the two towns were major tourist attractions in the 1920s and '30s. Cruise ships from Baltimore carried passengers to the Twin Beaches' boardwalks, where music, dancing, carnival rides and swimming provided wholesome family entertainment. The construction of the Chesapeake Bay Bridge in the 1950s brought the Atlantic beaches into the range of weekend vacationers and destroyed the Twin Beaches' reason for existence. There followed several decades of decay during which the increasingly dilapidated Twin Beaches became slums notorious as a major hangout for Hell's Angels and a center for the regional trade in heroin and prostitutes.

But as Washington D.C. grew apace, the worm eventually turned. By the 1990s the Twin Beaches were being turned into prime exurban real estate with a high-rise resort, a water park, miles of upscale refurbished housing and all the rest of the human drama.

If you visit the area, you'll find much to enjoy. You can stroll the boardwalk of North Beach while gazing out at the pylons that once supported the docks for the long ago cruise ships. North Beach also offers a protected swimming area, white sand, antique shops, a history museum and several cozy restaurants. Chesapeake Beach supports the lovely resort, several waterside restaurants, a railroad museum, a hiking trail that follows the old rail line and the afore mentioned water park.

And if you look closely, you may see Sam and Tucker, the models for Rory and Al, strolling the North Beach boardwalk.

Book Club Discussion Questions

1. Kim's Aunt Emerald can't tell the difference between real diamonds and imitation. Even so, she refuses to wear man-made diamonds, calling them inferior. Do you agree? Why or why not?

2. Kim's grandfather plays a special role in her life, offering encouragement and nonjudgmental support. This role is often played by aunts, uncles or even family friends. Who were the special adults from your childhood? What life lessons did they instill in you?

3. Though Kim loves her family, she worried that moving back to a Osprey Beach would destroy her privacy. Yet small-town living also offers opportunities not found in big cities. Discuss the advantages and disadvantages to living in a small town. Which would you prefer? Why?

4. In *The Blue Diamond*, Kim struggles against her attraction to "bad boys" like Lieutenant Brockley and Jason, the fellow from her high school. She's not alone; women have claimed attraction to "bad boys" from the moment James Dean donned a leather jacket. How would you define a "bad boy"? Why do women find them attractive?

5. Psychologists have determined that people are better able to process information if it is told in story form. Throughout the book, the author weaves stories about gemstone history, legend and lore. What were your favorite gemstone stories from the book? Which stories surprised you?

6. Just for Fun: The author uses the two dogs to provide comic relief in the book. Yet Rorschach clearly plays a major role in Kim's life. What are the dogs or pets in your life? How do they help you cope with life's ups and downs?

ACKNOWLEDGEMENTS

It is sometimes surprising how much investigating and fact-checking goes into a work of fiction. At the same time, that's where much of the fun can be found. I'm thinking, for instance, of the rainy day I spent with Sam Dunaway at the Morefield Amazonite Mine in North Carolina. Mr. Dunaway graciously donned rain gear and spent several hours showing me the workings of a real, operating gem mine.

Then there was the weekend with Lee Lofland and the amazing instructors of the Writers Police Academy. Not only did these stalwart folks attempt to teach us correct police procedure, they didn't even flinch at our blood-thirsty questions. Any procedural mistakes in this book are mine alone.

And speaking of the police academy, I need to thank my firearms training simulator partner, Cailin Garfunkel, for her amazing dead-eye accuracy and for keeping us safe while I (unintentionally) shot squirrels.

Kim Garland, Park Interpreter at Crater of Diamonds, graciously shared the park's history, geology and stories of the diamonds found there.

Larry Larson of the Gemological Institute of America had the tough job of answering my off-topic questions while I studied for my jewelry accreditation.

Author Hank Phillippi Ryan provided a needed confidence boost when she expressed interest in my story and posed a critical question that helped me deepen it.

The internet discussion groups for The Mystery Writers of America, Sisters in Crime, DorothyL, Murder Must Advertise and Kiss of Death (don't you love the name?) offered guidance and encouragement from other mystery lovers.

Thank you to the folks at WriteWay Pro for creating a software program that allows writers to focus on their work instead of worrying about glitches in the software.

On a more personal level, Charlene Dunlap, fellow artist and standard poodle lover, offered valuable input on the final draft and long-distance emotional support.

Virginia Reinhart not only proofed the manuscript, but served as the model for Aunt Ginny.

Joan Rose discovered a few minor plot glitches, then did such an amazing job copy editing that there were few problems for the proof-reader to find. Joan also served as photographer on my fact-finding trips and allowed me to fashion Al after her two delightful longhaired dachshunds, Tucker and Clifford.

And while we're on the topic of dogs, I'd like to offer a special thank you to Nancy McGee for breeding Paradigm Sam Clemens, the role model for Rorschach. Nancy, please don't ever stop breeding these delightful standard poodles.

Author Mary Buckham, editor extraordinaire, helped me think through the story, pointed out places where I could "dig deeper" and pushed me to make this book the best it could possibly be. Mary's honest appraisal was worth its weight in gold.

This book would never have been written without the support of my husband, author Jon Franklin. Thank you, honey, for thirty years of writing instruction, witty banter, exotic adventures and endless love.

Finally, I must acknowledge the ghost my Grandpa, Max Bahler. Grandpa, you may be physically gone, but you will live on in my mind and in these pages.

ABOUT THE AUTHOR

Lynn Franklin's five-star mystery series brings to life gemstone history, legend and lore. From childhood, gemstones, writing and mysteries have been an integral part of Lynn's life. After 30 years of teaching and writing for newspapers, magazines and the internet, she became an accredited jewelry professional and began writing the Jeweler's Gemstone stories.

Although Lynn's books are set in the Chesapeake Bay

area, researching the third book, The Carolina Emerald, offered the rare opportunity to tour a privately owned commercial emerald mine. Lynn uses these kinds of experiences to draw her readers into a fictional world populated with strong characters, quirky relatives and endearing dogs.

To learn more about Lynn's adventures – from dancing with swallows to flunking out of the writers' police academy to wrestling with Empress Josephine (the antique rose, not Napoleon's wife) – go to **LynnFranklin.com** and sign up for her Diamond Digest.

Made in the USA
Middletown, DE
25 February 2021